From Enlightenment
to Romanticism

ANTHOLOGY I

This Anthology is dedicated to the memory
of our colleague Stephanie Clennell (1921–2000)

From Enlightenment to Romanticism

ANTHOLOGY I

edited by
Ian Donnachie and Carmen Lavin

MANCHESTER UNIVERSITY PRESS
Manchester and New York
distributed exclusively in the USA by Palgrave
Published in association with

The Open University

Published by Manchester University Press
Oxford Road, Manchester M13 9NR, UK
and Room 400, 175 Fifth Avenue, New York, NY 10010, USA
www.manchesteruniversitypress.co.uk

Distributed exclusively in the USA by
Palgrave, 175 Fifth Avenue, New York, NY 10010, USA

Distributed exclusively in Canada by
UBC Press, University of British Columbia, 2029 West Mall,
Vancouver, BC, Canada, V6T 1Z2

British Library Cataloguing-in-Publication Data
A catalogue record for this book is available from the British Library

Library of Congress Cataloging-in-Publication Data applied for

ISBN 978 0 7190 6671 9 paperback

First published 2003
First reprinted 2007

This publication forms part of an Open University course A207 *From Enlightenment to Romanticism, c.1780–1830*. Details of this and other Open University courses can be obtained from the Course Information and Advice Centre, PO Box 724, The Open University, Milton Keynes MK7 6ZS, United Kingdom: tel. +44 (0)1908 653231, e-mail general-enquiries@open.ac.uk. Alternatively, you may visit the Open University website at http://www.open.ac.uk where you can learn more about the wide range of courses and packs offered at all levels by The Open University.

Typeset in Sabon
by Northern Phototypesetting Co. Ltd, Bolton
Printed in Great Britain
by the MPG Books Group

Contents

Contents

Acknowledgements

The editors and publisher would like to thank the following for help in preparing this anthology: *Wolfgang Amadeus Mozart, Don Giovanni*, prepared by Donald Burrows; *Faith and death in the late Enlightenment*, prepared by Alex Barber; *The French Revolution* and *Documentary extracts on Napoleon*, prepared by Antony Lentin; *Documents relating to a painting competition, 1807*, prepared and translated by Emma Barker; *Slave writings*, prepared by David Johnson; *John Newton, William Cowper and others: the* Olney Hymns *in context* and *William Wilberforce*, prepared by John Wolffe.

The editors and publisher would also like to thank the following for permission to publish the enclosed documents: *Memoirs of Lorenzo da Ponte*, from Broadway Diaries, Memoirs and Letters, ed. and trans. L. A. Sheppard, 1929, Routledge & Sons; reproduced with kind permission. David Hume, *Of the Immortality of the Soul* and *Of Suicide*, reproduced with the kind permission of the National Library of Scotland. Jean-Jacques Rousseau, *Profession of Faith of a Savoyard Vicar* in *Emile*. From *Emile, or, On Education* by Jean-Jacques Rousseau, translated by Allan Bloom. Copyright © 1979 by Basic Books, Inc; reprinted by permission of Basic Books, a member of Perseus Books, L. L. C. Marquis de Sade, *Dialogue between a Priest and a Dying Man*, from *The Misfortunes of Virtue and Other Early Tales*, translated and edited by David Coward, 1992, Oxford University Press; reprinted by permission of Oxford University Press. Abbé Siéyès, *What is the Third Estate?*, from *The Enlightenment*, ed. David Williams, 1999, Cambridge University Press; reproduced with kind permission. Edmund Burke, *Reflections on the Revolution in France*, Everyman, Dent, 1910 (1955 edition). Copyright © Everyman's Library; reproduced with kind permission. *Decree on the Death Penalty*, 1792, from *A Documentary Survey of the French Revolution*, ed. John Hall Stewart, 1951, Macmillan; reproduced with kind permission from Pearson Education Inc. 'Farewell letter to his son, 1793' by Olympe de Gourges from *Last Letters* by Oliver Blanc. Translation copyright © 1987 by André Deutsch Limited. Reproduced by permission of Farrar, Straus and Giroux, LLC. Robespierre, 'Report on the principles of revolutionary government', 1793, translated by Patsy Peel for the Courseware for History Implementation Consortium, from *Textes choises*, ed. J. Poperen, 1957, Editions Sociales; reproduced with kind permission. Robespierre, 'Speech on the reign of eternal justice, 1794', from

The Press in the French Revolution, J. Gilchrist and W. J. Murray, 1971, Cheshire Ginn; reproduced with kind permission. Jacques Godechot, *Considérations sur la Révolution Française*, translated by A. Lentin © Tallandier, 1983; reproduced with kind permission. Extracts by Quobna Ottobah Cugoano, from *Thoughts and Sentiments on the Evil of Slavery and Other Writings*, ed. Vincent Carretta, 1999, Penguin; reproduced with kind permission. Extracts by Robert Wedderburn, from *The Horrors of Slavery and Other Writings by Robert Wedderburn*, ed. Iain McCalman, 1991, Edinburgh University Press; reproduced with kind permission. Mary Prince, *The History of Mary Prince, a West Indian Slave*, ed. Sara Salih, 2000, Harmondsworth, Penguin; reproduced with kind permission. Extracts from the *Olney Hymns*: reprinted from *Olney Hymns, in Three Books*, first edition 1779, facsimile edition 1979; by kind permission of the Trustees of The Cowper and Newton Museum, Olney, Bucks.

Introduction

This is the first of two anthologies designed to accompany the Open University course *From Enlightenment to Romanticism*, an interdisciplinary second-level course exploring changes and transitions in European culture between 1780 and 1830. The course supports the Arts Faculty's acknowledged commitment to inter-disciplinary teaching and draws on the disciplines of music, philosophy, religious studies, history, literature, history of art and history of science. These different disciplines allow insights into the breadth of major cultural shifts in Europe during a period of unprecedented turbulence and change.

Momentous historical events erupted at the end of the eighteenth century and the early part of the nineteenth century. The French Revolution of 1789 and the excesses of the Terror unleashed new forces within society, and the conquests of Napoleon altered the social structure of European nations. By 1830 the last of the Bourbons had been driven from the throne of France. These political convulsions were going on at the very same time that the developments of the industrial revolution decisively changed the balance of urban and rural life and work in Britain. Meanwhile advances in social and scientific knowledge in the late eighteenth century broke down old ideas about how the world worked and how society operated. Primarily secular energies ran alongside a new evangelicalism and a quest for a different kind of transcendentalism. From all sides, Enlightenment confidence in reason and empiricism was challenged in contradictory impulses. The voices of slaves were heard while at the same time colonialism was making footholds in other continents. Freedom found new forms of expression, breaking down barriers in life and in art with fresh emphasis on the spontaneous and the intuitive, and a delight in imagination and exoticism. New perceptions of human aspirations brought a significant shift in thinking of human beings first and foremost as members of society to human beings as individuals, radically altering conceptions of human nature. There was suddenly a whole different way of looking at life. Romanticism came as a reaction to the mechanistic and the urban, bringing an emphasis on wildness and the sublime in nature. The impetus came separately during this period in each European country in a different momentum within each of the arts and within science and society. French hegemony at the beginning of this period gave way to German and British hegemony by the end of it.

The universal theme through this age is the emergence of human individuality, the essential feature of Romanticism. The spiritual, intellectual
and moral conflicts – between sense and sensibility, personal aspirations
and social integration – are the critical dilemmas whose repercussions are
still with us today.

The collection of extracts in this anthology provides primary sources
which offer perspectives to complement the course *From Enlightenment to
Romanticism*. They are grouped in accordance with particular sections of
the course but do not necessarily reflect the balance and arrangement of the
whole course. In this first anthology you will find readings ranging from
documentation on the widespread effects of the French Revolution to com-
peting representations of Napoleon, from questions from David Hume and
the Marquis de Sade about the nature of God and religion to affirmation of
faith in the hymns of Cowper and Newton and the practical Christianity of
William Wilberforce, from the claims of feeling expounded by Rousseau
and the personal accounts of black slaves to the genesis and synopsis of
Mozart's opera *Don Giovanni*.

Like the course itself, extracts in the anthology stimulate questions rather
than provide reassuring answers. A companion volume offers readings
which accompany the remainder of the course.

The introduction to each group of texts is intended to provide a useful
context for the general reader as well as for Open University students.
Editorial additions are enclosed in square brackets and deletions within the
texts are indicated by an ellipsis within square brackets. Unless otherwise
indicated, footnotes have been provided by the contributors and editors.
Footnotes by originating authors or editors are identified by an asterisk at
the close of the note.

We would like to express our thanks to the members of the course team
in the preparation of these anthologies. Each anthology is a collaborative
venture and the contributors to this first volume are Alex Barber, Emma
Barker, Donald Burrows, David Johnson, Antony Lentin and John Wolffe.
We would particularly like to register our appreciation to Nancy Marten
for editorial advice and guidance, Dorothy Calderwood for her editorial
support, Yvette Purdy for invaluable administrative support and
Carol Green for secretarial assistance. We would also like to thank Denise
Hall for her expertise in preparing the manuscript of the anthology.

Ian Donnachie and Carmen Lavin

PART I

Death of the
Old Regime?

Wolfgang Amadeus Mozart, *Don Giovanni*

In 1787 Mozart received an invitation from Prague to compose a new opera, and the result was *Don Giovanni*, which was first performed there on 29 October 1787. The libretto was provided by the Viennese court theatre poet Lorenzo da Ponte (1749–1838), and the first extract is taken from his memoirs, written in New York towards the end of his life. Da Ponte was a colourful character: he naturally tried to present himself to best advantage and his memoirs, written many years afterwards, may not be an entirely accurate recollection.

Da Ponte took as his starting-point another recent operatic text from an opera which had been produced in Venice earlier in 1787 with words by Giovanni Bertati (1735–1815). He rewrote the text both in its literary aspects and its dramatic content. The story of the opera was one which had seen many previous stage versions, including comedies in French by Molière (1665) and in Italian by Goldoni (1736), with a separate history in popular stage traditions.

Together Da Ponte and Mozart created one of the richest works in the Italian genre of *opera buffa* (the term used by Da Ponte on the printed libretto was 'Dramma giocosa'). The second extract presents the synopsis of their lively treatment of the characters and the situations, which turned a simple morality tale – of the debauchee who is eventually brought to judgement by the arrival of a 'stone guest' – into a complex human drama which raises questions about social and political issues, such as the nature of the dependence between men and women, and between the individual and society.

Lorenzo da Ponte, *Memoirs of Lorenzo da Ponte*

I thought it time, however, to exert my poetic powers again. [. . .] The opportunity was presented to me by the three above-mentioned composers, Martín [y Soler], Mozart and Salieri, who all came to me at once asking me for a play. I liked and esteemed all three, and hoped with their aid to make amends for past failures and to increase my modest theatrical fame. I considered whether it would not be possible to satisfy them all three and write three operas at one and the same time. Salieri did not ask me for an original play. At Paris he had written the music for the opera "Tarar";[1] he now wanted to remodel words and music in the Italian style, so he only asked me for a free translation. Mozart and Martín left the choice entirely to me. For the former I chose "Don Giovanni," a subject which pleased him exceedingly, while for Martín, for whom I wished to find a theme of delicate charm suitable to the sweetness of his inimitable and soul-penetrating melodies, I chose "L'Arbore di Diana."

Having found these three subjects, I went to the Emperor, put my ideas before him and informed him that I intended to write these three operas contemporaneously.

"You won't succeed," he replied.

"Perhaps not," I answered, "but I shall make the attempt. At night I shall write for Mozart, and I shall regard it as reading Dante's Inferno; in the morning I shall write for Martín, and that will be like reading Petrarch; in the evening for Salieri, and that will be my Tasso." He thought my parallel very good.

Directly I reached home I set to work.

I sat down at my writing table and stayed there for twelve hours on end, with a little bottle of Tokay on my right hand, an inkstand in the middle, and a box of Seville tobacco on the left. A beautiful young girl of sixteen was living in my house with her mother, who looked after the household. (I should have wished to love her only as a daughter— but—.) She came into my room whenever I rang the bell, which in truth was fairly often, and particularly when my inspiration seemed to begin to cool. [. . .] At first I allowed her visits to be very frequent, but in the end I had to make them much less so, in order not to lose too much time in the tendernesses of love, of which she was complete mistress.

On the first day, however, between the Tokay, the Seville tobacco, the coffee, the bell and the young Muse, I wrote the first two scenes of "Don Giovanni," two scenes of "L'Arbore di Diana," and more than half the first act of "Tarar," a title which I changed to "Assur." In the morning I took these scenes to the three composers, who could hardly believe their own eyes, and in sixty-three days the first two operas were quite finished, and nearly two-thirds of the last.

"L'Arbore di Diana" was the first to be produced. [. . .] After only one performance of this opera, I was obliged to set out for Prague where

---

[1] "Tarar" was produced in Paris in June, 1787.*

Mozart's "Don Giovanni" was to be played for the first time on the arrival of the Princess of Tuscany in that city.[2] I stayed there a week to direct the rehearsals, but before it was produced I was obliged to go back to Vienna. [. . .]

I had not seen "Don Giovanni" performed at Prague [1788], but Mozart quickly informed me of its wonderful reception, while Guardassoni wrote to me, "Long live Da Ponte! Long live Mozart! All impresari and performers ought to bless you. As long as you two live, hard times will be unknown in the theatre." The Emperor sent for me, and with many gracious expressions of praise made me a present of another hundred sequins, and told me he very much wanted to see 'Don Giovanni.' Mozart came back and at once gave the score to the copyist who hurriedly copied out the parts, as Joseph had to go away.[3] It was staged, and—must I say it?—"Don Giovanni" did not please. Everyone, except Mozart, thought something was wanting. Additions were made, some of the airs were changed, and it was then produced again—and still "Don Giovanni" did not please. And what did the Emperor say of it? "The opera is divine. It is almost certainly better than 'Figaro,' but it is not meat for the teeth of my Viennese." I told this to Mozart, who imperturbably replied, "Let us leave them time to chew it." He was not mistaken. On his advice, I managed to get the opera repeated frequently. At every performance the applause was greater, and little by little even the Viennese with their bad teeth came to enjoy it and appreciate its beauties, and counted "Don Giovanni" one of the finest operas performed in any theatre.

Source: Memoirs of Lorenzo da Ponte, Broadway Diaries, Memoirs and Letters, ed. and trans. L. A. Sheppard, London, Routledge & Sons, 1929, pp. 152–5.

Donald Burrows, Don Giovanni synopsis

Operatic Comedy in Two Acts
Libretto by Lorenzo da Ponte
Music by Wolfgang Amadeus Mozart

[2] "Don Giovanni" was played for the first time 29 October, 1787. Prince Anton and his bride left Prague on 15 October. Jahn. III, 132n.*
[3] Joseph left Vienna for Army Headquarters 28 February, 1788. "Don Giovanni" was first played in Vienna, 7 May of the same year.*

The principal source for the opera's text, which conveys the plot and the stage action, is the printed libretto for the original performances, *Il Dissoluto punito. O sia il D. Giovanni. Dramma Giocoso in due atti*, Prague, 1787; reference has also been made to the libretto for Mozart's performances at Vienna in 1788. The Vienna production differed from the version as originally composed and performed in Prague; in particular the sequence at Act II Scena 9/10 was rewritten and Act II Scena Ultima was shortened. Although these variations are not included here, references to two arias composed for the Vienna version, which are often included in modern performances, are incorporated in square brackets. Scenic and stage directions included in this synopsis are taken from the printed libretti or Mozart's autograph score of the opera.

It is modern practice to refer to sequences of action that take place within a single stage set as 'scenes', but the convention in Italian opera was for 'Scena' to refer to a sequence defined by the combination of characters on stage. In the following synopsis the distinction has been made by using 'Scene' for the former and 'Scena' for the latter, following the numbering of the original libretto. Musical movements are identified by the numbering given in the modern collected edition of Mozart's works: Wolfgang Amadeus Mozart, *Neue Ausgabe sämtlicher Werke*, Serie II *Bühnenwerke*, Werkgruppe 5 Band 17, *Il dissoluto punito ossia il Don Giovanni*, ed. Wolfgang Plath und Wolfgang Rehm (Kassel, 1968). Following the movement number, the participating characters, the type of movement (e.g. 'Aria'), and the first line of Italian text are listed in each case. The honorific titles 'Don' and 'Donna' are omitted from the synopsis.

Dramatis personae

Don Giovanni	An extremely licentious young nobleman	Baritone
Donna Anna	A lady, betrothed to	Soprano
Don Ottavio		Tenor
The Commendatore	[Father to Donna Anna]	Bass
Donna Elvira	A lady from Burgos, abandoned by Don Giovanni	Soprano
Leporello	Don Giovanni's servant	Bass
Masetto	[Peasant] in love with	Bass
Zerlina	Country girl	Soprano

Chorus of peasants and girls; servants; subterranean chorus; ministers of justice (non-singing).

Orchestra: 2 Flutes, 2 Oboes, 2 Clarinets, 2 Bassoons, 2 Trumpets, Timpani, 3 Trombones (entering Act II Scene 11), Violins, Violas, Cellos,

Double Basses. The *semplice* recitatives are accompanied by a keyboard instrument (probably originally harpsichord). Aria no. 16 includes a Mandolin in the accompaniment. The finale to Act I includes three on-stage orchestras (Oboes, Horns and Strings/Strings/Strings); the finale to Act II has an on-stage orchestra of Oboes, Clarinets, Bassoons, Horns and a Cello.

The action takes place in a city in Spain.

Synopsis

Ouvertura (andante, leading to allegro)

The overture opens with a reference to the 'statue' music in Act II. The ensuing faster movement leads straight into the first scena: the stage curtain would have probably been raised in one of the louder passages near the end of the overture.

ACT ONE

SCENE I

A garden. Night.

Scena 1 (No. 1, Introduction. Leporello: Aria 'Notte e giorno faticar'. The scene then proceeds continuously as other characters enter, culminating in a trio for Giovanni, Leporello and the Commendatore: Mozart's heading 'Introduzione' probably refers to the chain of musical movements, matching the 'Finale' structures at the ends of the Acts.) Leporello, wearing a cloak, paces up and down in front of Anna's house, where Giovanni has left him to give protection against disturbance; he complains about the life that he has to lead as Giovanni's servant. Giovanni is pursued from the house by Anna, who tries to uncover his face in order to identify her intruder. He angrily attempts to shake her off, but Anna only releases him and returns indoors when she hears her father (the Commendatore) approaching. The Commendatore provokes Giovanni to a sword-fight, in which the younger and more agile man is quickly victorious, delivering a final thrust which proves to be fatal. During the Commendatore's dying moments, Leporello is horrified and even Giovanni is momentarily taken aback. (Trio 'Ah, soccorso?')

Scena 2 Giovanni seeks out Leporello (who had presumably hidden himself away during the sword-fight), who is ironically critical of his master's 'exploits'. Giovanni will not listen to this criticism, and the two men go off together.

7

Scena 3 Anna returns with Ottavio, bringing him to give assistance to her father against his assailant, but they discover the Commendatore's dead body. (No. 2, Anna and Ottavio: Accompanied Recitative 'Ma qual mai s'offre, O Dei' and Duet 'Fuggi, crudele'.) Anna faints; Ottavio summons assistance and orders the body to be removed. When Anna revives she seems to reject Ottavio's approaches, possibly mistaking him for her father's murderer. When she comes to her senses she begs his forgiveness, and demands that he proves his devotion by taking vengeance on her father's murderer. The oath is sealed in the duet.

SCENE II

A street, in the pale light of dawn [the following morning].

Scena 4 Leporello protests at Giovanni's way of life, but Giovanni brushes the familiar criticism aside and begins to tell of a new lady that he has invited to his villa. Suddenly he smells the presence of a woman, and the two men hide.

Scena 5 Elvira enters in travelling clothes. (No. 3, Elvira: Aria 'Ah chi mi dice mai quel barbaro dov'è'.) She is looking for the man she loved, but who has betrayed her: she threatens to kill him if he will not return to her. During the later part of the aria Giovanni (still hidden) promises to 'console' the lady, with Leporello commenting 'as he's consoled eighteen hundred others'. At the end of the aria Giovanni approaches her, and is immediately recognised by Elvira as her deceiver. She accuses him of seducing her in her home, promising marriage, then deserting her. After a short exchange Giovanni escapes, leaving Leporello to explain his behaviour. Leporello assures her that Giovanni is not worth pursuit: he has a whole book-full of names of Giovanni's women. (No. 4, Leporello: Aria 'Madamina, il catalogo è questo' – the 'catalogue' aria.) He enumerates Giovanni's women: 640 in Italy, 231 in Germany, 100 in France, 91 in Turkey, and 1003 in Spain, so far. The women are diverse – the blonde, the brunette, the plump, the slender, the tall, the short, and, particularly, the young and untried: 'so long as they wear a skirt, you know what will happen'.

Scena 6 After Leporello has left, Elvira expresses her outrage and distress, and then departs.

Scena 7 [By now day has broken.] A festive party of peasants appears, playing instruments, dancing, and singing in anticipation of the wedding of Zerlina and Masetto. (No. 5, Chorus, led by Zerlina and Masetto: 'Giovinette che fate all'amore'.)

Scena 8 Giovanni and Leporello join the group. Giovanni offers to 'take the bride under his protection', and invites everyone to feast at his palace. Leporello is commanded to order chocolate, coffee, wines and ham, and to show everyone the house and gardens, leaving Zerlina with Giovanni. Masetto objects that his bride cannot remain without him, though she seems all too content to remain 'in the hands of a cavalier': Giovanni threatens him into compliance. (No. 6, Masetto: Aria 'Ho capito, signor, si'.) Masetto ironically accepts that Giovanni, as a 'gentleman' (cavalier), can do as he pleases, and taunts Zerlina: 'stay, and see if he makes you a lady.'

Scena 9 After the others have left, Giovanni quickly overcomes Zerlina's protestations of duty and her doubts as to his sincerity: he says that she is too good for such a bumpkin, and he will marry her himself. (No. 7, Don Giovanni and Zerlina: Duet 'Là ci darem la mano'.) Zerlina eventually accepts the invitation to Giovanni's villa, apparently without reservation.

Scena 10 Elvira desperately intercepts Giovanni as they leave, anxious to protect Zerlina and to reveal Giovanni's character. Giovanni dismisses Elvira as a person who is deranged on account of her infatuation with him, but she warns Zerlina against involvement with him and leads her away. (No. 8, Elvira: Aria 'Ah, fuggi il traditor'.)

Scena 11 Giovanni, left alone, is so discomposed by the energy of Elvira's intervention that he is uncharacteristically reduced to grumbling that his plans are going wrong. Anna and Ottavio enter, in search of assistance in tracing the Commendatore's unidentified assailant. They address Giovanni as someone well known to them, and as a gallant man who will help them; Giovanni is relieved that he himself is not suspected, and offers his support in rather exaggerated terms, asking Anna what has upset her.

Scena 12 Before Anna can reply, Elvira bursts in once more, accosts Giovanni and then addresses the others. (No. 9, Elvira, Anna, Ottavio, Giovanni: Quartet 'Non ti fidar, o misera, di quel ribaldo cor'.) Elvira urges Anna to place no confidence in such a villain. Anna and Ottavio are startled, but at once perceive Elvira's earnestness and noble bearing. Giovanni tries to persuade Anna and Ottavio that Elvira is mad, but she overhears and denounces him. Anna and Ottavio are perplexed, but Anna remarks that Elvira does not appear to be mad. Giovanni and Elvira exchange abuse, and eventually Elvira leaves.

Scena 13 (No. 10, Anna and Ottavio: Accompanied Recitative 'Don Ottavio, son morta', and Anna: Aria 'Or sai chi l'onore'.) In Giovanni's parting words Anna recognises the voice of her intruder from the previous evening. She describes to an incredulous Ottavio how the man (who at first she took to be Ottavio) had entered her room, and had tried to stifle her cries for help, before her escape. Now that she knows his identity, she renews her appeal for vengeance.

9

Scena 14 Ottavio, alone, is reluctant to believe that a nobleman like Giovanni would commit such a crime. ('Come mai creder deggio di sì nero delitto capece un cavaliero'.) He determines to establish the truth, so that he can undeceive Anna or avenge her. [In the Vienna 1788 version, an aria for Ottavio follows, No. 10a: 'Dalla sua pace'.] Ottavio leaves.

Scena 15 Leporello reports to Giovanni that he took the peasants back to Giovanni's home, did all he could to placate Masetto, and gave everyone a lot of drink. All was going well until Elvira turned up with Zerlina and shouted denunciations against Giovanni. However Leporello contrived to lock her out of the house. Giovanni looks forward to entertaining the country girls until nightfall. (No. 11, Giovanni: Aria 'Fin ch'an dal vino'.) Leporello is instructed to let the wine flow freely and to bring in all the girls he can find. Let the dances be arranged simultaneously, to cause confusion: tomorrow there will be another ten names on Giovanni's list.

SCENE III

Garden of Giovanni's mansion with two doors locked from the
outside and two alcoves. [Probably, early afternoon.] Masetto,
Zerlina and villagers are scattered about, some sleeping, some
sitting on the grassy banks.

Scena 16 Masetto is sullen and accusing; Zerlina tries to convince him that nothing happened between her and the cavalier, and she uses all her charm to win him over. (No. 12, Zerlina: Aria with cello obbligato, 'Batti, batti, o bel Masetto'.) Masetto is placated, but then Giovanni's voice is heard within. Zerlina is frightened and confused, and Masetto's suspicions instantly revive. (No. 13, Finale: this comprises a succession of musical movements, and covers the remaining scenes to the end of the Act.) Masetto decides to spy, hidden in one of the alcoves, and Zerlina's attempt to dissuade him only increases his jealous rage.

Scena 17 Giovanni enters with four servants. He invites the company into the house; the servants echo him in a brief chorus, and the stage is cleared but for Giovanni and Zerlina.

Scena 18 Zerlina makes futile efforts to hide, but Giovanni renews his attempt at seduction and draws her towards the niche in which Masetto is concealed: after a short hesitation he yields Zerlina to Masetto in an ironic exchange. Sounds of a ball are heard within the house, and the three go in together.

Scena 19 Ottavio, intent on the pursuit of Giovanni, enters with Anna and Elvira; all three are masked. Elvira intends to expose Giovanni's wrongdoing: she urges courage and prudence, and Ottavio supports her.

Anna, clearly nervous, thinks of the danger to them all, but to Ottavio in particular. From inside the house Leporello opens a window, and the dancing is heard. Giovanni instructs him to invite the maskers in. Ottavio accepts with grave formality, and the three maskers together commend their enterprise to Heaven.

SCENE IV

A hall [in Don Giovanni's house], lit up and prepared for a grand festive ball. [The stage was probably divided into different areas, possibly even separated by partitions.]

Scena 20 ('Riposate, vezzose ragazze'.) A dance has just finished; Giovanni and Leporello invite the company to rest, and refreshments are served. Masetto cautions Zerlina to be careful, but she does not turn away as Giovanni begins to flirt with her. (Leporello meanwhile is pursuing some other girls.) Masetto's jealousy is apparent to everyone. The three maskers enter and are greeted ('Venite pur avanti'). They return the greeting, and join Giovanni and Leporello in a toast to 'Libertà'. Giovanni orders the dancing to recommence. Three contrasted dances, played by onstage bands, are introduced cumulatively. Ottavio and Anna dance the aristocratic Minuet, in the course of which Elvira points out Zerlina to them as Giovanni's intended victim. Giovanni's remark that all is going well ('Va bene') is ironically echoed by the watchful Masetto. A second dance ensemble is heard tuning up. Leporello is ordered to keep Masetto occupied; Giovanni approaches Zerlina and they dance a Contredanse. The third ensemble is heard tuning. While Ottavio and Elvira are occupied with supporting Anna, who is feeling faint, Leporello bullies a reluctant Masetto into partnering him in the third dance, a 'Teitsch' ('German Dance'). Three dances in different metres are now taking place simultaneously, creating a distracting environment in which Giovanni is able to drag Zerlina, resisting, from the room. Masetto notices this, breaks free from Leporello, and runs out in pursuit. Leporello, foreseeing trouble, leaves as well, presumably in order to be on hand if Giovanni is challenged by Masetto. From behind the scenes Zerlina screams and sounds of struggle are heard. The dances stop abruptly; the musicians and villagers leave in confusion. Anna, Ottavio and Elvira break down the door in an effort to reach Zerlina, but she enters from the other side of the stage. Masetto joins them, and then Giovanni, with his hand on his sword, drags Leporello on, shamelessly accusing him of the attack on Zerlina. ('Ecco il birbo che t'ha offesa'.) Ottavio, pistol in hand, stops Giovanni in his tracks: he and the ladies unmask in turn and, with Zerlina and Masetto, call him a traitor, saying that everyone now

11

knows of his villainy ('Tutto, tutto già si sà'). Giovanni makes no reply and the five together threaten Giovanni with exposure and revenge. ('Trema, trema, o scellarato'.) At first Giovanni seems to be cowed, but his courage re-asserts itself and the act ends with him matching with defiance their cries for retribution, while Leporello can only echo his master's changing moods.

ACT TWO

SCENE I

A street. [Outside Elvira's lodging; early evening.]

Scena 1 (No. 14, Giovanni and Leporello: Duet 'Eh via buffone, non mi seccar'.) Leporello is seriously considering leaving the service of Giovanni, who tries to dissuade him by offering money. Leporello agrees to stay, but asks Giovanni to promise that he will stop pursuing women. However Giovanni replies that women are more necessary to him than the bread he eats and the air he breathes: 'It is all love; to be faithful to one is to be cruel to the rest'. His next plan is the seduction of Elvira's maid; as Elvira appears at the window [of a balcony above] he exchanges cloaks and hats with Leporello. Darkness begins to fall.

Scena 2 (No. 15, Elvira, Leporello and Giovanni: Trio 'Ah, taci, ingiusto core'.) Elvira tries to remain firm against Giovanni, but feels the former attraction return when he addresses her. (In this trio Giovanni stands and sings behind Leporello, who is impersonating him.) Giovanni asks her to come down ('Discendi, o gioia bella', anticipating the music of the following serenade). She angrily refuses, but Giovanni responds with growing urgency, threatening suicide, at which Leporello nearly bursts with laughter. Elvira gives in, though she reproaches herself with weakness, and she moves away from the window. While she comes down Giovanni forces Leporello, at pistol-point, to agree to lead her away, and Giovanni stands aside to watch.

Scena 3 Elvira arrives. After a nervous start Leporello (as 'Giovanni') warms to his role and Elvira seems convinced by his protestations of fidelity. Giovanni shouts out as if killing somebody; the other pair run away and he comes forward laughing. Giovanni, dressed as Leporello, sings a serenade to attract the attention of Elvira's maid. (No. 16, Giovanni, with mandolin obbligato, the instrument held by the singer: Canzonetta, 'Deh vieni alla finestra'.)

Scena 4 Giovanni sees someone at the window, but before he can proceed further Masetto is heard approaching with an armed gang of villagers. Giovanni quickly sizes up the situation and plays the role of a servant willing to betray his odious master. (No. 17, Giovanni: Aria 'Metà di voi qua vadano'.) Giovanni directs half of the peasants to go to the right, half to the left, instructing them to look for a man with a girl and to attack him. Maliciously he describes his own white-plumed hat, the cloak and sword, now worn by Leporello. He hustles the peasants off, and persuades Masetto to leave separately with him.

Scena 5 Giovanni immediately re-enters with Masetto, who he disarms and beats soundly with the flat of his sword. When Masetto has been subdued, Giovanni leaves.

Scena 6 Zerlina, with a lantern, comes upon the groaning Masetto. She comforts him and determines to take him home, promising to make him feel better, provided he will be less jealous. (No. 18, Zerlina: Aria 'Vedrai, carino'.) She has a very special remedy, which she indicates by allowing him to place his hand on her heart, and they go off together, fully reconciled.

SCENE II

A dark entrance courtyard at Donna Anna's house, with three doors.

Scena 7 Leporello, trying to shake off Elvira, enters the enclosed court because he has seen lights approaching on the road. He asks her to wait in the courtyard, but she does not want to be left there alone. (No. 19, Elvira, Leporello, Ottavio and Anna, joined by Zerlina and Masetto: Sextet 'Sola, sola in bujo loco'; the movement continues into Scena 8.) Elvira expresses her fear, as Leporello leaves to try and make his escape through one of the doorways. His progress is interrupted as Ottavio and Anna enter, and Leporello has to hide. Oblivious of the presence of the others, Ottavio tries to calm Anna, who at first rejects his attempts at consolation. Elvira and Leporello both hope to slip away through one of the doors: Leporello gets there first, but runs into Zerlina and Masetto as they enter.

Scena 8 With Anna and Ottavio, Zerlina and Masetto quickly surround Leporello and threaten to execute him on the spot. Elvira steps forward to plead for the life of her 'husband', but the four cry 'No! he must die!' Ottavio is about to act on this when 'Giovanni' falls to his knees and reveals himself as Leporello, uttering an exaggeratedly lachrymose plea for mercy. Leporello is really afraid, Elvira is deeply humiliated, and the others are stupefied. Anna, unable to take any more, goes off with her servants. [The Vienna version is different for the rest of this scene.]

Scena 9 The remaining characters upbraid Leporello – Elvira on account of his deceit, the peasants for beating up Masetto. (No. 20, Lep-

13

orello: Aria 'Ah, pietà, Signori miei'.) Running from one to another, apologising (to Elvira), denying knowledge of the crime (to Zerlina), and explaining his trespass (to Ottavio), Leporello contrives to reach the door and escape.

Scena 10 Elvira, Masetto and Zerlina accept that pursuit of Leporello would be impractical, and Ottavio announces his belief that there can by now be no doubt that Giovanni was the murderer of Anna's father. He asks them to remain in the house, while he goes to the authorities. (No. 21, Ottavio: Aria 'Il mio tesoro intanto'.) [A scene for Elvira, composed for Vienna in 1788, is sometimes inserted here: it comprises No. 21, Accompanied Recitative 'In quali eccessi, o numi' and Aria 'Mi tradì quell'alma ingrata'.]

SCENE III

An enclosed place in the form of a cemetery. Various equestrian statues, and the statue of the Commendatore. [Night, with moonlight, about 10 p.m.]

Scena 11 Giovanni leaps over the wall, laughing, having just escaped from an indignant woman. He wonders how Leporello has fared and, hearing his voice outside, calls him in. [The Vienna libretto indicates that they change back to their own clothes and has some additional recitative.] Giovanni hears with amusement that Leporello was nearly killed as a result of being taken for his master, and then relates that he has been getting on very well with a lady who mistook him for Leporello. The latter is disturbed that the lady in question might have been his own wife, but Giovanni merely laughs at this. His merriment is interrupted by a sepulchral voice: 'Your laughter will be over before dawn.' Leporello says that this is a 'voice from the other world', but Giovanni is more inclined to look for a human protagonist. The statue speaks again: 'Bold scoundrel, leave the dead in peace.' Giovanni suspects a practical joke, but notices the statue of the Commendatore and asks Leporello to read the inscription. After some protest, he does so: 'Dell'empio, che mi trasse al passo estremo, qui attendo la vendetta' – 'Here I await vengeance upon the evil man who brought me to my death.' Leporello is apprehensive, while Giovanni becomes more brazen and, still probably in the spirit of a jest, forces Leporello to invite the statue to dinner. (No. 22, Leporello and Giovanni: Duet 'O statua gentilissima'.) Leporello approaches the statue, recoils, and is forced forward again by Giovanni; eventually he stammers out the invitation on behalf of his master. The statue nods, much to the dread of Leporello. Giovanni at first mocks Leporello, but is persuaded to see for himself, and when the statue nods again he addresses the invitation himself, receiving the answer 'Sì' ('yes'). Leporello, severely frightened, is anxious to get away as soon as possible, but Giovanni rather relishes the strange adventure, and the two go off to arrange the meal.

SCENE IV

A dimly-lit room in Donna Anna's house.

Scena 12 Having alerted the proper authorities, Ottavio asks Anna to marry him tomorrow, but she replies that she is not yet ready. (No. 23, Anna: Accompanied Recitative 'Crudele! Ah nò mio bene' and Aria 'Non mi dir, bell'idol mio'.) Anna insists that she is not being cruel to Ottavio: she desires their union, but the world would look askance at this during her time of mourning. After she has departed, Ottavio resolves to help her bear the burden of sorrow.

SCENE V

A room in Giovanni's house, with a table set for supper.

The rest of the opera constitutes the Second Act Finale, No. 24.

Scena 13 Giovanni looks forward to a good supper, with music in the background provided by an onstage band. Servants bring in food; Leporello is starving, and also acutely jealous of his master. As Giovanni eats, he hears the band play excerpts from the latest operas. The first is from *Una cosa rara* (libretto by Da Ponte, music by Martín y Soler). Giovanni seems to be enjoying Leporello's discomfiture. The second extract is from *I due litiganti* (libretto based on Goldoni, music by Giuseppe Sarti). Leporello pours wine, changes the dishes, and snatches a mouthful of food, which Giovanni notices. The third musical extract is a tune from *The Marriage of Figaro*, the recent opera by Da Ponte and Mozart that had been popular in Prague. In order to catch Leporello with a mouthful of food, Giovanni asks him to whistle a tune from the opera. The ensuing exchange is interrupted by the arrival of Elvira.

Scena 14 An animated trio for Elvira, Leporello and Giovanni ensues ('L'ultima prova dell'amor mio'). She entreats Giovanni to give up his profligate life-style and declares her fidelity to him, but he reacts with mockery (at one stage kneeling with her) and returns to the table, inviting her to join him. He raises a toast to wine and women, the support and glory of mankind. ('Vivan le femmine, viva il buon vino, sostegno e gloria d'umanità!') Elvira runs out in despair: she is heard screaming outside, and rushes back to escape by another door. (The stage musicians also leave at this point.) Leporello is sent to see what the fuss was about:

he too cries out and returns quaking with fear. In the following duet ('Ah, Signor, per carità') Leporello gasps out that the stone statue is approaching with huge strides (which he imitates), but Giovanni declares that he is mad. Knocking is heard at the door: Leporello refuses to answer it, so Giovanni takes a lamp and goes himself. Leporello hides under the table, and from there he maintains a frightened commentary on what follows.

Scena 15 (Commendatore, Giovanni and Leporello: Trio 'Don Giovanni, a cenar teco'.) When Giovanni opens the door he is faced with the statue: this movement is marked by the first use of the trombones in the opera. Giovanni, apparently taking the situation in his stride, orders Leporello to provide another meal for the guest, but as he is about to arrange this the Commendatore stops him: he cannot now eat mortal food. Instead, the Commendatore solemnly says that he has another mission: to invite Giovanni to dine with him. Leporello intervenes to say that his master is busy, but Giovanni accepts the invitation fearlessly. The statue demands his hand as pledge: the cold grip freezes Giovanni and he struggles in vain to free himself. ('Ohimè! Cos'hai? Che gelo è questo mai?') The statue declares that he has come to call Giovanni to repentance and to change his life, but Giovanni rejects this final opportunity and the statue leaves. Now Giovanni feels fear for the first time as flames spring up and the earth shakes ('Da quel tremore insolito'). From underground a chorus 'with hollow voices' proclaims that no punishment is too great for him, and worse torments await him with them. Giovanni cries out, the flames increase and he disappears below. Leporello, having witnessed Giovanni's end, echoes his master to the last with a cry of despair. The flames subside and the hall returns to normal.

Scena ultima The other five characters enter ('Ah, dov'è il perfido') with ministers of justice, still searching to apprehend Giovanni. Leporello says his master is now far away and, although still rather incoherent, manages to convey what he has witnessed: Elvira confirms that she had seen the 'spectre' earlier. The characters work out how they will resume their lives. Ottavio entreats Anna to agree to marry him at last, now that heaven has taken the vengeance on Giovanni ('Or che tutti, o mio tesoro'), but she insists on a year's mourning first. Elvira briefly announces that she will retire to a convent; Zerlina and Masetto will go home to celebrate; Leporello will go to the inn to find a better master. Led by Zerlina, Masetto and Leporello, the six remaining characters cheerfully repeat the 'ancient song' (i.e. moral): evil-doers always come to an evil end, in life or death:

> Questo è il fin di chi fà mal,
> E de' perfidi la morte all vita è sempre ugual.

Faith and death in the late Enlightenment

David Hume, *Of the Immortality of the Soul*

Of the Immortality of the Soul was due to go into a collection of short essays by Hume (1711–76) called *Five Dissertations*. Hume argues that there are no grounds, whether metaphysical, moral or physical, for supposing we have an afterlife. ('Metaphysical' grounds have to do with the soul's immateriality and its capacity to survive the body's demise; 'moral' grounds have to do with God's need for a time and place where justice can be done for acts committed in this life; 'physical' grounds are grounds that respect Hume's empiricist scruples.)

Pre-publication copies proved so controversial that it was replaced, along with another essay (*Of Suicide*, the next item in this anthology), by a single essay on aesthetic judgement. The collection was renamed *Four Dissertations* (1757). The contents of both essays circulated as rumour and in a small number of clandestine copies of the original *Five Dissertations*, then anonymously in French, then anonymously and posthumously in English. Only in 1783 did an edition appear under Hume's name as *Two Essays* – and even then it was surrounded by a hostile editor's comments, 'intended as an antidote to the poison contained in these performances'.

The text below is based on Hume's hand-corrected copy of the 1755 proofs, now in the National Library of Scotland (MS 509). These corrections are missing from previously available editions. Spelling and punctuation have been modernised, with some paragraphs split for ease of comprehension.

By the mere light of reason it seems difficult to prove the immortality of the soul. The arguments for it are commonly derived either from *metaphysical* topics, or *moral* or *physical*. But in reality it is the gospel and the gospel alone that has brought life and immortality to light.

I

1   *Metaphysical* topics are founded on the supposition that the soul is immaterial, and that it is impossible for thought to belong to a material substance.

2   But just metaphysics teach us that the notion of substance is wholly confused and imperfect, and that we have no other idea of any substance than as an aggregate of particular qualities, inhering in an unknown something. Matter, therefore, and spirit, are at bottom equally unknown, and we cannot determine what qualities may inhere in the one or in the other.

3   They likewise teach us that nothing can be decided *a priori* concerning any cause or effect; and that experience being the only source of our judgements of this nature, we cannot know from any other principle whether matter, by its structure or arrangement, may not be the cause of thought. Abstract reasonings cannot decide any question of fact or existence.

4   But admitting a spiritual substance to be dispersed throughout the universe, like the ethereal fire of the Stoics,[1] and to be the only inherent subject of thought, we have reason to conclude from analogy that nature uses it after the manner she does the other substance, matter. She employs it as a kind of paste or clay; modifies it into a variety of forms and existences; dissolves after a time each modification, and from its substance erects a new form. As the same material substance may successively compose the bodies of all animals, the same spiritual substance may compose their minds. Their consciousness, or that system of thought which they formed during life, may be continually dissolved by death. And nothing interests them in the new modification. The most positive asserters of the mortality of the soul never denied the immortality of its substance. And that an immaterial substance, as well as a material, may lose its memory or consciousness appears, in part, from experience, if the soul be immaterial.

5   Reasoning from the common course of nature, and without supposing any new interposition of the supreme cause, which ought always to be excluded from philosophy, what is incorruptible must also be ingenerable.[2] The soul therefore, if immortal, existed before our birth; and if the former existence no wise[3] concerned us, neither will the latter.

[1] *Stoics*: members of a school of philosophy founded *c.* 300 BC in Athens and committed to the ideals of virtue, endurance and self-sufficiency.

[2] *ingenerable*: incapable of being generated.

[3] *no wise*: in no way.

6   Animals undoubtedly feel, think, love, hate, will, and even reason, though in a more imperfect manner than men. Are their souls also immaterial and immortal?

II

7 Let us now consider the *moral* arguments, chiefly those derived from the justice of God, which is supposed to be farther interested in the farther punishment of the vicious and reward of the virtuous.

8   But these arguments are grounded on the supposition that God has attributes beyond what he has exerted in this universe, with which alone we are acquainted. Whence do we infer the existence of these attributes? It is very safe for us to affirm that whatever we know the Deity to have actually done, is best; but it is very dangerous to affirm that he must always do what to us seems best. In how many instances would this reasoning fail us with regard to the present world?

9   But if any purpose of nature be clear, we may affirm that the whole scope and intention of man's creation, so far as we can judge by natural reason, is limited to the present life. With how weak a concern, from the original inherent structure of the mind and passions, does he ever look farther? What comparison either for steadiness or efficacy, between so floating an idea, and the most doubtful persuasion of[4] any matter of fact that occurs in common life? There arise indeed in some minds some unaccountable terrors with regard to futurity;[5] but these would quickly vanish were they not artificially fostered by precept and education. And those who foster them, what is their motive? Only to gain a livelihood, and to acquire power and riches in this world. Their very zeal and industry therefore is an argument against them.

10   What cruelty, what iniquity, what injustice in nature, to confine all our concern, as well as all our knowledge, to the present life, if there be another scene still awaiting us, of infinitely greater consequence? Ought this barbarous deceit to be ascribed to a beneficent and wise being?

11   Observe with what exact proportion the task to be performed and the performing powers are adjusted throughout all nature. If the reason of man gives him great superiority above other animals, his necessities are proportionably multiplied upon him. His whole time, his whole capacity, activity, courage, and passion, find sufficient

---

[4] *doubtful persuasion of*: weakly held opinion concerning.
[5] *futurity*: the future.

19

employment in fencing against the miseries of his present condition, and frequently, nay almost always, are too slender for the business assigned them. A pair of shoes perhaps was never yet wrought to the highest degree of perfection which that commodity is capable of attaining. Yet it is necessary, at least very useful, that there should be some politicians and moralists, even some geometers,[6] historians, poets, and philosophers among mankind. The powers of men are no more superior to their wants, considered merely in this life, than those of foxes and hares are, compared to their wants and to their period of existence. The inference from parity of reason is therefore obvious. On the theory of the soul's mortality, the inferiority of women's capacity is easily accounted for. Their domestic life requires no higher faculties, either of mind or body. This circumstance vanishes and becomes absolutely insignificant, on the religious theory: the one sex has an equal task to perform with the other; their powers of reason and resolution ought also to have been equal, and both of them infinitely greater than at present.

12   As every effect implies a cause, and that another, till we reach the first cause of all, which is the Deity; everything that happens is ordained by him, and nothing can be the object of his punishment or vengeance. By what rule are punishments and rewards distributed? What is the divine standard of merit and demerit? Shall we suppose that human sentiments have place in the Deity? How bold that hypothesis. We have no conception of any other sentiments.

13   According to human sentiments, sense, courage, good manners, industry, prudence, genius, etc. are essential parts of personal merits. Shall we therefore erect an Elysium[7] for poets and heroes like that of the ancient mythology? Why confine all rewards to one species of virtue?

14   Punishment, without any proper end or purpose, is inconsistent with our ideas of goodness and justice, and no end can be served by it after the whole scene is closed.

15   Punishment, according to our conception, should bear some proportion to the offence. Why then eternal punishment for the temporary offences of so frail a creature as man? Can any one approve of Alexander's rage, who intended to exterminate a whole nation because they had seized his favourite horse Bucephalus?[8]

---

[6] *geometers*: engineers, surveyors, designers, architects or geometrists.
[7] *Elysium*: heaven in ancient Greek religion or mythology.
[8] Alexander the Great (356–323 BC): king of Macedonia, and conqueror of much of Asia Minor. The nation referred to is Lydia, east of the Caspian; the incident is described in Quintus Curtis's *History of Alexander*, 6.5.

16   Heaven and hell suppose two distinct species of men, the good and the bad; but the greatest part of mankind float between vice and virtue. Were one to go round the world with an intention of giving a good supper to the righteous, and a sound drubbing to the wicked, he would frequently be embarrassed in his choice, and would find that the merits and the demerits of most men and women scarcely amount to the value of either.

17   To suppose measures of approbation and blame different from the human confounds every thing. Whence do we learn that there is such a thing as moral distinctions, but from our own sentiments? What man who has not met with personal provocation (or what good-natured man who has) could inflict on crimes, from the sense of blame alone, even the common, legal, frivolous punishments? And does anything steel the breast of judges and juries against the sentiments of humanity but reflection on necessity and public interest? By the Roman law those who had been guilty of parricide[9] and confessed their crime, were put into a sack alone with an ape, a dog, and a serpent, and thrown into the river. Death alone was the punishment of those who denied their guilt, however fully proved. A criminal was tried before Augustus and condemned after a full conviction; but the humane emperor, when he put the last interrogatory, gave it such a turn as to lead the wretch into a denial of his guilt. *You surely*, said the prince, *did not kill your father.*[10] This lenity[11] suits our natural ideas of right even towards the greatest of all criminals, and even though it prevents so inconsiderable a sufferance. Nay even the most bigoted priest would naturally without reflection approve of it—provided the crime was not heresy or infidelity, for as these crimes hurt himself in his temporal interest and advantages, perhaps he may not be altogether so indulgent to them. The chief source of moral ideas is the reflection on the interest of human society. Ought these interests, so short, so frivolous, to be guarded by punishments eternal and infinite? The damnation of one man is an infinitely greater evil in the universe, than the subversion of a thousand millions of kingdoms. Nature has rendered human infancy peculiarly frail and mortal, as it were on purpose to refute the notion of a probationary state;[12] the half of mankind die before they are rational creatures.

[9] *parricide*: murder of one's father.

[10] The incident is described in Suetonius, *Lives of the Caesars*, 'Life of Augustus', ch. 3. Gaius Julius Caesar Octavianus Augustus (27 BC–14 AD) was the first emperor of Rome.

[11] *lenity*: leniency.

[12] *probationary state*: period in which assessment or testing takes place prior to punishment or reward.

III

18 The *physical* arguments from the analogy of nature are strong for the mortality of the soul, and are really the only philosophical arguments which ought to be admitted with regard to this question, or indeed any question of fact. Where any two objects are so closely connected that all alterations which we have ever seen in the one, are attended with proportionable alterations in the other, we ought to conclude by all rules of analogy, that, when there are still greater alterations produced in the former, and it is totally dissolved, there follows a total dissolution of the latter.

19 Sleep, a very small effect on the body, is attended with a temporary extinction, at least a great confusion in the soul. The weakness of the body and that of the mind in infancy are exactly proportioned: their vigour in manhood, their sympathetic disorder in sickness, their common gradual decay in old age. The step further seems unavoidable: their common dissolution in death. The last symptoms which the mind discovers are disorder, weakness, insensibility, and stupidity, the fore-runners of its annihilation. The farther progress of the same causes increasing, the same effects totally extinguish it.

20 Judging by the usual analogy of nature, no form can continue when transferred to a condition of life very different from the original one, in which it was placed. Trees perish in the water, fishes in the air, animals in the earth. Even so small a difference as that of climate is often fatal. What reason then to imagine that an immense alteration, such as is made on the soul by the dissolution of its body and all its organs of thought and sensation, can be effected without the dissolution of the whole? Everything is in common between soul and body. The organs of the one are all of them the organs of the other. The existence therefore of the one must be dependent on that of the other. The souls of animals are allowed to be mortal; and these bear so near a resemblance to the souls of men, that the analogy from one to the other forms a very strong argument. Their bodies are not more resembling; yet no one rejects the argument drawn from comparative anatomy. The metempsychosis[13] is therefore the only system of this kind that philosophy can so much as hearken to. Nothing in this world is perpetual, everything however seemingly firm is in contin-

---

[13] The (theory of) metempsychosis holds that souls pass from body to body ('transmigrate') upon the death of a body. In particular, that they can pass across species boundaries. Hume's point is not that he accepts this thesis, but that even this non-Christian view is better supported than the Christian one in which souls leave the material world entirely.

ual flux and change. The world itself gives symptoms of frailty and dissolution. How contrary to analogy, therefore, to imagine that one single form, seemingly the frailest of any, and from the slightest causes subject to the greatest disorders, is immortal and indissoluble? What daring theory is that! How lightly, not to say how rashly entertained!

21   How to dispose of the infinite number of posthumous existences ought also to embarrass the religious theory. Every planet in every solar system we are at liberty to imagine peopled with intelligent mortal beings, at least we can fix on no other supposition. For these, then, a new universe must every generation be created beyond the bounds of the present universe, or one must have been created at first so prodigiously wise as to admit of this continual influx of beings. Ought such bold suppositions to be received by any philosophy, and that merely on the pretence of a bare possibility? When it is asked whether *Agamemnon, Thersites, Hannibal, Varro*,[14] and every stupid clown that ever existed in Italy, Scythia, Bactria, or Guinea, are now alive, can any man think that a scrutiny of nature will furnish arguments strong enough to answer so strange a question in the affirmative? The want of argument without revelation sufficiently establishes the negative.

22   *Quanto facilius*, says Pliny,[15] *certiusque sibi quemque credere, ac specimen securitatis antigentali sumere experimento*. Our insensibility before the composition of the body, seems to natural reason a proof of a like state after dissolution.

23   Were our horrors of annihilation an original passion, not the effect of our general love of happiness, it would rather prove the mortality of the soul. For as nature does nothing in vain, she would never give us a horror against an impossible event. She may give us a horror against an unavoidable; yet the human species could not be preserved had not nature inspired us with an aversion toward it. All doctrines are to be suspected which are favoured by our passions, and the hopes and fears which gave rise to this doctrine are very obvious.

---

[14] Agamemnon and Thersites were Greeks who according to legend fought against Troy; Hannibal (247–183 BC) was the Carthaginian commander who, in the Second Punic War, led his army, with its elephants, across the Alps to invade Italy (218 BC); Gaius Terentius Varro was a Roman general defeated by Hannibal at Cannae in 216 BC.

[15] Pliny the Elder (23–79 AD): Roman administrator. This quotation (from his *Natural History* 7: 56) translates as: 'How much easier and more certain for each of us to trust in ourselves, and to derive our example of tranquility from our experience before birth.'

24   It is an infinite advantage in every controversy to defend the negative. If the question be out of the common experienced course of nature, this circumstance is almost, if not altogether, decisive. By what arguments or analogies can we prove any state of existence which no one ever saw, and which no way resembles any that ever was seen? Who will repose such trust in any pretended philosophy as to admit upon its testimony the reality of so marvellous a scene? Some new species of logic is requisite for that purpose, and some new faculties of the mind that may enable us to comprehend that logic.

25   Nothing could set in a fuller light the infinite obligations which mankind have to divine revelation, since we find that no other medium could ascertain this great and important truth.

Source: David Hume, *Of the Immortality of the Soul*, reproduced with the kind permission of the National Library of Scotland.

David Hume, *Of Suicide*

At the heart of this essay by Hume is a criticism of the 'sanctity of life' argument, widely appealed to in the moral condemnation of those who commit suicide. According to this, to take one's own life is to take a decision that belongs to God and to God alone. Hume was in fact an agnostic; but here he is trying to show that *even if* one adopts a religious stance, suicide must be regarded as morally permissible.

The essay opens with some general thoughts about the relation between religion, philosophy, and our ordinary emotions, viewpoints, and drives. It ends by rejecting several other reasons for condemning acts of suicide.

The text is based on Hume's hand-corrected proofs from the aborted 1755 publication (see the introduction to *Of the Immortality of the Soul*, the previous item in this anthology).

1   One considerable advantage that arises from philosophy consists in the sovereign antidote which it affords to superstition and false religion. All other remedies against that pestilent distemper are vain, or at least uncertain. Plain good sense and the practice of the world, which alone serve most purposes of life, are here found ineffectual.

History as well as daily experience afford instances of men endowed with the strongest capacity for business and affairs, who have all their lives crouched under slavery to the grossest superstition. Even gaiety and sweetness of temper, which infuse a balm into every other wound, afford no remedy to so virulent a poison, as we may particularly observe of the fair sex, who, though commonly possessed of their rich presents of nature, feel many of their joys blasted by this importunate intruder.

2   But when sound philosophy has once gained possession of the mind, superstition is effectually[16] excluded, and one may fairly affirm that her triumph over this enemy is more complete than over most of the vices and imperfections incident to human nature. Love or anger, ambition or avarice, have their root in the temper and affection, which the soundest reason is scarce ever able fully to correct, but superstition being founded on false opinion, must immediately vanish when true philosophy has inspired juster sentiments of superior powers. The contest is here more equal between the distemper and the medicine, and nothing can hinder the latter from proving effectual but its being false and sophisticated.

3   It will here be superfluous to magnify the merits of philosophy by displaying the pernicious tendency of that vice of which it cures the human mind. The superstitious man, says Tully, is miserable in every scene, in every incident in life.[17] Even sleep itself, which banishes all other cares of unhappy mortals, affords to him matter of new terror, while he examines his dreams, and finds in those visions of the night prognostications of future calamities.

4   I may add that though death alone can put a full period to his misery, he dares not fly to this refuge, but still prolongs a miserable existence from a vain fear lest he offend his Maker by using the power with which that beneficent being has endowed him. The presents of God and nature are ravished from us by this cruel enemy, and notwithstanding that one step would remove us from the regions of pain and sorrow, her menaces still chain us down to a hated being which she herself chiefly contributes to render miserable. It is observed by such as have been reduced by the calamities of life to the necessity of employing this fatal remedy, that if the unseasonable care of their friends deprive them of that species of death which they proposed to themselves, they seldom venture upon any other, or can

---

[16] *effectually*: effectively.

[17] Tully (106–43 BC): Roman statesman and philosopher, also known as (Marcus Tullius) Cicero. The passage cited is from *On Divination* 2:72.

summon up so much resolution a second time as to execute their purpose. So great is our horror of death that when it presents itself under any form besides that to which a man has endeavoured to reconcile his imagination, it acquires new terrors and overcomes his feeble courage. But when the menaces of superstition are joined to this natural timidity, no wonder it quite deprives men of all power over their lives, since even many pleasures and enjoyments, to which we are carried by a strong propensity, are torn from us by this inhuman tyrant. Let us here endeavour to restore men to their native liberty by examining all the common arguments against Suicide, and showing that that action may be free from every imputation of guilt or blame, according to the sentiments of all the ancient philosophers.

5   If suicide be criminal, it must be a transgression of our duty either to God, our neighbour, or ourselves.

6   To prove that suicide is no transgression of our duty to God, the following considerations may perhaps suffice. In order to govern the material world, the almighty Creator has established general and immutable laws, by which all bodies, from the greatest planet to the smallest particle of matter, are maintained in their proper sphere and function. To govern the animal world, he has endowed all living creatures with bodily and mental powers; with senses, passions, appetites, memory, and judgement, by which they are impelled or regulated in that course of life to which they are destined. These two distinct principles of the material and animal world, continually encroach upon each other, and mutually retard or forward each other's operation. The powers of men and of all other animals are restrained and directed by the nature and qualities of the surrounding bodies, and the modifications and actions of these bodies are incessantly altered by the operation of all animals. Man is stopped by rivers in his passage over the surface of the earth; and rivers, when properly directed, lend their force to the motion of machines, which serve to the use of man. But though the provinces of the material and animal powers are not kept entirely separate, there results from thence no discord or disorder in the creation; on the contrary, from the mixture, union, and contrast of all the various powers of inanimate bodies and living creatures, arises that sympathy, harmony, and proportion, which affords the surest argument of supreme wisdom.

7   The providence of the Deity appears not immediately in any operation, but governs everything by those general and immutable laws, which have been established from the beginning of time. All events, in one sense, may be pronounced the action of the Almighty. They all

proceed from those powers with which he has endowed his creatures. A house which falls by its own weight, is not brought to ruin by his providence more than one destroyed by the hands of men; nor are the human faculties less his workmanship than the laws of motion and gravitation. When the passions play, when the judgement dictates, when the limbs obey, this is all the operation of God, and upon these animate principles, as well as upon the inanimate, has he established the government of the universe. Every event is alike important in the eyes of that infinite being, who takes in at one glance the most distant regions of space and remotest periods of time. There is no event, however important to us, which he has exempted from the general laws that govern the universe, or which he has peculiarly reserved for his own immediate action and operation. The revolution of states and empires depends upon the smallest caprice or passion of single men; and the lives of men are shortened or extended by the smallest accident of air or diet, sunshine or tempest. Nature still continues her progress and operation; and if general laws be ever broke by particular volitions of the Deity, it is after a manner which entirely escapes human observation. As, on the one hand, the elements and other inanimate parts of the creation carry on their action without regard to the particular interest and situation of men, so men are entrusted to their own judgement and discretion in the various shocks of matter, and may employ every faculty with which they are endowed, in order to provide for their ease, happiness, or preservation.

8   What is the meaning then of that principle that a man who, tired of life and hunted by pain and misery, bravely overcomes all the natural terrors of death and makes his escape from this cruel scene; that such a man I say, has incurred the indignation of his Creator by encroaching on the office of divine providence, and disturbing the order of the universe? Shall we assert that the Almighty has reserved to himself in any peculiar manner the disposal of the lives of men, and has not submitted that event, in common with others, to the general laws by which the universe is governed? This is plainly false. The lives of men depend upon the same laws as the lives of all other animals, and these are subjected to the general laws of matter and motion. The fall of a tower, or the infusion of a poison, will destroy a man equally with the meanest creature. An inundation sweeps away every thing without distinction that comes within the reach of its fury. Since therefore the lives of men are forever dependent on the general laws of matter and motion, is a man's disposing of his life criminal, because in every case it is criminal to encroach upon these

laws, or disturb their operation? But this seems absurd. All animals are entrusted to their own prudence and skill for their conduct in the world, and have full authority as far as their power extends, to alter all the operations of nature. Without the exercise of this authority they could not subsist a moment. Every action, every motion of a man, innovates on the order of some parts of matter, and diverts from their ordinary course the general laws of motion. Putting together, therefore, these conclusions, we find that human life depends upon the general laws of matter and motion, and that it is no encroachment on the office of providence to disturb or alter these general laws. Has not every one, of consequence, the free disposal of his own life? And may he not lawfully employ that power with which nature has endowed him?

9   In order to destroy the evidence of this conclusion, we must show a reason why this particular case is excepted. Is it because human life is of such great importance that it is a presumption for human prudence to dispose of it? But the life of a man is of no greater importance to the universe than that of an oyster. And were it of ever so great importance, the order of human nature has actually submitted it to human prudence, and reduced us to a necessity, in every incident, of determining concerning it. Were the disposal of human life so much reserved as the peculiar province of the Almighty that it were an encroachment on his right for men to dispose of their own lives, it would be equally criminal to act for the preservation of life as for its destruction. If I turn aside a stone which is falling upon my head, I disturb the course of nature, and I invade the peculiar province of the Almighty, by lengthening out my life beyond the period which by the general laws of matter and motion he had assigned to it. A hair, a fly, an insect is able to destroy this mighty being whose life is of such importance. Is it an absurdity to suppose that human prudence may lawfully dispose of what depends on such insigni-ficant causes? It would be no crime in me to divert the Nile or Danube from its course, were I able to effect such purposes. Where then is the crime of turning a few ounces of blood from their natural channel?

10   Do you imagine that I repine at providence or curse my creation, because I go out of life, and put a period to a being, which, were it to continue, would render me miserable? Far be such sentiments from me; I am only convinced of a matter of fact, which you your-self acknowledge possible, that human life may be unhappy, and that my existence, if further prolonged, would become ineligible. But I thank providence, both for the good which I have already enjoyed, and for the power with which I am endowed of escaping the ill that

threatens me.[18] To you it belongs to repine at providence, who foolishly imagine that you have no such power, and who must still prolong a hated being, though loaded with pain and sickness, with shame and poverty.

11   Do not you teach that when any ill befalls me, though by the malice of my enemies, I ought to be resigned to providence; and that the actions of men are the operations of the Almighty as much as the actions of inanimate beings? When I fall upon my own sword, therefore, I receive my death equally from the hands of the Deity as if it had proceeded from a lion, a precipice, or a fever. The submission which you require to providence, in every calamity that befalls me, excludes not human skill and industry, if possible by their means I can avoid or escape the calamity. And why may I not employ one remedy as well as another? If my life be not my own, it were criminal for me to put it in danger, as well as to dispose of it. Nor could one man deserve the appellation of hero, whom glory or friendship transports into the greatest dangers, and another merit the reproach of wretch or miscreant who puts a period to his life, from the same or like motives. There is no being which possesses any power or faculty that it receives not from its Creator; nor is there anyone which, by ever so irregular an action, can encroach upon the plan of his providence, or disorder the universe. Its operations are his works equally with that chain of events which it invades, and whichever principle prevails, we may for that very reason conclude it to be most favoured by him. Be it animate or inanimate, rational or irrational, it is all a case: its power is still derived from the supreme Creator, and is alike comprehended in the order of his providence. When the horror of pain prevails over the love of life, when a voluntary action anticipates the effects of blind causes, it is only in consequence of those powers and principles which he has implanted in his creatures. Divine providence is still inviolate, and placed far beyond the reach of human injuries.

12   It is impious, says the old *Roman* superstition, to divert rivers from their course, or invade the prerogatives of nature.[19] It is impious says the *French* superstition, to inoculate for the smallpox, or usurp the business of providence by voluntarily producing distemper and maladies. It is impious, says the modern *European* superstition,

---

[18] *Agamus Deo gratius, quod nemo in vita teneri potest.*, *Letters from a Stoic*, 12.* (Translation: 'Let us thank God that no one can be held a prisoner in life.' Lucius Annaeus Seneca, 4 BC–65 AD, was a Roman statesman and philosopher who was required to commit suicide by the Roman emperor, Nero, a few years after writing these words.)

[19] Tacitus, *Annals* 1: 79.*

to put a period to our own life and thereby rebel against our Creator; and why not impious, say I, to build houses, cultivate the ground, or sail upon the ocean? In all these actions we employ our powers of mind and body, to produce some innovation in the course of nature; and in none of them do we any more. They are all of them, therefore, equally innocent or equally criminal.

13   *But you are placed by providence, like a sentinel, in a particular station, and when you desert it without being recalled, you are equally guilty of rebellion against your almighty sovereign, and have incurred his displeasure.* I ask, why do you conclude that providence has placed me in this station? For my part I find that I owe my birth to a long chain of causes, of which many and even the principal depended upon voluntary actions of men. *But providence guided all these causes, and nothing happens in the universe without its consent and co-operation.* If so, then neither does my death, however voluntary, happen without its consent; and whenever pain or sorrow so far overcome my patience as to make me tired of life, I may conclude that I am recalled from my station in the clearest and most express terms. It is providence, surely, that has placed me at this present in this chamber; but may I not leave it when I think proper, without being liable to the imputation of having deserted my post or station? When I shall be dead, the principles of which I am composed will still perform their part in the universe, and will be equally useful in the grand fabric as when they composed this individual creature. The difference to the whole will be no greater than between my being in a chamber and in the open air. The one change is of more importance to me than the other; but not more so to the universe.

14   It is a kind of blasphemy to imagine that any created being can disturb the order of the world, or invade the business of Providence! It supposes, that that being possesses powers and faculties, which it received not from its creator, and which are not subordinate to his government and authority. A man may disturb society no doubt, and thereby incur the displeasure of the Almighty. But the government of the world is placed far beyond his reach and violence. And how does it appear that the Almighty is displeased with those actions that disturb society? By the principles which he has implanted in human nature, and which inspire us with a sentiment of remorse if we ourselves have been guilty of such actions, and with that of blame and disapprobation if we ever observe them in others. Let us now examine, according to the method proposed, whether Suicide be of this kind of actions, and be a breach of our duty to our neighbour and to society.

15   A man who retires from life does no harm to society: he only ceases to do good, which, if it is an injury, is of the lowest kind. All our obligations to do good to society seem to imply something reciprocal. I receive the benefits of society, and therefore ought to promote its interests; but when I withdraw myself altogether from society, can I be bound any longer? But allowing that our obligations to do good were perpetual, they have certainly some bounds. I am not obliged to do a small good to society at the expense of a great harm to myself. Why then should I prolong a miserable existence because of some frivolous advantage which the public may perhaps receive from me? If upon account of age and infirmities I may lawfully resign any office and employ my time altogether in fencing against these calamities, and alleviating, as much as possible, the miseries of my future life, why may I not cut short these miseries at once by an action which is no more prejudicial to society? But suppose that it is no longer in my power to promote the interest of the public; suppose that I am a burden to it; suppose that my life hinders some person from being much more useful to the public. In such cases, my resignation of life must not only be innocent, but laudable. And most people who lie under any temptation to abandon existence are in some such situation; those who have health, or power, or authority, have commonly better reason to be in humour with the world.

16   A man is engaged in a conspiracy for the public interest; is seized upon suspicion; is threatened with the rack, and knows from his own weakness that the secret will be extorted from him. Could such a one consult the public interest better than by putting a quick period to a miserable life? This was the case of the famous and brave Strozzi of Florence.[20]

17   Again, suppose a malefactor is justly condemned to a shameful death; can any reason be imagined, why he may not anticipate his punishment, and save himself all the anguish of thinking on its dreadful approaches? He invades the business of providence no more than the magistrate did, who ordered his execution; and his voluntary death is equally advantageous to society, by ridding it of a pernicious member.

18   That suicide may often be consistent with interest and with our duty to ourselves, no one can question, who allows that age, sickness, or misfortune, may render life a burden, and make it worse

---

[20] Filippo Strozzi (1488–1538) is alleged to have committed suicide rather than abandon the republican cause against the Medici dynasty.

even than annihilation. I believe that no man ever threw away life while it was worth keeping. For such is our natural horror of death that small motives will never be able to reconcile us to it; and though perhaps the situation of a man's health or fortune did not seem to require this remedy, we may at least be assured that any one who, without apparent reason, has had recourse to it, was cursed with such an incurable depravity or gloominess of temper as must poison all enjoyment, and render him equally miserable as if he had been loaded with the most grievous misfortunes.

19   If suicide be supposed a crime, it is only cowardice can impel us to it. If it be no crime, both prudence and courage should engage us to rid ourselves at once of existence when it becomes a burden. It is the only way that we can then be useful to society, by setting an example which, if imitated, would preserve to everyone his chance for happiness in life, and would effectually free him from all danger of misery.[21]

Source: David Hume, *Of Suicide*, reproduced with the kind permission of the National Library of Scotland.

---

[21] It would be easy to prove that suicide is as lawful under the Christian dispensation as it was to the heathens. There is not a single text of scripture which prohibits it. That great and infallible rule of faith and practice, which must control all philosophy and human reasoning, has left us in this particular to our natural liberty. Resignation to providence is indeed recommended in scripture; but that implies only submission to ills that are unavoidable, not to such as may be remedied by prudence or courage. *Thou shalt not kill* is evidently meant to exclude only the killing of others, over whose life we have no authority. That this precept, like most of the scripture precepts, must be modified by reason and common sense, is plain from the practice of magistrates, who punish criminals capitally, notwithstanding the letter of the law. But were this commandment ever to express against suicide, it would now have no authority. For all the law of Moses is abolished, except so far as it is established by the law of nature; and we have already endeavoured to prove that suicide is not prohibited by that law. In all cases Christians and heathens are precisely upon the same footing. Cato and Brutus, Arria and Portia acted heroically; those who imitate their example ought to receive the same praises from posterity. The power of committing suicide is regard by Pliny as an advantage which men possess even above the deity himself. *Deus non sibi potest mortem consciscere, si velit, quod homini dedit optimum in tantis vitae poenis.* ['God cannot, even if wishes, commit suicide, the supreme boon that he has bestowed on man among all the penalties of life'] *Natural History*, 2.5.77.*

Jean-Jacques Rousseau, extracts from *Profession of Faith of a Savoyard Vicar*

The *Profession de foi d'un vicaire savoyard* is embedded in Book IV of Rousseau's influential work on education, *Émile*. It figures within this larger book as a discussion of religious education, but is in effect a self-contained statement of Rousseau's religious attitude. It is this segment of the book that led to *Émile* being condemned and even burned in several European cities, forcing its author into exile from France.

The profession is recollected, by the narrator of *Émile*, as having been made to him as a young boy in the Italian Alps by an exiled priest from the Savoy region of what are now the French Alps. Rousseau, in his *Confessions*, does describe having met and been profoundly influenced by two priests in his own youth. But in several letters he says that the profession of faith is in effect his own.

There are two parts to the profession. In the first, the priest offers a unique form of deism as an alternative to agnosticism, appealing to inner sentiment as much as the outer senses as his guide. In the second he rejects revealed religion, and in particular Catholicism, though at the same time endorses many of the non-revelatory elements of the New Testament. The first half alienated him from the mainstream of the Enlightenment; the second led to his condemnation by Church authorities.

The extracts below are drawn mainly from the first half; the final one is from the second. The subheadings have been added.

The priest's journey

My child, do not expect either learned speeches or profound reasonings from me. I am not a great philosopher, and I care little to be one. But I sometimes have good sense, and I always love the truth. I do not want to argue with you or even attempt to convince you. It is enough for me to reveal to you what I think in the simplicity of my heart. Consult yours during my speech. This is all I ask of you. If I am mistaken, it is in good faith. That is enough for my error not to be imputed to crime. If you were to be similarly mistaken, there would be little evil in that. Reason is common to us, and we have the same interest in listening to it. If I think well, why would you not think as do I?

I was born poor and a peasant, destined by my station to cultivate the earth. But it was thought to be a finer thing for me to learn to earn my bread in the priest's trade, and the means were found to permit me to study. Certainly neither my parents nor I thought very much of seeking what was good, true, and useful, but rather we thought of what had to be known in order to be ordained. I learned what I was supposed to learn; I said what I was supposed to say. I committed myself as I was supposed to, and I was made a priest. But it was not long before I sensed that in obliging myself not to be a man I had promised more than I could keep.

[. . .]

From my youth on I have respected marriage as the first and the holiest institution of nature. Having taken away my right to submit myself to it, I resolved not to profane it; for in spite of my classes and studies, I had always led a uniform and simple life, and I had preserved all the clarity of the original understanding in my mind. The maxims of the world had not obscured it, and my poverty removed me from the temptations dictated by the sophisms of vice.

This resolve was precisely what destroyed me. My respect for the bed of others left my faults exposed. The scandal had to be expiated. Arrested, interdicted, driven out, I was far more the victim of my scruples than of my incontinence; and I had occasion to understand, from the reproaches with which my disgrace was accompanied, that often one need only aggravate the fault to escape the punishment.

A few such experiences lead a reflective mind a long way. Seeing the ideas that I had of the just, the decent, and all the duties of man overturned by gloomy observations, I lost each day one of the opinions I had received. Since those opinions that remained were no longer sufficient to constitute together a self-sustaining body, I felt the obviousness of the principles gradually becoming dimmer in my mind. And finally reduced to no longer knowing what to think, I reached the same point where you are, with the difference that my incredulity, the late fruit of a riper age, had been more painfully formed and ought to have been more difficult to destroy.

[. . .]

I meditated therefore on the sad fate of mortals, floating on this sea of human opinions without rudder or compass and delivered to their stormy passions without any other guide than an inexperienced pilot who is ignorant of his route and knows neither where he is coming from nor where he is going. I said to myself, "I love the truth, I seek it and cannot recognize it. Let it be revealed to me, and I shall remain attached to it. Why must it hide itself from the eagerness of a heart made to adore it?"

Although I have often experienced greater evils, I have never led a life so constantly disagreeable as during those times of perplexity and anxiety, when I ceaselessly wandered from doubt to doubt and brought back from my long meditations only uncertainty, obscurity, and contradictions about the cause of my being and the principle of my duties.

[. . .]

What doubled my confusion was that I was born in a church which decides everything and permits no doubt; therefore, the rejection of a single point made me reject all the rest, and the impossibility of accepting so many absurd decisions also detached me from those which were not absurd. By being told "Believe everything," I was prevented from believing anything, and I no longer knew where to stop.

I consulted the philosophers. I leafed through their books. I examined their various opinions. I found them all to be proud, assertive, dogmatic (even in their pretended skepticism), ignorant of nothing, proving nothing, mocking one another; and this last point, which was common to all, appeared to me the only one about which they are all right. Triumphant when they attack, they are without force in defending themselves. If you ponder their reasoning, they turn out to be good only at destructive criticism. If you count votes, each is reduced to his own. They agree only to dispute. Listening to them was not the means of getting out of my uncertainty.

[. . .]

If the philosophers were in a position to discover the truth, who among them would take an interest in it? Each knows well that his system is no better founded than the others. But he maintains it because it is his. There is not a single one of them who, if he came to know the true and the false, would not prefer the lie he has found to the truth discovered by another. Where is the philosopher who would not gladly deceive mankind for his own glory? Where is the one who in the secrecy of his heart sets himself any other goal than that of distinguishing himself? Provided that he raises himself above the vulgar, provided that he dims the brilliance of his competitors, what more does he ask? The essential thing is to think differently from others. Among believers he is an atheist; among atheists he would be a believer.

The first fruit I drew from these reflections was to learn to limit my researches to what was immediately related to my interest, to leave myself in a profound ignorance of all the rest, and to worry myself to the point of doubt only about things it was important for me to know.

I understood further that the philosophers, far from delivering me from my useless doubts, would only cause those which tormented me to multiply and would resolve none of them. Therefore, I took another guide, and I said to myself, "Let us consult the inner light; it will lead me

35

astray less than they lead me astray; or at least my error will be my own, and I will deprave myself less in following my own illusions than in yielding to their lies."

[. . .]

Taking the love of the truth as my whole philosophy, and as my whole method an easy and simple rule that exempts me from the vain subtlety of arguments, I pick up again on the basis of this rule the examination of the knowledge that interests me. I am resolved to accept as evident all knowledge to which in the sincerity of my heart I cannot refuse my consent; to accept as true all that which appears to me to have a necessary connection with this first knowledge; and to leave all the rest in uncertainty without rejecting it or accepting it and without tormenting myself to clarify it if it leads to nothing useful for practice.

A sensing self

[. . .]

My glance must first be turned toward myself in order to know the instrument I wish to use and how far I can trust its use.

I exist, and I have senses by which I am affected. This is the first truth that strikes me and to which I am forced to acquiesce.

[. . .]

My sensations take place in me, since they make me sense my existence; but their cause is external to me, since they affect me without my having anything to do with it, and I have nothing to do with producing or annihilating them. Therefore, I clearly conceive that my sensation, which is in me, and its cause or its object, which is outside of me, are not the same thing.

Thus, not only do I exist, but there exist other beings—the objects of my sensations; and even if these objects were only ideas, it is still true that these ideas are not me.

Now, all that I sense outside of me and which acts on my senses, I call *matter*; and all the portions of matter which I conceive to be joined together in individual beings, I call *bodies*. Thus all the disputes of idealists and materialists signify nothing to me. Their distinctions concerning the appearance and reality of bodies are chimeras.

Already I am as sure of the universe's existence as of my own. Next, I reflect on the objects of my sensations; and, finding in myself the faculty of comparing them, I sense myself endowed with an active force which I did not before know I had.

To perceive is to sense; to compare is to judge. Judging and sensing are not the same thing. By sensation, objects are presented to me separated, isolated, such as they are in nature. By comparison I move them, I transport them, and, so to speak, I superimpose them on one another in order to pronounce on their difference or their likeness and generally on all their relations. [. . .] This passive being will sense each object separately, or it will even sense the total object formed by the two; but, having no force to bend them back on one another, it will never compare them, it will not judge them.

To see two objects at once is not to see their relations or to judge their differences. To perceive several objects as separate from one another is not to number them. I can at the same instant have the idea of a large stick and of a small stick without comparing them and without judging that one is smaller than the other, just as I can see my entire hand at once without making the count of my fingers. These comparative ideas, *larger* and *smaller*, just like the numerical ideas of *one*, *two*, etc., certainly do not belong to the sensations, although my mind produces them only on the occasion of my sensations.

[. . .]

Add to that a reflection I am sure will strike you when you have thought about it. It is that if we were purely passive in the use of our senses, there would be no communication among them. It would be impossible for us to know that the body we touch and the object we see are the same. Either we would never sense anything outside of us, or there would be five sensible substances for us whose identity we would have no means of perceiving.

Let this or that name be given to this force of my mind which brings together and compares my sensations; let it be called *attention*, *meditation*, *reflection*, or whatever one wishes. [. . .] Without being master of sensing or not sensing, I am the master of giving more or less examination to what I sense.

Therefore, I am not simply a sensitive and passive being but an active and intelligent being; and whatever philosophy may say about it, I shall dare to pretend to the honor of thinking. [. . .]

God and His properties

Having, so to speak, made certain of myself, I begin to look outside of myself, and I consider myself with a sort of shudder, cast out and lost in this vast universe, as if drowned in the immensity of beings, without knowing anything about what they are either in themselves or in relation to me. I study them, I observe them, and the first object which presents itself to me for comparison with them is myself.

37

Everything I perceive with the senses is matter; and I deduce all the essential properties of matter from the sensible qualities that make me perceive it and are inseparable from it. I see it now in motion and now at rest, from which I infer that neither rest nor motion is essential to it. But motion, since it is an action, is the effect of a cause of which rest is only the absence. Therefore, when nothing acts on matter, it does not move; and by the very fact that it is neutral to rest and to motion, its natural state is to be at rest.

I perceive in bodies two sorts of motion—communicated motion and spontaneous or voluntary motion. In the first the cause of motion is external to the body moved; and in the second it is within it.

[. . .]

You will ask me how I know that there are spontaneous motions. I shall tell you that I know it because I sense it. I want to move my arm, and I move it without this movement's having another immediate cause than my will. It would be vain to try to use reason to destroy this sentiment in me. It is stronger than any evidence. One might just as well try to prove to me that I do not exist.

If there were no spontaneity in the actions of men or in anything which takes place on earth, one would only be more at a loss to imagine the first cause of all motion. As for me, I sense myself to be so persuaded that the natural state of matter is to be at rest and that by itself it has no force for acting, that when I see a body in motion, I judge immediately either that it is an animate body or that this motion has been communicated to it. My mind rejects all acquiescence to the idea of unorganized matter moving itself or producing some action.

Meanwhile, this visible universe is matter, scattered and dead matter which [. . .] is in motion; and in its motion, which is regular, uniform, and subjected to constant laws, it contains nothing of that liberty appearing in the spontaneous motions of man and the animals. [. . .] Therefore there is some cause of its motions external to it, one which I do not perceive. But inner persuasion makes this cause so evident to my senses that I cannot see the sun rotate without imagining a force that pushes it; or if the earth turns, I believe I sense a hand that makes it turn.

[. . .]

The first causes of motion are not in matter. It receives motion and communicates it, but it does not produce it. The more I observe the action and the reaction of the forces of nature acting on one another, the more I find that one must always go back from effects to effects to some will as first cause; for to suppose an infinite regress of causes is to suppose no cause at all. In a word, every motion not produced by another

38

can come only from a spontaneous, voluntary action. Inanimate bodies act only by motion, and there is no true action without will. This is my first principle. I believe therefore that a will moves the universe and animates nature. This is my first dogma, or my first article of faith.

How does a will produce a physical and corporeal action? I do not know, but I experience within myself that it does so. I want to act, and I act. I want to move my body, and my body moves. But that an inanimate body at rest should succeed in moving itself or in producing motion—that is incomprehensible and without example. The will is known to me by its acts, not by its nature. I know this will as a cause of motion; but to conceive of matter as productive of motion [. . .] is to conceive of absolutely nothing.

[. . .]

If moved matter shows me a will, matter moved according to certain laws shows me an intelligence. This is my second article of faith. To act, to compare, and to choose are operations of an active and thinking being. Therefore this being exists. "Where do you see him existing?" you are going to say to me. Not only in the heavens which turn, not only in the star which gives us light, not only in myself, but in the ewe which grazes, in the bird which flies, in the stone which falls, in the leaf carried by the wind.

[. . .]

Let us compare the particular ends, the means, the ordered relations of every kind. Then let us listen to our inner sentiment. What healthy mind can turn aside its testimony; to which unprejudiced eyes does the sensible order not proclaim a supreme intelligence; and how many sophisms must be piled up before it is impossible to recognize the harmony of the beings and the admirable concurrences of each piece in the preservation of the others? They can talk to me all they want about combination and chance. Of what use is it to you to reduce me to silence if you cannot lead me to persuasion, and how will you take away from me the involuntary sentiment that always gives you the lie in spite of myself? If organized bodies were combined fortuitously in countless ways before taking on constant forms, if at the outset there were formed stomachs without mouths, feet without heads, hands without arms, imperfect organs of every kind which have perished for want of being able to preserve themselves, why do none of these unformed attempts strike our glance any longer, why did nature finally prescribe laws to itself to which it was not subjected at the outset? I should not, I agree, be surprised that a thing happens, if it is possible and the difficulty of its occurrence is compensated for by the number of throws of the dice. Nevertheless, if someone were to come to me and say that print thrown around at random had produced the *Aeneid* all in order,

I would not deign to take a step to verify the lie. "You forget," I shall be told, "the number of throws." But how many of those throws must I assume in order to make the combination credible? As for me, seeing only a single throw, I can give odds of infinity to one that what it produced is not the result of chance. [. . .]

I believe therefore that the world is governed by a powerful and wise will. I see it or, rather, I sense it; and that is something important for me to know. But is this same world eternal or created? Is there a single principle of things? Or, are there two or many of them, and what is their nature? I know nothing about all this, and what does it matter to me? As soon as this knowledge has something to do with my interests, I shall make an effort to acquire it. Until then I renounce idle questions which may agitate my *amour-propre* but are useless for my conduct and are beyond my reason.

Always remember that I am not teaching my sentiment; I am revealing it. Whether matter is eternal or created, whether there is or is not a passive principle, it is in any event certain that the whole is one and proclaims a single intelligence; for I see nothing which is not ordered according to the same system and does not contribute to the same end—namely, the preservation of the whole in its established order. This Being which wills and is powerful, this Being active in itself, this Being, whatever it may be, which moves the universe and orders all things, I call *God*. I join to this name the ideas of intelligence, power, and will which I have brought together, and that of goodness which is their necessary consequence. But I do not as a result know better the Being to which I have given them; it is hidden equally from my senses and from my understanding. The more I think about it, the more I am confused. I know very certainly that it exists, and that it exists by itself. I know that my existence is subordinated to its existence, and that all things known to me are in absolutely the same situation. I perceive God everywhere in His works. I sense Him in me; I see Him all around me. But as soon as I want to contemplate Him in Himself, as soon as I want to find out where He is, what He is, what His substance is, He escapes me, and my clouded mind no longer perceives anything.

[. . .]

Our position in the universe and in society

After having discovered those attributes of the divinity by which I know its existence, I return to myself and I try to learn what rank I occupy in the order of things that the divinity governs and I can examine. I find myself by my species incontestably in the first rank; for by my will and by the instruments in my power for executing it, I have more force for acting on all the bodies surrounding me, for yielding to or eluding their actions as I please, than any of them has for acting on me against my will by physical impulsion alone; and by my intelligence I am the only one that has a view of the whole. What being here on earth besides man is able to observe all the others, to measure, calculate, and foresee their movements and their effects, and to join, so to speak, the sentiment of common existence to that of its individual existence? What is there so ridiculous about thinking that everything is made for me, if I am the only one who is able to relate everything to himself?

[. . .]

The effect of this reflection is less to make me proud than to touch me; for this state is not of my choice, and it was not due to the merit of a being who did not yet exist. Can I see myself thus distinguished without congratulating myself on filling this honorable post and without blessing the hand which placed me in it? From my first return to myself there is born in my heart a sentiment of gratitude and benediction for the Author of my species; and from this sentiment my first homage to the beneficent divinity. I adore the supreme power, and I am moved by its benefactions. I do not need to be taught this worship: it is dictated to me by nature itself. Is it not a natural consequence of self-love to honor what protects us and to love what wishes us well?

But when next I seek to know my individual place in my species, and I consider its various ranks and the men who fill them, what happens to me? What a spectacle! Where is the order I had observed? The picture of nature had presented me with only harmony and proportion; that of mankind presents me with only confusion and disorder! Concert reigns among the elements, and men are in chaos! The animals are happy; their king alone is miserable. O wisdom, where are your laws? O providence, is it thus that you rule the world? Beneficent Being, what has become of your power? I see evil on earth.

Would you believe, my good friend, that from these gloomy reflections and these apparent contradictions there were formed in my mind the sublime ideas of the soul which had not until then resulted from my researches? In meditating on the nature of man, I believed I discovered in it two distinct principles; one of which raised him to the study of eternal truths, to the love of justice and moral beauty, and to the regions of the intellectual world whose contemplation is the wise man's delight; while the other took him basely into himself, subjected him to the empire of the senses and to the passions which are their ministers, and by means of these hindered all that the sentiment of the former inspired in him.

[. . .]

41

The more I reflect on thought and on the nature of the human mind, the more I find that the reasoning of materialists resembles that of [a] deaf man. They are indeed deaf to the inner voice crying out to them in a tone difficult not to recognize. A machine does not think; there is neither motion nor figure which produces reflection. Something in you seeks to break the bonds constraining it. [. . .] Your sentiments, your desires, your uneasiness, even your pride have another principle than this narrow body in which you sense yourself enchained.

No material being is active by itself, and I am. One may very well argue with me about this; but I sense it, and this sentiment that speaks to me is stronger than the reason combating it. I have a body on which other bodies act and which acts on them. This reciprocal action is not doubtful. But my will is independent of my senses; I consent or I resist; I succumb or I conquer; and I sense perfectly within myself when I do what I wanted to do or when all I am doing is giving way to my passions. I always have the power to will, I do not always have the force to execute. When I abandon myself to temptations, I act according to the impulsion of external objects. When I reproach myself for this weakness, I listen only to my will. I am enslaved because of my vices and free because of my remorse. The sentiment of my freedom is effaced in me only when I become depraved and finally prevent the voice of the soul from being raised against the law of the body.

[. . .]

Doubtless, I am not free not to want my own good; I am not free to want what is bad for me. But it is in this precisely that my freedom consists—my being able to will only what is suitable to me, or what I deem to be such, without anything external to me determining me. Does it follow that I am not my own master, because I am not the master of being somebody else than me?

The principle of every action is in the will of a free being. [. . .] Man is therefore free in his actions and as such is animated by an immaterial substance. This is my third article of faith. From these three you will easily deduce all the others without my continuing to count them out.

If man is active and free, he acts on his own. All that he does freely does not enter into the ordered system of providence and cannot be imputed to it. Providence does not will the evil a man does in abusing the freedom it gives him; but it does not prevent him from doing it, whether because this evil, coming from a being so weak, is nothing in its eyes, or because it could not prevent it without hindering his freedom and doing a greater evil by degrading his nature. It has made him free in order that by choice he do not evil but good. It has put him in a position to make this choice by using well the faculties with which it has endowed him. But it has limited his strength to such an extent that the abuse of the freedom it reserves for him cannot disturb the general order. The evil that man does falls back on him without changing anything in the system of the world, without preventing the human species from preserving itself in spite of itself. To complain about God's not preventing man from doing evil is to complain about His having given him an excellent nature, about His having put in man's actions the morality which ennobles them, about His having given him the right to virtue. The supreme enjoyment is in satisfaction with oneself; it is in order to deserve this satisfaction that we are placed on earth and endowed with freedom, that we are tempted by the passions and restrained by conscience. What more could divine power itself do for us? Could it make our nature contradictory and give the reward for having done well to him who did not have the power to do evil? What! To prevent man from being wicked, was it necessary to limit him to instinct and make him a beast? No, God of my soul, I shall never reproach You for having made him in Your image, so that I can be free, good, and happy like You!

[. . .]

Man, seek the author of evil no longer. It is yourself. No evil exists other than that which you do or suffer, and both come to you from yourself. [. . .]

God [. . .] owes His creatures [. . .] all He promises them in giving them being. Now, to give them the idea of a good and to make them feel the need of it is to promise it to them. The more I return within myself, and the more I consult myself, the more I see these words written in my soul: *Be just and you will be happy.* That simply is not so, however, considering the present state of things: the wicked man prospers, and the just man remains oppressed. Also, see what indignation is kindled in us when this expectation is frustrated! Conscience is aroused and complains about its Author. It cries out to Him in moaning, "Thou hast deceived me!"

"I have deceived you, rash man! And who told you so? Is your soul annihilated? Have you ceased to exist? [. . .] No, you are going to live, and it is then that I shall keep all the promises I have made you."

From the complaints of impatient mortals, one would say that God owes them the recompense before they have deserved it, and that He is obliged to pay their virtue in advance. O, let us be good in the first place, and then we shall be happy. Let us not demand the prize before the victory nor the wage before the work. It is not at the starting block, said Plutarch, that the victors in our sacred games are crowned; it is after they have gone around the track.

If the soul is immaterial, it can survive the body; and if it survives the body, providence is justified. If I had no proof of the immateriality of the soul other than the triumph of the wicked and the oppression of the just in this world, that alone would prevent me from doubting it. So shocking a dissonance in the universal harmony would make me seek to resolve it. I would say to myself, "Everything does not end with life for us; everything returns to order at death." [. . .]

But what is this life, and is the soul immortal by its nature? My limited understanding conceives nothing without limits. All that is called infinite escapes me. What can I deny and affirm, what argument can I make about that which I cannot conceive? I believe that the soul survives the body long enough for the maintenance of order. Who knows whether that is long enough for it to last forever? However, whereas I can conceive how the body wears out and is destroyed by the division of its parts, I cannot conceive of a similar destruction of the thinking being; and, not imagining how it can die, I presume that it does not die. Since this presumption consoles me and contains nothing unreasonable, why would I be afraid of yielding to it?

[. . .]

[The good] will be happy, because their Author, the Author of all justice, having created them as sensitive beings did not create them to suffer; and since they did not abuse their freedom on earth, they did not fail to attain their destiny due to their own fault. Nevertheless they suffered in this life; therefore they will be compensated in another. This sentiment is founded less on the merit of man than on the notion of goodness which seems to me inseparable from the divine essence. I am only supposing that the laws of order are observed and that God is constant to Himself.

Do not ask me whether the torments of the wicked will be eternal. I do not know that either and do not have the vain curiosity to clarify useless questions. What difference does it make to me what will become of the wicked? I take little interest in their fate. However, I have difficulty in believing that they are condemned to endless torments. If supreme justice does take vengeance, it does so beginning in this life. O nations, you and your errors are its ministers. Supreme justice employs the evils that you do to yourselves to punish the crimes which brought on those evils. It is in your insatiable hearts, eaten away by envy, avarice, and ambition, that the avenging passions punish your heinous crimes in the bosom of your false prosperity. What need is there to look for hell in the other life? It begins in this one in the hearts of the wicked.

[. . .]

How we should live

After having thus deduced the principal truths that it mattered for me to know from the impression of sensible objects and from the inner sentiment that leads me to judge of causes according to my natural lights, I still must investigate what manner of conduct I ought to draw from these truths and what rules I ought to prescribe for myself in order to fulfill my destiny on earth according to the intention of Him who put me there. In continuing to follow my method, I do not draw these rules from the principles of a high philosophy, but find them written by nature with ineffaceable characters in the depth of my heart. I have only to consult myself about what I want to do. Everything I sense to be good is good; everything I sense to be bad is bad. The best of all casuists is the conscience; and it is only when one haggles with it that one has recourse to the subtleties of reasoning. The first of all cares is the care for oneself. Nevertheless how many times does the inner voice tell us that, in doing our good at another's expense, we do wrong! We believe we are following the impulse of nature, but we are resisting it. In listening to what it says to our senses, we despise what it says to our hearts; the active being obeys, the passive being commands. Conscience is the voice of the soul; the passions are the voice of the body. Is it surprising that these two languages often are contradictory? And then which should be listened to? Too often reason deceives us. We have acquired only too much right to challenge it. But conscience never deceives; it is man's true guide. It is to the soul what instinct is to the body; he who follows conscience obeys nature and does not fear being led astray. This point is important. [. . .] Allow me to tarry a bit to clarify it.

All the morality of our actions is in the judgment we ourselves make of them. If it is true that the good is good, it must be so in the depths of our hearts as it is in our works, and the primary reward for justice is to sense that one practices it. If moral goodness is in conformity with our nature, man could be healthy of spirit or well constituted only to the extent that he is good. If it is not and man is naturally wicked, he cannot cease to be so without being corrupted, and goodness in him is only a vice contrary to nature. If he were made to do harm to his kind, as a wolf is made to slaughter his prey, a humane man would be an animal as depraved as a pitying wolf, and only virtue would leave us with remorse.

Let us return to ourselves, my young friend! Let us examine, all personal interest aside, where our inclinations lead us. Which spectacle gratifies us more—that of others' torments or that of their happiness? Which is sweeter to do and leaves us with a more agreeable impression after having done it—a beneficent act or a wicked act? In whom do you take an interest in your theaters? Is it in heinous crimes that you take pleasure? Is it to their authors when they are punished that you give your tears? It is said that we are indifferent to everything outside of our interest; but, all to the contrary, the sweetness of friendship and of humanity

45

consoles us in our suffering; even in our pleasures we would be too alone, too miserable, if we had no one with whom to share them. If there is nothing moral in the heart of man, what is the source of these transports of admiration for heroic actions, these raptures of love for great souls? What relation does this enthusiasm for virtue have to our private interest? Why would I want to be Cato, who disembowels himself, rather than Caesar triumphant? Take this love of the beautiful from our hearts, and you take all the charm from life. He whose vile passions have stifled these delicious sentiments in his narrow soul, and who, by dint of self-centeredness, succeeds in loving only himself, has no more transports. His icy heart no longer palpitates with joy; a sweet tenderness never moistens his eyes; he has no more joy in anything. This unfortunate man no longer feels, no longer lives. He is already dead.

But however numerous the wicked are on the earth, there are few of these cadaverous souls who have become insensitive, except where their own interest is at stake, to everything which is just and good. Iniquity pleases only to the extent one profits from it; in all the rest one wants the innocent to be protected. One sees some act of violence and injustice in the street or on the road. Instantly an emotion of anger and indignation is aroused in the depths of the heart, and it leads us to take up the defense of the oppressed; but a more powerful duty restrains us, and the laws take from us the right of protecting innocence. On the other hand, if some act of clemency or generosity strikes our eyes, what admiration, what love it inspires in us! Who does not say to himself, "I would like to have done the same"? It is surely of very little importance to us that a man was wicked or just two thousand years ago; nevertheless, we take an interest in ancient history just as if it all had taken place in our day. What do Catiline's crimes do to me? Am I afraid of being his victim? Why, then, am I as horrified by him as if he were my contemporary? We do not hate the wicked only because they do us harm, but because they are wicked. Not only do we want to be happy; we also wish for the happiness of others. And when this happiness does not come at the expense of our own, it increases it. Finally, in spite of oneself, one pities the unfortunate; when we are witness to their ills, we suffer from them. The most perverse are unable to lose this inclination entirely. Often it puts them in contradiction with themselves. The robber who plunders passers-by still covers the nakedness of the poor, and the most ferocious killer supports a fainting man.

We speak of the cry of remorse which in secret punishes hidden crimes and so often brings them to light. Alas, who of us has never heard this importunate voice? We speak from experience, and we would like to stifle this tyrannical sentiment that gives us so much torment. Let us obey nature. We shall know with what gentleness it reigns, and what charm one finds, after having hearkened to it, in giving favorable testimony on our own behalf. The wicked man fears and flees himself. He cheers himself up by rushing outside of himself. His restless eyes rove around him and seek an object that is entertaining to him. Without bitter satire, without insulting banter, he would always be sad. The mocking laugh is his only pleasure. By contrast, the serenity of the just man is internal. His is not a malignant laugh but a joyous one; he bears its source in himself. He is as gay alone as in the midst of a circle. He does not draw his contentment from those who come near him; he communicates it to them.

[. . .]

There is in the depths of souls, then, an innate principle of justice and virtue according to which, in spite of our own maxims, we judge our actions and those of others as good or bad. It is to this principle that I give the name *conscience*.

[. . .]

It is said that everyone contributes to the public good for his own interest. But what then is the source of the just man's contributing to it to his prejudice? What is going to one's death for one's interest? No doubt, no one acts for anything other than for his good; but if there is not a moral good which must be taken into account, one will never explain by private interest anything but the action of the wicked. It is not even likely that anyone will attempt to go farther. This would be too abominable a philosophy—one which is embarrassed by virtuous actions, which could get around the difficulty only by fabricating base intentions and motives without virtue, which would be forced to vilify Socrates and calumniate Regulus. If ever such doctrines could spring up among us, the voice of nature as well as that of reason would immediately be raised against them and would never leave a single one of their partisans the excuse that he is of good faith.

It is not my design here to enter into metaphysical discussions which are out of my reach and yours, and which, at bottom, lead to nothing. I have already told you that I wanted not to philosophize with you but to help you consult your heart. Were all the philosophers to prove that I am wrong, if you sense that I am right, I do not wish for more.

For that purpose I need only to make you distinguish our acquired ideas from our natural sentiments; for we sense before knowing, and since we do not learn to want what is good for us and to flee what is bad for us but rather get this will from nature, by that very fact love of the good and hatred of the bad are as natural as the love of ourselves. The acts of the conscience are not judgments but sentiments. Although all our ideas come to us from outside, the sentiments evaluating them are within

47

us, and it is by them alone that we know the compatibility or incompatibility between us and the things we ought to seek or flee.

[. . .]

Conscience, conscience! Divine instinct, immortal and celestial voice, certain guide of a being that is ignorant and limited but intelligent and free; infallible judge of good and bad which makes man like unto God; it is you who make the excellence of his nature and the morality of his actions. Without you I sense nothing in me that raises me above the beasts, other than the sad privilege of leading myself astray from error to error with the aid of an understanding without rule and a reason without principle.

Thank heaven, we are delivered from all that terrifying apparatus of philosophy. We can be men without being scholars. Dispensed from consuming our life in the study of morality, we have at less expense a more certain guide in this immense maze of human opinions. But it is not enough that this guide exists; one must know how to recognize it and to follow it. If it speaks to all hearts, then why are there so few of them who hear it? Well, this is because it speaks to us in nature's language, which everything has made us forget. Conscience is timid; it likes refuge and peace. The world and noise scare it; the prejudices from which they claim it is born are its cruelest enemies. It flees or keeps quiet before them. Their noisy voices stifle its voice and prevent it from making itself heard. Fanaticism dares to counterfeit it and to dictate crime in its name. It finally gives up as a result of being dismissed. It no longer speaks to us. It no longer responds to us. And after such long contempt for it, to recall it costs as much as banishing it did.

[. . .]

O my child! May you one day sense what a weight one is relieved of when, after having exhausted the vanity of human opinions and tasted the bitterness of the passions, one finally finds so near to oneself the road of wisdom, the reward of this life's labors, and the source of the happiness of which one has despaired. All the duties of the natural law, which were almost erased from my heart by the injustice of men, are recalled to it in the name of the eternal justice which imposes them on me and sees me fulfill them. I no longer sense that I am anything but the work and the instrument of the great Being who wants what is good, who does it, and who will do what is good for me through the conjunction of my will and His and through the good use of my liberty.

[. . .]

Revealed religion and the model of Jesus

[. . .]

I have told you nothing up to now which I did not believe could be useful to you and of which I was not profoundly persuaded. The examination which remains to be made (of revelation, of the scriptures, of those obscure dogmas through which I have been wandering since childhood) is very different. I see in it only perplexity, mystery, and obscurity. I bring to it only uncertainty and distrust. I decide only in trembling, and I tell you my doubts rather than my opinions. [. . .]

You see in my exposition only natural religion. It is very strange that any other is needed! How shall I know this necessity? What can I be guilty of in serving God according to the understanding He gives to my mind and the sentiments He inspires in my heart? What purity of morality, what dogma useful to man and honorable to his Author can I derive from a positive doctrine which I cannot derive without it from the good use of my faculties? Show me what one can add, for the glory of God, for the good of society, and for my own advantage, to the duties of the natural law, and what virtue you produce from a new form of worship that is not a result of mine? The greatest ideas of the divinity come to us from reason alone. View the spectacle of nature; hear the inner voice. Has God not told everything to our eyes, to our conscience, to our judgment? What more will men tell us? Their revelations have only the effect of degrading God by giving Him human passions. I see that particular dogmas, far from clarifying the notions of the great Being, confuse them; that far from ennobling them, they debase them; that to the inconceivable mysteries surrounding the great Being they add absurd contradictions; that they make man proud, intolerant, and cruel; that, instead of establishing peace on earth, they bring sword and fire to it. I ask myself what good all this does, without knowing what to answer. I see in it only the crimes of men and the miseries of mankind.

I am told that a revelation was needed to teach men the way God wanted to be served. They present as proof the diversity of bizarre forms of worship which have been instituted, and do not see that this very diversity comes from the fancifulness of revelations. As soon as peoples took it into their heads to make God speak, each made Him speak in its own way and made Him say what it wanted. If one had listened only to what God says to the heart of man, there would never have been more than one religion on earth.

There had to be uniformity of worship. Very well. But was this point so important that the whole apparatus of divine power was needed to establish it? Let us not confuse the ceremony of religion with religion itself. The worship God asks for is that of the heart. And that worship, when it is sincere, is always uniform. One must be possessed of a mad vanity indeed to imagine that God takes so great an interest in the form of the priest's costume, in the order of the words he pronounces, in the gestures he makes at the altar, and in all his genuflexions. Ah, my friend, remain upright! You will always be near enough to the earth. God wants to be revered in spirit and in truth. This is the duty of all religions, all countries, all men. As to the external worship, if it must be uniform for the sake of good order, that is purely a question of public policy; no revelation is needed for that.

[. . .]

Regarding the point at which I had arrived as the common point from which all believers start in order to arrive at a more enlightened form of worship, I found nothing in natural religion but the elements of every religion. I considered this diversity of sects which reign on earth, and which accuse each other of lying and error. I asked, "Which is the right one?" Each answered, "It is mine." Each said, "I and my partisans alone think rightly; all the others are in error." "And how do you know that your sect is the right one?" "Because God said so." "And who told you that God said so?" "My pastor, who certainly knows. My pastor told me this is what to believe, and this is what I believe. He assures me that all those who say something other than he does are lying, and I do not listen to them."

What, I thought, is the truth not one, and can what is true for me be false for you? If the methods of the man who follows the right road and of the man who goes astray are the same, what merit or what fault belongs to one of these men more than the other? Their choice is the effect of chance; to blame them for it is iniquitous. It is to reward or punish them for being born in this or in that country. To dare to say that God judges us in this way is to insult His justice.

Either all religions are good and agreeable to God; or if there is one which He prescribes to men and punishes them for refusing to recognize, He has given it certain and manifest signs so that it is distinguished and known as the only true one. These signs exist in all times and all places, equally to be grasped by all men, great and small, learned and ignorant, Europeans, Indians, Africans, savages. If there were a religion on earth outside of whose worship there was only eternal suffering, and if in some place in the world a single mortal of good faith had not been struck by its obviousness, the God of that religion would be the most iniquitous and cruel of tyrants.

Are we, then, sincerely seeking the truth? Let us grant nothing to the right of birth and to the authority of fathers and pastors, but let us recall for the examination of conscience and reason all that they have taught us from our youth. They may very well cry out, "Subject your reason." He who deceives me can say as much. I need reasons for subjecting my reason.

All the theology that I can acquire on my own from the inspection of the universe and by the good use of my faculties is limited to what I have explained to you previously. To know more one must have recourse to extraordinary means. These means could not be the authority of men; for since no man belongs to a different species from me, all that a man knows naturally I too can know, and another man can be mistaken as well as I. When I believe what he says, it is not because he says it but because he proves it. Therefore the testimony of men is at bottom only that of my own reason and adds nothing to the natural means God gave me for knowing the truth.

Apostle of the truth, what then have you to tell me of which I do not remain the judge? "God Himself has spoken. Hear His revelation." That is something else. God has spoken! That is surely a great statement. To whom has He spoken? "He has spoken to men." Why, then, did I hear nothing about it? "He has directed other men to give you His word." I understand: it is men who are going to tell me what God has said. I should have preferred to have heard God Himself. It would have cost Him nothing more, and I would have been sheltered from seduction. "He gives you a guarantee in making manifest the mission of his messengers." How is that? "By miracles." And where are these miracles? "In books." And who wrote these books? "Men." And who saw these miracles? "Men who attest to them." What! Always human testimony? Always men who report to me what other men have reported! So many men between God and me! Nevertheless let us see, examine, compare, verify. Oh, if God had deigned to relieve me of all this labor, would I have served him any less heartily?

Consider, my friend, in what a horrible discussion I am now engaged, what immense erudition I need to go back to the most remote antiquity—to examine, weigh, and compare the prophecies, the revelations, the facts, all the monuments of faith put forth in every country of the world, to fix times, places, authors, occasions! What critical precision is necessary for me to distinguish the authentic documents from the forged ones; to compare the objections to the responses, the translations to the originals; to judge of the impartiality of witnesses, of their good sense, of their understanding; to know whether anything has been suppressed, anything added, anything transposed, changed, falsified; to resolve the contradictions which remain; to judge what weight should be given to the silence of adversaries concerning facts alleged against them; whether these allegations were known to them; whether they took them seriously enough to deign to respond; whether books were common enough for ours to reach them; whether we have been of good enough faith to allow their books to circulate among us and to let remain their strongest objections just as they made them.

Once all these monuments are recognized as incontestable, one must next move on to the proofs of their authors' mission. One must have a good knowledge of all of the following: the laws of probability and the likelihood of events, in order to judge which predictions cannot be fulfilled without a miracle; the particular genius of the original languages, in order to distinguish what is prediction in these languages and what is only figure of speech; which facts belong to the order of nature and which other facts do not, so as to be able to say to what extent a skillful man can fascinate the eyes of simple people and can amaze even enlightened ones; how to discern to which species a miracle ought to belong and what authenticity it ought to have—not only for it to be believed, but for it to be a punishable offense to doubt it; how to compare the proof of true and false miracles and how to find certain rules for discerning them; and, finally, how to explain why God chose, for attesting to His word, means which themselves have so great a need of attestation, as though He were playing on men's credulity and intentionally avoiding the true means of persuading them.

Let us suppose that the divine Majesty were to design to lower itself sufficiently to make a man the organ of its sacred will. Is it reasonable, is it just to demand that all of mankind obey the voice of this minister without making him known to it as such? Is there equity in providing this minister as his only credentials some special signs given to a few obscure people, signs of which all the rest of men will never know anything except by hearsay? In every country in the world, if one were to accept the truth of all the miracles which the people and the simple folk say they have seen, every sect would be the right one; there would be more miracles than natural events, and the greatest of all miracles would be if there were not miracles wherever fanatics are persecuted. It is the unalterable order of nature which best shows the Supreme Being. If many exceptions took place, I would no longer know what to think; and as for me, I believe too much in God to believe in so many miracles that are so little worthy of Him.

Let a man come and use this language with us: "Mortals, I announce the will of the Most High to you. Recognize in my voice Him who sends me. I order the sun to change its course, the stars to form another arrangement, the mountains to become level, the waters to rise up, the earth to change its aspect." At these marvels who will not instantly recognize the Master of nature? It does not obey impostors. Their miracles are worked at crossroads, in deserts, within the confines of a room; it is there that they have an easy time with a small number of spectators already disposed to believe everything. Who will dare to tell me how many eyewitnesses are needed in order to make a miracle worthy of faith? If your miracles, which are performed to prove your doctrine, themselves need to be proved, of what use are they? You might as well perform none.

[. . .]

Doctrine coming from God ought to bear the sacred character of the divinity. Not only should it clarify for us the confused ideas which reasoning draws in our mind, but it should also propound a form of worship, a morality, and maxims that are suitable to the attributes with which we conceive His essence on our own. If it taught us only things that are absurd and without reason, if it inspired in us only sentiments of aversion for our fellows and terror for ourselves, if it depicted for us only a god who is angry, jealous, vengeful, partisan, one who hates men, a god of war and battles always ready to destroy and strike down, always speaking of torments and suffering, and boasting of punishing even the innocent, my heart would not be attracted toward this terrible god, and I would take care not to give up the natural religion for this one. For you surely see that one must necessarily choose. Your God is not ours, I would say to its sectarians. He who begins by choosing a single people for Himself and proscribing the rest of mankind is not the common Father of men. He who destines the great majority of His creatures to eternal torment is not the clement and good God my reason has shown me.

With respect to dogmas, my reason tells me that they ought to be clear, luminous, and striking by their obviousness. If natural religion is insufficient, this is due to the obscurity in which it leaves the great truths it teaches us. It is for revelation to teach us these truths in a manner evident to man's mind, to put them within his reach, to make him conceive them in order that he may believe them. Faith is given certainty and solidity by the understanding. The best of all religions is infallibly the clearest. He who burdens the worship he teaches me with mysteries and contradictions teaches me thereby to distrust it. The God I worship is not a god of shadows. He did not endow me with an understanding in order to forbid me its use. To tell me to subject my reason is to insult its Author. The minister of the truth does not tyrannize my reason; he enlightens it.

[. . .]

If the eternal truths which my mind conceives could be impaired, there would no longer be any kind of certainty for me, and far from being sure that you speak to me on behalf of God, I would not even be sure that He exists.

[. . .]

There is often nothing which is more deceptive than books, and which renders less faithfully the sentiments of those who wrote them. [. . .]

In the three revelations the sacred books are written in languages unknown to the people who follow them. The Jews no longer understand Hebrew; the Christians understand neither Hebrew nor Greek; neither the Turks nor the Persians understand Arabic, and the modern Arabs themselves no longer speak the language of Mohammed. Is this not a simple way of instructing men—always speaking to them in a language they do not understand? These books are translated, it will be said. A fine answer! Who will assure me that these books are faithfully translated, that it is even possible that they be? And if God has gone so far as to speak to men, why must He need an interpreter?

I shall never be able to conceive that what every man is obliged to know is confined to books, and that someone who does not have access to these books, or to those who understand them, is punished for an ignorance which is involuntary. Always books! What a mania. Because Europe is full of books, Europeans regard them as indispensable, without thinking that in three-quarters of the earth they have never been seen. Were not all books written by men? Why, then, would man need them to know his duties, and what means had he of knowing them before these books were written? Either he will learn these duties by himself, or he is excused from knowing them.

Our Catholics make a great to-do about the authority of the Church; but what do they gain by that, if they need as great an apparatus of proofs to establish this authority as other sects need for establishing their doctrine directly? The Church decides that the Church has the right to decide. [. . .]

Do you know many Christians who have taken the effort to examine with care what Judaism alleges against them? If some individuals have seen something of this, it is in the books of Christians. A good way of informing oneself about their adversaries' arguments! But what is there to do? If someone dared to publish among us books in which Judaism were openly favored, we would punish the author, the publisher, the bookseller. This is a convenient and sure policy for always being right. There is a pleasure in refuting people who do not dare to speak.

Those among us who have access to conversation with Jews are not much farther advanced. These unfortunates feel themselves to be at our mercy. The tyranny practiced against them makes them fearful. They know how little troubled Christian charity is by injustice and cruelty.

What will they dare to say without laying themselves open to our accusing them of blasphemy? Greed gives us zeal, and they are too rich not to be wrong. The most learned, the most enlightened among them are always the most circumspect. You will convert some miserable fellow, who is paid to calumniate his sect. You will put words into the mouths of some vile old-clothes dealers, who will yield in order to flatter you. You will triumph over their ignorance or their cowardice, while their learned men will smile in silence at your ineptitude. But do you believe that in places where they feel secure you would win out over them so cheaply? At the Sorbonne it is as clear as day that the predictions about the Messiah relate to Jesus Christ. Among the Amsterdam rabbis it is just as clear that they do not have the least relation to Jesus. I shall never believe that I have seriously heard the arguments of the Jews until they have a free state, schools, and universities, where they can speak and dispute without risk. Only then will we be able to know what they have to say.

At Constantinople the Turks state their arguments, but we do not dare to state our own. There it is our turn to crawl. If the Turks demand from us the same respect for Mohammed that we demand for Jesus Christ from the Jews, who do not believe in him any more than we believe in Mohammed, are the Turks wrong? Are we right? According to what equitable principle shall we resolve this question?

Two-thirds of mankind are neither Jews nor Mohammedans nor Christians, and how many million men have never heard of Moses, Jesus Christ, or Mohammed? This is denied; it is maintained that our missionaries go everywhere. That is easily said. But do they go into the still unknown heart of Africa, where no European has ever penetrated up to now? Do they go to deepest Tartary, to follow on horseback the wandering hordes who are never approached by a foreigner, and who, far from having heard of the Pope, hardly even know of the Grand Lama? Do they go into the immense continents of America, where whole nations still do not know that peoples from another world have set foot in theirs? Do they go to Japan, from which their maneuvers got them thrown out forever, and where their predecessors are known to the generations now being born only as guileful intriguers who came with a hypocritical zeal to take hold of the empire by stealth? Do they go into the harems of the princes of Asia to proclaim the Gospel to thousands of poor slaves? What have the women of this part of the world done to prevent any missionary from preaching the faith to them? Will they all go to hell for having been recluses?

Even if it were true that the Gospel has been proclaimed everywhere on earth, what would be gained by it? Surely on the eve of the day that the first missionary arrived in some country, someone died there who was not able to hear him. Now tell me what we are going to do with that person? If there were only a single man in the whole universe who had never been preached to about Jesus Christ, the objection would be as strong for that single man as for a quarter of mankind.

Even if the ministers of the Gospel have made themselves heard by distant peoples, what have they told them which could reasonably be accepted on their word and which did not demand the most exact verification? You proclaim to me a God born and dead two thousand years ago at the other end of the world in some little town, and you tell me that whoever has not believed in this mystery will be damned. These are very strange things to believe so quickly on the sole authority of a man whom I do not know! Why did your god make these events take place so far from me, if he wanted me to be under an obligation to be informed of them? Is it a crime not to know what takes place at the antipodes? Can I divine that there were a Hebrew people and a city of Jerusalem in another hemisphere? I might as well be obliged to know what is happening on the moon! You say that you come to teach this to me. But why did you not come to teach it to my father, or why do you damn this good old man for never having known anything about it? Ought he to be eternally punished for your laziness, he who was so good and beneficent, and who sought only the truth? Be of good faith; then put yourself in my place. See if I ought to believe on your testimony alone all the unbelievable things you tell me and to reconcile so many injustices with the just God whom you proclaim to me. I beg you, let me go and see this distant country where so many marvels take place that are unheard of in this one. Let me go and find out why the inhabitants of this Jerusalem treated God like a thief. They did not, you say, recognize him as god? What shall I do then, I who have never even heard Him mentioned except by you? You add that they were punished, dispersed, oppressed, enslaved, that none of them comes near that city anymore. Surely they well deserved all that. But what do today's inhabitants say of the deicide committed by their predecessors? They deny it; they, too, do not recognize God as God. The children of the others, then, might as well have been left there.

What! In the very city where God died, neither the old nor the new inhabitants acknowledged him, and you want me to acknowledge him, me who was born two thousand years after and two thousand leagues away? Do you not see that before I put faith in this book which you call sacred, and of which I understand nothing, I must be informed by people other than you when and by whom it was written, how it was preserved, how it was transmitted to you, what arguments are given by those in your country who reject it, although they know as well as you all that

56

you teach me? You are well aware that I must necessarily go to Europe, Asia, and Palestine and examine everything for myself. I would have to be mad to listen to you prior to that time.

Not only does this discourse appear reasonable to me, but I maintain that every man in his senses ought to speak thus in a similar case and dismiss without more ado the missionary who is in a hurry to instruct and baptize him before verification of the proofs. Now, I maintain that there is no revelation against which the same objections do not have as much strength as, or more strength than, against Christianity. From this it follows that if there is only one true religion and every man is obliged to follow it under penalty of damnation, one's life must be spent in studying them all, in going deeper into them, in comparing them, in roaming around the country where each is established. No one is exempt from the first duty of man; no one has a right to rely on the judgment of others. The artisan who lives only by his work, the laborer who does not know how to read, the delicate and timid maiden, the invalid who can hardly leave his bed—all without exception must study, meditate, engage in disputation, travel, roam the world. There will no longer be any stable and settled people; the whole earth will be covered only with pilgrims going at great expense and with continuous hardships to verify, to compare, and to examine for themselves the various forms of worship that people observe. Then it will be goodbye to the trades, the arts, the humane sciences, and all the civil occupations. There can no longer be any other study than that of religion. He who has enjoyed the most robust health, best employed his time, best used his reason, and lived the most years will hardly know what to think in his old age; and it will be a great deal if he learns before his death in what worship he ought to have lived.

[. . .]

You see, my son, to what absurdity pride and intolerance lead, when each man is so sure of his position and believes he is right to the exclusion of the rest of mankind. All my researches have been sincere—I take as my witness that God of peace Whom I adore and Whom I proclaim to you. But when I saw that these researches were and always would be unsuccessful, and that I was being swallowed up in an ocean without shores, I retraced my steps and restricted my faith to my primary notions. I have never been able to believe that God commanded me, under penalty of going to hell, to be so learned. I therefore closed all the books. There is one open to all eyes: it is the book of nature. It is from this great and sublime book that I learn to serve and worship its divine Author. No one can be excused for not reading it, because it speaks to all men a language that is intelligible to all minds. Let us assume that I was born on a desert island, that I have not seen any man other than myself, that I have never learned what took place in olden times in some corner of the world; nonetheless, if I exercise my reason, if I cultivate it, if I make good use of my God-given faculties which require no intermediary, I would learn of myself to know Him, to love Him, to love His works, to want the good that He wants, and to fulfill all my duties on earth in order to please Him. What more will all the learning of men teach me?

[. . .]

I also admit that the majesty of the Scriptures amazes me, and that the holiness of the Gospel speaks to my heart. Look at the books of the philosophers with all their pomp. How petty they are next to this one! Can it be that a book at the same time so sublime and so simple is the work of men? Can it be that he whose history it presents is only a man himself? Is his the tone of an enthusiast or an ambitious sectarian? What gentleness, what purity in his morals! What touching grace in his teachings! What elevation in his maxims! What profound wisdom in his speeches! What presence of mind, what finesse, and what exactness in his responses! What a dominion over his passions! Where is the man, where is the sage who knows how to act, to suffer, and to die without weakness and without ostentation? When Plato depicts his imaginary just man, covered with all the opprobrium of crime and worthy of all the rewards of virtue, he depicts Jesus Christ feature for feature. The resemblance is so striking that all the Fathers have sensed it; it is impossible to be deceived about it. What prejudices, what blindness one must have to dare to compare the son of Sophroniscus to the son of Mary? What a distance from one to the other! Socrates, dying without pain and without ignominy, easily sticks to his character to the end; and if this easy death had not honored his life, one would doubt whether Socrates, for all his intelligence, were anything but a sophist. He invented morality, it is said. Others before him put it into practice; all he did was to say what they had done; all he did was to draw the lesson from their examples. Aristides was just before Socrates said what justice is. Leonidas died for his country before Socrates had made it a duty to love the fatherland. Sparta was sober before Socrates had praised sobriety. Before he had defined virtue, Greece abounded in virtuous men. But where did Jesus find among his own people that elevated and pure morality of which he alone gave the lessons and the example? From the womb of the most furious fanaticism was heard the highest wisdom, and the simplicity of the most heroic virtues lent honor to the vilest of all peoples. The death of Socrates, philosophizing tranquilly with his friends, is the sweetest one could desire; that of Jesus, expiring in torment, insulted, jeered at, cursed by a whole people, is the most horrible one could fear. Socrates, taking the poisoned cup, blesses the man who gives it to him and who is crying.

Jesus, in the midst of a frightful torture, prays for his relentless executioners. Yes, if the life and death of Socrates are those of a wise man, the life and death of Jesus are those of a god. Shall we say that the story of the Gospel was wantonly contrived? My friend, it is not thus that one contrives; the facts about Socrates, which no one doubts, are less well attested than those about Jesus Christ. At bottom, this is to push back the difficulty without doing away with it. It would be more inconceivable that many men in agreement had fabricated this book than that a single one provided its subject. Never would Jewish authors have found either this tone or this morality; and the Gospel has characteristics of truth that are so great, so striking, so perfectly inimitable that its contriver would be more amazing than its hero. With all that, this same Gospel is full of unbelievable things, of things repugnant to reason and impossible for any sensible man to conceive or to accept! What is to be done amidst all these contradictions? One ought always to be modest and cirumspect, my child—to respect in silence what one can neither reject nor understand, and to humble oneself before the great Being who alone knows the truth.

[. . .]

My son, keep your soul in a condition where it always desires that there be a God, and you shall never doubt it. What is more, whatever decision you may make, bear in mind that the true duties of religion are independent of the institutions of men; that a just heart is the true temple of the divinity; that in every country and in every sect the sum of the law is to love God above everything and one's neighbor as oneself; that no religion is exempt from the duties of morality; that nothing is truly essential other than these duties; that inner worship is the first of these duties; and that without faith no true virtue exists.

Flee those who sow dispiriting doctrines in men's hearts under the pretext of explaining nature. Their apparent skepticism is a hundred times more assertive and more dogmatic than the decided tone of their adversaries. Under the haughty pretext that they alone are enlightened, true, and of good faith, they imperiously subject us to their peremptory decisions and claim to give us as the true principles of things the unintelligible systems they have built in their imaginations. Moreover, by overturning, destroying, and trampling on all that men respect, they deprive the afflicted of the last consolation of their misery, and the powerful and the rich of the only brake on their passions. They tear out from the depths of our hearts remorse for crime and hope of virtue, and yet boast that they are the benefactors of mankind. They say that the truth is never harmful to men. I believe it as much as they do, and in my opinion this is a great proof that what they teach is not the truth.

59

Good young man, be sincere and true without pride. Know how to be ignorant. You will deceive neither yourself nor others. If ever you have cultivated your talents and they put you in a position to speak to men, never speak to them except according to your conscience, without worrying whether they will applaud you. The abuse of learning produces incredulity. Every learned man disdains the common sentiment; each wants to have his own. Proud philosophy leads to freethinking as blind devoutness leads to fanaticism. Avoid these extremes. Always remain firm in the path of truth (or what in the simplicity of your heart appears to you to be the truth), without ever turning away from it out of vanity or weakness. Dare to acknowledge God among the philosophers; dare to preach humanity to the intolerant. You will perhaps be the only member of your party, but you will have within yourself a witness which will enable you to do without the witness of men. Whether they love you or hate you, whether they read or despise your writings, it does not matter: speak the truth; do the good. What does matter for man is to fulfill his duties on earth, and it is in forgetting oneself that one works for oneself. My child, private interest deceives us. It is only the hope of the just which never deceives.

Source: J.-J. Rousseau, *Emile, or, On Education*, trans. A. Bloom, London, Harmondsworth, Penguin, 1991/© 1979, pp. 266–9, 270–2, 272–7, 277–8, 280–4, 286–92, 294, 295–308, 311, 313.

Marquis de Sade, *Dialogue between a Priest and a Dying Man*

Dialogue entre un prêtre et un moribund was written by Sade (1740–1814) in his fourth year in the Royal Prison in Vincennes in 1782, where he was being held under one of Louis XVI's *lettres de cachet*, as orchestrated by Sade's mother-in-law as a means of avoiding a scandalous trial for sodomy, poisoning and blasphemy. In the dialogue, rather than making a final confession for caving in to earthly temptations, a dying man expresses regret at having not caved in often enough. He then presents the priest with some familiar and new objections to both natural and established religion, and outlines his (and Sade's) sensualist credo as an alternative. The dialogue ends with the dying man inviting the priest to follow his own true nature.

The final scene aside, this dialogue is atypical for Sade. It was probably written with a view to establishing his intellectual credentials, as someone capable of carrying out a considered and sober discussion.

PRIEST. Now that the fatal hour is upon you wherein the veil of illusion is torn aside only to confront every deluded man with the cruel tally of his errors and vices, do you, my son, earnestly repent of the many sins to which you were led by weakness and human frailty?

DYING MAN. Yes, I do so repent.

PRIEST. Then in the short space you have left, profit from such timely remorse to ask that you be given general absolution of your sins, believing that only by considering the reverence of the most comfortable and holy sacrament of penitence may you hope for forgiveness at the hand of Almighty God our Eternal Father.

DYING MAN. I understand you no better than you have understood me.

PRIEST. What's that?

DYING MAN. I said I repented.

PRIEST. I heard you.

DYING MAN. Yes, but you did not understand what I meant.

PRIEST. But what other interpretation . . . ?

DYING MAN. The one I shall now give. I was created by Nature with the keenest appetites and the strongest of passions and was put on this earth with the sole purpose of placating both by surrendering to them. They are components of my created self and are no more than mechanical parts necessary to the functioning of Nature's basic purposes. Or if you prefer, they are incidental effects essential to her designs for me and conform entirely to her laws. I repent only that I never sufficiently acknowledged the omnipotence of Nature and my remorse is directed solely against the modest use I made of those faculties, criminal in your eyes but perfectly straightforward in mine, which she gave me to use in her service. I did at times resist her, and am heartily sorry for it. I was blinded by the absurdity of your doctrines to which I resorted to fight the violence of desires planted in me by a power more divinely inspired by far, and I now repent of having done so. I picked only flowers when I could have gathered in a much greater harvest of ripe fruits. Such is the proper cause of my regret; respect me enough to impute no other to me.

PRIEST. To what a pass have you been brought by your errors! How misled you have been by such sophisms! You attribute to the created world all the power of the Creator! Do you not see that the lamentable tendencies which have misdirected your steps are themselves no more than effects of that same corrupt Nature to which you attribute omnipotence?

DYING MAN. It seems to me that your reasoning is as empty as your head. I wish that you would argue more rationally or else just let me alone to die in peace. What do you mean by 'Creator'? What do you understand by 'corrupt Nature'?

PRIEST. The Creator is the Master of the Universe. All that was created was created by Him, everything was made by His hand, and His creation is maintained as a simple effect of His omnipotence.

DYING MAN. Well now, He must be a very great man indeed! In which case, tell me why this man of yours, who is so powerful, nevertheless made Nature 'corrupt', as you put it.

PRIEST. But what merit would men have had if God had not given them free will? What merit would there be in its exercise if, in this life, it were not as possible to choose good as it were to avoid evil?

DYING MAN. So your God proceeded to make the world askew simply to tempt and test man. Did He then not know His creature? And did He not know the outcome?

PRIEST. Of course He knew His creature but, in addition, He wished to leave him the merit of choosing wisely.

DYING MAN. But what for? He knew all along what His creature would choose and it was within His power—for you say that He is all-powerful—well within His power, say I, to see to it that he chose correctly?

PRIEST. Who can comprehend the vast and infinite purpose which God has for man? Where is even the man who understands all things visible?

DYING MAN. Anyone who sees things simply, and especially the man who does not go looking for a multiplicity of causes with which to obscure the effects. Why do you need a second difficulty when you cannot explain the first? If we admit it is possible that Nature alone is responsible for creating what you attribute to your God, why do you insist on looking for a master hand? The cause of what you do not comprehend may be the simplest thing there is. Study physics and you will understand Nature better; learn to think clearly, cast out your preconceived ideas and you will have no need of this God of yours.

PRIEST. Miserable sinner! I understood you were no more than a Socinian[22] and came armed with weapons to fight you. But since I see

[22] *a Socinian*: Socinianism was the doctrine of two Italian heresiarchs, Lælus Socinus (1525–62) and his nephew Faustus (1539–1604), which, with some differences, resembles that of modern Unitarianism. It argued that the only foundation on which Protestantism should be based was human reason, and Faustus combated the principal dogmas of the Church: the

now that you are an atheist whose heart is closed to the authentic and innumerable proofs which are daily given us of the existence of the Creator, there is no point in my saying anything more. Sight cannot be restored to a blind man.

DYING MAN. Admit one thing: is not the blinder of two men surely he who puts a blindfold on his eyes, not he who removes it? You edify, you fabricate reasons, you multiply explanations, whereas I destroy and simplify the issues. You pile error on error, and I challenge all errors. So which of us is blind?

PRIEST. So you do not believe in God?

DYING MAN. No, and for a very simple reason: it is impossible to believe what one does not understand. There must always be an obvious connection between understanding and belief. Understanding is the prime condition of faith. Where there is no understanding, faith dies and those who do not understand yet say they believe are hypocrites. I defy you to say that you believe in the God whose praises you sing, because you cannot demonstrate His existence nor is it within your capacities to define His nature, which means that you do not understand Him and since you do not understand you are incapable of furnishing me with reasoned arguments. In other words, anything which is beyond the limits of human reason is either illusion or idle fancy, and since your God must be either one or the other, I should be mad to believe in the first and stupid to believe in the second.

Prove to me that matter is inert, and I shall grant you a Creator. Show me that Nature is not sufficient unto herself, and I shall gladly allow you to give her a Master. But until you can do this, I shall not yield one inch. I am convinced only by evidence, and evidence is provided by my senses alone. Beyond their limits, I am powerless to believe in anything. I believe the sun exists because I can see it: I take it to be the centre where all of Nature's flammable matter is gathered together and I am charmed but in no wise astonished by its regular courses. It is a phenomenon of physics, perhaps no more complex than the workings of electricity, which it is not given to us to understand. Need I say more? You can construct your God and set Him above such phenomena, but does that take me any further forward? Am I not required to make as much effort to understand the workman as to define His handiwork?

---

divinity of Christ, original sin, propitiatory sacrifice, and everything which could not be justified in rational terms. The Socinians were admired by Enlightenment *philosophes* who saw in them early exponents of deism, or natural religion.

Consequently, you have done me no service by erecting this illusion of yours. You have confused but not enlightened my mind and I owe you not gratitude but hatred. Your God is a machine which you have built to serve your own passions and you have set it to run according to their requirements. But you must see that I had no choice but to jettison your model the instant it fell out of step with my passions? At this moment, my weak soul stands in need of peace and philosophy: why do you now try to alarm it with your sophistry which will strike it with terror but not convert it, inflame it without making it better? My soul is what it pleased Nature to be, which is to say a consequence of the organs which Nature thought fit to implant in me in accordance with her purposes and needs. Now, since Nature needs vice as much as she needs virtue, she directed me towards the first when she found it expedient, and when she had need of the second, she filled me with the appropriate desires to which I surrendered equally promptly. Do not seek further than her laws for the cause of our human inconsistency, and to explain her laws look not beyond her will and her needs.

PRIEST. And so everything in the world is necessary?

DYING MAN. Of course.

PRIEST. But if all is necessary, there must be order in everything?

DYING MAN. Who argues that there is not?

PRIEST. But who or what is capable of creating the order that exists if not an all-powerful, supremely wise hand?

DYING MAN. Will not gunpowder explode of necessity when lit by a match?

PRIEST. Yes.

DYING MAN. And where is the wisdom in that?

PRIEST. There isn't any.

DYING MAN. So you see it is possible that there are things which are necessary but were not wisely made, and it follows that it is equally possible that everything derives from a first cause in which there may be neither reason nor wisdom.

PRIEST. What are you driving at?

DYING MAN. I want to prove to you that it is possible that everything is simply what it is and what you see it to be, without its being the effect of some cause which was reasonable and wisely directed; that natural effects must have natural causes without there being any need to suppose that they had a non-natural origin such as your God who, as I have already observed, would require a good deal of explaining but would not of Himself explain anything; that therefore once it is conceded that God serves no useful purpose, He becomes completely irrelevant; that there is every likelihood that what is irrelevant is of no account and what is of no account is as nought. So, to convince myself that your God is an illusion, I need no other argument than that which is supplied by my certain knowledge that He serves no useful purpose.

PRIEST. If that is your attitude, I cannot think that there is any reason why I should discuss religion with you.

DYING MAN. Why ever not? I know nothing more entertaining than seeing for myself to what extravagant lengths men have taken fanaticism and imbecility in religious matters—excesses so unspeakable that the catalogue of aberrations, though ghastly, is, I always think, invariably fascinating to contemplate. Answer me this frankly, and above all, do not give self-interested responses! If I were to be weak enough to let myself be talked into believing your ludicrous doctrines which prove the incredible existence of a being who makes religion necessary, which form of worship would you advise me to offer up to Him? Would you have me incline towards the idle fancies of Confucius or the nonsense of Brahma? Should I bow down before the Great Serpent of the Negro, the Moon and Stars of the Peruvian, or the God of Moses' armies? Which of the sects of Muhammad would you suggest I join? Or which particular Christian heresy would you say was preferable to all the others? Think carefully before you answer.

PRIEST. Can there be any doubt about my reply?

DYING MAN. But that is a self-interested answer.

PRIEST. Not at all. In recommending my own beliefs to you, I love you as much as I love myself.

DYING MAN. By heeding such errors, you show little enough love for either of us.

PRIEST. But who can be blind enough not to see the miracles of our Divine Redeemer?

DYING MAN. He who sees through Him as the most transparent of swindlers and the most tiresome of humbugs.

PRIEST. *O Lord, thou hearest but speakest not with a voice of thunder!*

DYING MAN. Quite so, and no voice is heard for the simple reason that your God, perhaps because He cannot or because He has too much sense or for whatever other reason you care to impute to a being whose existence I acknowledge only out of politeness or, if you prefer, to be as accommodating as I can to your petty views, no voice, I say, is heard because this God, if He exists as you are mad enough to believe, cannot possibly have set out to convince us by using means as ludicrous as those employed by your Jesus.

PRIEST. But what of the prophets, the miracles, the martyrs? Are not all these proofs?

DYING MAN. How, in terms of strict logic, can you expect me to accept as proof something which itself first needs to be proved? For a prophecy to be a proof, I must first be completely convinced that what was foretold was in fact fulfilled. Now since prophecies are part of history, they can have no more force in my mind than all other historical facts, of which three-quarters are highly dubious. If to this I were to add further the possibility, or rather the likelihood, that they were transmitted to me solely by historians with a vested interest, I should be, as you see, more than entitled to be sceptical. Moreover, who will reassure me that such and such a prophecy was not made after the event, or that it was not just politically or self-fulfillingly contrived, like the prediction which foretells a prosperous reign under a just king or forecasts frost in winter? If all this is in fact the case, how can you argue that prophecies, which stand in dire need of proof, can themselves ever become a proof?

As for your miracles, I am no more impressed by them than by prophecies. All swindlers have worked miracles and the stupid have believed in them. To be convinced of the truth of a miracle, I should have to be quite certain that the event which you would call miraculous ran absolutely counter to the laws of Nature, since only events occurring outside Nature can be deemed a miracle. But there, who is so learned in her ways to dare state at what point Nature ends and at what precise moment Nature is violated? Only two things are required to accredit an alleged miracle: a mountebank and a crowd of spineless lookers-on. There is absolutely no point looking for any other kind of origin for your miracles. All founders of new sects have been miracle-workers and, what is decidedly odder, they have always found imbeciles who believed them. Your Jesus never managed anything more prodigious than Apollonius of Tyana,[23] and it would never enter anyone's head to claim that he was a god. As to your martyrs, they are by far the weakest of all your arguments. Zeal and obstinacy are all it takes to make a martyr and if an alternative cause were to furnish me with as many martyred saints as you claim for yours, I should never have proper grounds for believing the one to be any better than the other but, on the contrary, should be very inclined to think that both were woefully inadequate.

---

[23] *Apollonius of Tyana*: Apollonius of Tyana (4 BC–97 AD) was a celebrated disciple of Pythagoras. He travelled widely and preached moral reform and the adoption of neo-Pythagorean ideas. He was one of the most virtuous and learned men of his day, and was popularly regarded as a worker of miracles and a divine being. In England, Charles Blount (1654–93) compared him with Jesus as did, nearer Sade's day, Jean Meslier (1664–1729), Voltaire and Diderot.

My dear fellow, if it were true that the God you preach really existed, would He need miracles, martyrs, and prophecies to establish His kingdom? And if, as you say, the heart of man is God's handiwork, would not men's hearts have been the temple He chose for His law? Surely this equitable law, since it emanates from a just God, would be equally and irresistibly imprinted in all of us, from one end of the universe to the other. All men, having in common this same delicate, sensitive organ, would also adopt a common approach to praising the God from whom they had received it. They would all have the same way of loving Him, the same way of adoring and serving Him, and it would be as impossible for them to mistake His nature as to resist the secret bidding of their hearts to praise Him. But instead of which, what do I find throughout the whole universe? As many gods as there are nations, as many ways of serving them as there are brains and fertile imaginations. Now, do you seriously believe that this multiplicity of opinions, among which I find it physically impossible to choose, is really the handiwork of a just God?

No, preacher, you offend your God by showing Him to me in this light. Allow me to deny Him altogether, for if He exists, I should offend Him much less by my unbelief than you by your blasphemies. Think, preacher! Your Jesus was no better than Muhammad, Muhammad was no better than Moses, and none of these three was superior to Confucius, though Confucius did set down a number of perfectly valid principles whereas the others talked nonsense. But they and their ilk are mountebanks who have been mocked by thinking men, believed by the rabble, and should have been strung up by due process of law.

PRIEST. Alas, such was only too true in the case of one of the four.

DYING MAN. Yes, He who deserved it most. He was a seditious influence, an agitator, a bearer of false witness, a scoundrel, a lecher, a showman who performed crude tricks, a wicked and dangerous man. He knew exactly how to set about hoodwinking the public and was therefore eminently punishable in the type of kingdom and state of which Jerusalem was then a part. It was a very sound decision to remove Him and it is perhaps the only case in which my principles, which are incidentally very mild and tolerant, could ever admit the application of the full rigour of Themis. I forgive all errors save those which may imperil the government under which we live; kings and their majesty are the only things that I take on trust and respect. The man who does not love his country and his King does not deserve to live.

PRIEST. But you do admit, do you not, that there is something after this life? It hardly seems possible that your mind has not on occasion

67

turned to piercing the mystery of the fate which awaits us. What concept have you found to be more convincing than that of a multitude of punishments for the man who has lived badly and an eternity of rewards for the man who has lived well?

DYING MAN. Why, my dear fellow, the concept of nothingness! The idea never frightened me; it strikes me as consoling and simple. All other answers are the handiwork of pride, but mine is the product of reason. In any case, nothingness is neither ghastly nor absolute. Is not Nature's never-ending process of generation and regeneration plain for my eyes to see? Nothing perishes, nothing on this earth is destroyed. Today a man, tomorrow a worm, the day after a fly—what is this if not eternal life? And why do you believe that I should be rewarded for virtues I possess through no merit of my own, and punished for criminal acts over which I have no control? How can you reconcile the goodness of your alleged God with this principle? Can He have created me solely in order to enjoy punishing me—and punish me for choosing wrongly while denying me the freedom to choose well?

PRIEST. But you are free to choose.

DYING MAN. I am—but only according to your assumptions which do not withstand examination by reason. The doctrine of free will was invented solely so that you could devise the principle of Divine Grace which validated your garbled presuppositions. Is there a man alive who, seeing the scaffold standing next to his crime, would willingly commit a crime if he were free not to commit it? We are impelled by an irresistible power and are never, not for a single instant, in a position to steer a course in any direction except down the slope on which our feet are set. There are no virtues save those which are necessary to Nature's ends and, reciprocally, no crime which she does not need for her purposes. Nature's mastery lies precisely in the perfect balance which she maintains between virtue and crime. But can we be guilty if we move in the direction in which she pushes us? No more than the wasp which punctures your skin with its sting.

PRIEST. So it follows that even the greatest crimes should not give us cause to fear anything?

DYING MAN. I did not say that. It is enough that the law condemns and the sword of justice punishes for us to feel aversion or terror for such crimes. But once they have, regrettably, been committed, we must accept the inevitable and not surrender to remorse which is pointless. Remorse is null since it did not prevent us from committing the crime, and void since it does not enable us to make amends: it would be absurd to surrender to it and absurder still to fear punishment in the next world if we have been fortunate enough to escape it in this. God forbid that anyone should think that in saying this I seek to give encouragement to crime! Of course we must do everything we can to avoid criminal acts—but we must learn to shun them through reason and not out of unfounded fears which lead nowhere, the effects of which are in any case neutralized in anyone endowed with strength of mind. Reason, yes reason alone must alert us to the fact that doing harm to others can never make us happy, and our hearts must make us feel that making others happy is the greatest joy which Nature grants us on this earth. All human morality is contained in these words: *make others as happy as you yourself would be*, and never serve them more ill than you would yourself be served. These, my dear fellow, are the only principles which we should follow. There is no need of religion or God to appreciate and act upon them: the sole requirement is a good heart.

But, preacher, I feel my strength abandon me. Put aside your prejudices, be a man, be human, have no fear and no hope. Abandon your divinities and your creeds which have never served any purpose save to put a sword into the hand of man. The mere names of horrible gods and hideous faiths have caused more blood to be shed than all other wars and scourges on earth. Give up the idea of another world, for there is none. But do not turn your back on the pleasure in this of being happy yourself and of making others happy. It is the only means Nature affords you of enlarging and extending your capacity for life. My dear fellow, sensuality was ever the dearest to me of all my possessions. All my life, I have bowed down before its idols and always wished to end my days in its arms. My time draws near. Six women more beautiful than sunlight are in the room adjoining. I was keeping them all for this moment. Take your share of them and, pillowed on their bosoms, try to forget, as I do, the vain sophisms of superstition and the stupid errors of hypocrisy.

NOTE

The Dying Man rang, the women entered the room, and in their arms the priest became a man corrupted by Nature—and all because he had been unable to explain what he meant by Corrupted Nature.

Source: *The Misfortunes of Virtue and Other Early Tales*, trans. D. Coward, Oxford, Oxford University Press, 1992, pp. 149–60.

The French Revolution

The twenty-two documents that follow have been selected as evidence illustrating salient turning points of the French Revolution across the epoch-making five years 1789 to 1794. The selection begins with sizeable extracts from Sieyès' *What is the Third Estate?*, the most influential of the many publications that appeared at the time of the summoning of the Estates-General in 1789. The documents bring out the rapidly unfolding events in France from the fall of the Bastille with the vacillating conduct of the king and the speedy radicalisation of the Revolution: the impact of the radical press, the rise of the Jacobins, the role of the *sans-culottes*. Evidence is also given of the Revolution's international dimension, the forebodings of Edmund Burke, the challenge to Europe as perceived by Austria and Prussia; and in turn evidence is given of the further radicalisation of the Revolution that resulted from foreign intervention and civil war with the institution of 'revolutionary government' 1793–94: the *levée en masse*, the law of suspects, the Terror (with testimony from its victims), and the ideological leadership of Robespierre. The selection ends with the uncompromising belligerence towards Old Regime Europe of the 'Marseillaise', anthem of the Revolution in arms.

Abbé Sieyès, *What is the Third Estate?*, 1789

The plan of this work is quite simple. We have three questions to ask ourselves.

1. What is the Third Estate? – *Everything*.
2. What has it been so far in the political order? – *Nothing*.
3. What does it ask to be? – *Something*.

We shall see if these are the right answers. Meanwhile, it would be wrong to say that these truths have been exaggerated when you have not yet seen the supporting evidence. Next we shall examine the measures that have been tried, and those that must [still] be taken, for the Third Estate to actually become *something*. Thus we shall state:

4. What ministers have tried to do in the interests of the Third Estate, and what the privileged themselves propose to do for it;
5. What should have been done;
6. And finally, what remains to be done for the Third Estate so that it can take up the place that is its due [. . .]

What is a nation? A body of people who join together to live under *common* laws and be represented by the same *legislative assembly*. It is only too clear, isn't it, that the nobility has privileges and exemptions it dares to call its rights that are separate from the rights of the main body of citizens. As a consequence of these special rights, it does not belong to the common order, [nor is it subject to] the common law. Thus its private rights already make the nobility into a separate people, a nation within a nation. [. . .]

With regard to its *political* rights, these also it exercises separately. It has its own representatives without any mandate from the people. Its corps of deputies sits separately, and even if it should sit in the same chamber as the deputies of ordinary citizens, its representative function would still be fundamentally distinct and separate. The nobility is alien to the nation, firstly from the standpoint of *principle*, since it does not derive its powers from the people; secondly from the standpoint of its objectives since these involve defending, not the general interest, but the private one.

The Third Estate thus contains everything proper to the nation; and those who do not belong to the Third Estate cannot be seen as part of the nation. What is the Third Estate? *Everything.* [*What is the third estate?* 1: 'The Third Estate is the complete nation']

We shall examine neither the servitude in which the people have suffered for so long, nor the restrictions and humiliations which still constrain it. Its civil status has changed; it must change still more. It is absolutely impossible for the nation as a whole, or even for any separate order, to be free, if the Third Estate is not. We do not get our freedom from privileges, but from our rights as citizens, rights which belong to everyone.

If the aristocrats seek to keep the people in a state of oppression at the expense of that very freedom of which they have proved themselves to be unworthy, the people may well ask on what grounds. If the answer is 'by right of conquest', you will agree that this means going back in time a bit. [. . .]

Sometimes, people seem surprised to hear complaints about the triple *aristocracy* of Church, Army and Law. They like to think that this is just a manner of speaking; but the phrase must be taken literally. If the Estates-General is the interpreter of the general will, and has legislative power in that capacity, then surely it is precisely this that makes the Estates-General, in as much as it is just a *clerical-noble-judicial* assembly, into a true aristocracy.

Add to this awful truth the fact that, in one way or another, every branch of the executive has fallen into the hands of the caste that supplies the Church, the Law and the Army with their members. Feelings of brotherhood or *comradeship* of some sort make nobles always prefer each other to the rest of the nation. The usurpation is total; they reign over us in every sense.

Read your history to check whether or not this statement fits the facts, and you will see, as I have seen, that it is a great mistake to think that France is governed as a monarchy. In the annals of our history, if you make an exception for a few years during the reign of Louis XI,[1] and of Richelieu,[2] and a few moments during Louis XIV's reign,[3] when it was a matter of despotism pure and simple, you will think you are reading the history of a *palace* autocracy. It is the court that reigns, not the monarch. The court has made and the court has unmade, has appointed ministers and dismissed them, has created posts and filled them, and so on. And what is the court but the head of this vast aristocracy overrunning the whole of France, which through its members seizes on everything and exercises total control over every essential aspect of public life. So in their muted complaints, the people has become used to distinguishing the monarch from those who exercise power. It has always looked upon the King as a man so thoroughly deceived and so defenceless in the midst of an active, all-powerful court that it has never thought of blaming him for all the evil that is done in his name. Finally, is it not enough to open people's eyes to what is happening around us at this very moment? What do you see? The aristocracy, isolated, fighting simultaneously against reason, justice, the people, the minister and the King. The outcome of this terrible struggle is still unclear; and to think that people say the aristocracy is just an illusion!

To sum up, so far the Third Estate has not had any true representatives in the Estates-General. Thus its political rights have been non-existent. [*What is the third estate?* 2: 'What has the Third Estate been until now? Nothing']

[1] Louis XI, reigned 1461–83.
[2] Richelieu governed France 1624–42.
[3] Louis XIV's reign 1643–1715.

The demands of the Third Estate must not be judged from the isolated observations of certain writers with some inklings of the rights of man. The Third Estate is still very backward in this respect, not only, I would say, by comparison with the enlightened views of students of the social order, but also with that mass of common ideas that forms public opinion. You can only make a judgment on the authentic petitions of the Third Estate through the formal demands which the great municipalities of the kingdom have addressed to the government. What do we see in these demands? That the people want to be *something* – to be honest, the least thing possible. First, it wants to have genuine representatives in the Estates-General, that is to say deputies *drawn from its own order*, able to interpret its wishes and defend its interests. But what would be the use of [the Third Estate] participating in the Estates-General if interests hostile to its own were to predominate? All it would do is sanction by its presence an oppression of which it would be the eternal victim. So it certainly cannot go and cast its vote in the Estates-General unless it exerted *an influence at least equal to that of the privileged orders*. Secondly, it demands that the number of its representatives be equal to that of the two other orders put together. However, this equality of representation would become a complete illusion if each chamber had its own separate vote. The Third Estate demands thirdly therefore that votes be counted *by heads and not by orders*. This is what these demands that have apparently set off alarm bells among the privileged orders boil down to. They thought that for this reason alone the reform of abuses was becoming indispensable.

The modest objective of the Third Estate is to have an influence in the Estates-General equal to that of the privileged orders. I repeat, could it ask for less? And is it not clear that if its influence is less than equal, it has no hope of emerging from its state of political non-existence, and of becoming *something*? [. . .]

SECOND DEMAND OF THE THIRD ESTATE

That the number of its deputies be equal to that of the two privileged orders.

Political rights, like civil rights, must derive from the status of being a citizen. This legal property is the same for everyone regardless of the amount of real property making up the wealth or income enjoyed by each individual. Any citizen fulfilling the conditions prescribed for becoming an elector has the right to be represented, and his representation cannot be a fraction of someone else's representation. This right is indivisible; everyone exercises it equally, just as everyone has equal protection under the law that they have agreed to make. How can you argue on the one hand that the law is the expression of the general will, that is to say of the plurality, and claim on the other that ten individual wills can cancel out a thousand other individual wills? Do we not then run the risk of having the law made by a minority? This is obviously contrary to the nature of things.

If these principles, certain as they are, seem to be derived too much from common ideas, I bring the reader back to a comparison right in front of his nose. Is it not true that everyone finds it fair for the huge bailiwick of Poitou to have more representatives in the Estates-General than the tiny bailiwick of Gex? Why is that? Because, they say, the population and tax revenue of Poitou are much higher than that of Gex. Thus principles are being accepted which permit you to determine the ratio of representatives. Do you want taxation to be the basis? Although we do not know precisely what the respective tax contribution of the different orders is, the Third Estate obviously bears more than half of the burden [. . .]

As far as population is concerned, the vast [numerical] superiority of the third order over the first two is well known. Like everybody else, I do not know what the real proportion is, but like anybody else I can do my sums [. . .] In total, there are less than two hundred thousand privileged persons in the first two orders. Compare that figure with a twenty-five to twenty-six million total population, and draw your own conclusions.

To get the same answer on the basis of different, but equally incontrovertible, principles, let us take the view that the privileged orders are to the great mass of citizens what exceptions are to the law. Every society must be regulated by common laws and be subject to a common order. If you make exceptions to that, they ought at the very least to be rare ones, and there can never be any question of the exception having the same weight and influence in public life as the norm. It is really insane to treat the interests of these exceptions as somehow balancing out those of the great mass of the people [. . .] In a few years time, when people come to look back on all the obstacles blocking this all too modest demand of the Third Estate, they will be surprised at the lack of substance in the arguments used against it, and even more surprised by the brazen effrontery of those who were bold enough to dig those excuses up.

The very people who invoke the authority of facts against the Third Estate could read in those facts a rule for their own conduct, if they were honest with themselves. The existence of a few loyal cities was enough to form a Chamber of Commons in the Estates-General under Philip the Fair.[4]

Since then, feudal servitude has disappeared, and rural areas have presented us with a large population of *new citizens*. Towns have multiplied

---

[4] Philip the Fair, reigned 1285–1314.

and grown. Commerce and the arts have created, as it were, a multitude of new classes with large numbers of prosperous families full of well-educated, public-spirited men. Why has this dual growth, so much greater than that of those loyal cities of earlier times, not encouraged this same authority to create two new chambers in favour of the Third Estate? Justice and sound politics alike require it. [. . .]

But I am using reason against people who can listen only to the voice of their own self-interest. Let us give them something to think about that might touch them more closely. Is it appropriate for today's nobility to hang on to the language and attitudes of the gothic age? Is it appropriate for the Third Estate, at the end of the eighteenth century, to stagnate in the sad, cowardly habits of the old servitude? If the Third Estate recognised and respected itself, then others would surely respect it too! People should note that the old relationship between the orders has been changed simultaneously on both sides. The Third Estate, which had been reduced to nothing, has regained, through its industry, part of what had been stolen from it by the offence [committed] against it by those who were stronger. Instead of demanding its rights back, it has consented to pay for them; they have not been restored to the Third Estate but sold back to it; and it has acquiesced in their purchase. But in the end, in one way or another, it can take possession of them. It must not forget that today it constitutes a reality in the nation, whereas before it was a shadow, [and] that, in the course of this long process of change, the nobility has ceased to be the monstrous feudal power that could oppress with impunity. It is the nobility that is now no more than the shadow of what it was, and this shadow is still trying to terrify a whole nation, but in vain – unless this nation wants to be regarded as the vilest on earth.

THIRD AND FINAL DEMAND OF THE THIRD ESTATE

That the Estates-General should vote, not by orders, but by heads.

[. . .]

The privileged orders fear the third order having equality of influence, and so they declare it to be unconstitutional. This behaviour is all the more remarkable for the fact that until now they have been two against one without finding anything unconstitutional in that unjust advantage. They feel very deeply the need to retain the veto over anything that could be against their interest.

Source: D. Williams (ed.), *The Enlightenment*, Cambridge, Cambridge University Press, 1999, pp. 494–5, 498–9, 504–6.

Gustav III of Sweden on the fall of the Bastille, 1789

Letter from Gustav III to Count Stendingk, his ambassador at St Petersburg, 7 August 1789

Nothing is more terrible than the events at Paris between 12th and 15th July: the *Invalides* broken into; canon and armed force used against the Bastille; this fortress taken by storm; the governor, Monsieur de Launay, dragged by the mob to the Place de Grève and decapitated; his head carried in triumph around the town; the same treatment meted out to the chief magistrate; the formation of a civil militia of 48,000 men; the French and Swiss guards joined with the people; Monsieur de Lafayette proclaimed commander-in-chief of the Paris militia; blue and red cockades raised,[5] the Estates declaring the King's ministers and the civil and military authorities to be responsible to the nation; and the King, alone with the Comte de Provence and the Comte d'Artois,[6] going on foot, without escort, to the Assembly, almost to apologise, and to request assistance to put down the disturbances: this is how weakness, uncertainty and an imprudent violence will overturn the throne of Louis XVI. I am still so disturbed by this news that I am afraid my letter shows it.

Source: A. Lentin (ed.), *Enlightened Absolutism (1760–1790). A Documentary Sourcebook*, Newcastle-upon-Tyne, Avero Publications, 1985, p. 281.

---

[5] Blue and red were the colours of the city of Paris. The tricolor (red, white and blue) devised by Lafayette, replaced the white fleur-de-lys of the house of Bourbon as the flag of Revolutionary France on 17 July 1789.

[6] The king's brothers, later Louis XVIII (1814–24) and Charles X (1824–30).

National Assembly, *Declaration of the Rights of Man and Citizen*, 1789

Declaration of the Rights of Man and Citizen, decreed by the National Assembly in the sessions of 20th, 21st, 23rd, 24th and 26th August, 1789, accepted by the King

INTRODUCTION

The representatives of the French people, constituted as a National Assembly, considering that ignorance, neglect or contempt for the rights of man are the sole causes of public misfortunes and the corruption of governments, have resolved to set forth in a solemn declaration the natural, inalienable and sacred rights of man, so that this declaration may serve as a constant reminder to all members of society of their rights and duties; so that the acts of the legislative power and of the executive power, being liable at any time to be compared with the purpose of all political institutions, may thereby be the more respected; so that the citizens' demands, henceforth founded on simple and incontrovertible principles, may always operate for the maintenance of the constitution and the good of all.

The National Assembly therefore recognises and declares, in the presence and under the auspices of the Supreme Being, the following rights of man and citizen:

1. Men are born and remain free and equal in respect of their rights; social distinctions can only be based on public utility.
2. The aim of every political association is the protection of the natural and imprescriptible rights of man; these rights are liberty, property, security and resistance to oppression.
3. The fundamental source of all sovereignty resides in the nation; no body of men, no individual can exercise an authority which does not expressly derive therefrom.
4. Liberty consists in being able to do whatever does not harm another. Thus, the exercise of each man's natural rights has no limits other than those which guarantee to the other members of society the enjoyment of these same rights; those limits can only be determined by the law.
5. The law can only forbid acts harmful to society. Whatever is not forbidden by the law cannot be prevented, and no-one can be forced to do what the law does not require.

6. The law is the expression of the general will; all citizens have the right to participate in lawmaking, personally or through their representatives; the law must be the same for all, whether it protects or punishes. All citizens being equal in its eyes, are equally eligible for all public honours, positions and duties, according to their ability, and without any distinction other than those of their virtues and talents.

7. No man may be charged, arrested or detained except under the circumstances laid down by the law and in accordance with the formalities prescribed therein. Those who solicit, promote, carry out or cause to be carried out any arbitrary orders, must be punished; but any citizen lawfully summonsed or arrested must instantly obey: he renders himself liable by resistance.

8. The penalties laid down by law should only be such as are strictly and manifestly necessary, and no-one may be punished except by virtue of an established law, promulgated before the commission of the offence, and lawfully applied.

9. Every man being presumed innocent until found guilty, if his arrest is considered essential, any harshness unnecessary to secure his arrest must be strictly forbidden by the law.

10. No man must be penalised for his opinions, even his religious opinions, provided that their expression does not disturb the public order established by the law.

11. The free expression of thoughts and opinions is one of the most precious of the rights of man; every citizen is therefore entitled to freedom of speech, of expression and of the press, save that he is liable for the abuse of this freedom in the circumstances laid down by the law.

12. The rights of man and of the citizen require a public force to guarantee them; this force is therefore established for the good of all, and not for the private benefit of those to whom it is entrusted.

13. A common tax is essential for the upkeep of the public force and for the costs of administration; it must be levied equally on the citizens in accordance with their capacity to pay.

14. The citizens are entitled, in person or through their representatives, to determine the need for public taxation, freely to consent to it, to control its use, and to fix the amount, basis, mode of collection and duration.

15. Society is entitled to require every public servant to give an account of his administration.

16. Any society which lacks a sure guarantee of rights or a fixed separation of powers, has no constitution.

17. Property being an inviolable and sacred right, no-one may be deprived of it save when this is clearly required by public necessity, lawfully determined, and only on condition of fair and prior compensation.

TO THE REPRESENTATIVES OF THE FRENCH PEOPLE

Source: Contemporary print of the *Declaration of the Rights of Man and Citizen* in the Musée Carnavalet, Paris. Reproduced in G. Duby, *Histoire de la France*, volume 2, Paris, Larousse, 1971, p. 306, trans. A. Lentin.

National Assembly, *Decree on the Abolition of the Nobility*, 19 June 1790

The National Assembly decrees that hereditary nobility is for all time abolished and that consequently no one whosoever shall use or be addressed by the titles of *prince, duc, comte, marquis, vicomte, vidame, baron, chevalier, messire, écuyer, noble* or any other similar title.

Every French citizen must use only the real surname of his family. He may no longer wear livery or cause it to be worn or possess armorial bearings. In church, incense will be burned only to honour the deity and will not be offered to anyone be he never so high.

No body or individual will be addressed by the titles *monseigneur* and *meisseigneurs* nor by those of *excellence, altesse, éminence* or *grandeur*. However, no citizen may choose to make the present decree a pretext for defacing monuments placed in churches, charters, titles and other documents of importance to families, property or the embellishments of any public or private building; nor may anyone at all proceed with or require the implementation of the provisions relating to liveries and to armorials on carriages before 14 July (for citizens resident in Paris) or before the expiry of three months (for those living in the provinces).

Source: J. Hardman (ed.), *The French Revolution Sourcebook*, London, Arnold, 1999, p. 113.

Edmund Burke on the French Revolution, 1790

It is now sixteen or seventeen years since I saw the queen of France, then the dauphiness, at Versailles; and surely never lighted on this orb, which she hardly seemed to touch, a more delightful vision. I saw her just above the horizon, decorating and cheering the elevated sphere she just began to move in,—glittering like the morning-star, full of life, and splendour, and joy. Oh! what a revolution! and what a heart must I have to contemplate without emotion that elevation and that fall![7] Little did I dream when she added titles of veneration to those of enthusiastic, distant, respectful love, that she should ever be obliged to carry the sharp antidote against disgrace concealed in that bosom; little did I dream that I should have lived to see such disasters fallen upon her in a nation of gallant men, in a nation of men of honour, and of cavaliers. I thought ten thousand swords must have leaped from their scabbards to avenge even a look that threatened her with insult. But the age of chivalry is gone. That of sophisters, economists, and calculators, has succeeded; and the glory of Europe is extinguished for ever. [. . .]

This mixed system of opinion and sentiment had its origin in the ancient chivalry; and the principle, though varied in its appearance by the varying state of human affairs, subsisted and influenced through a long succession of generations, even to the time we live in. If it should ever be totally extinguished, the loss I fear will be great. It is this which has given its character to modern Europe. It is this which has distinguished it under all its forms of government, and distinguished it to its advantage, from the states of Asia, and possibly from those states which flourished in the most brilliant periods of the antique world. It was this, which, without confounding ranks, had produced a noble equality, and handed it down through all the gradations of social life. It was this opinion which mitigated kings into companions, and raised private men to be fellows with kings. Without force or opposition, it subdued the fierceness of pride and power; it obliged sovereigns to submit to the soft collar of social esteem, compelled stern authority to submit to elegance, and gave a dominating vanquisher of laws to be subdued by manners.

But now all is to be changed. All the pleasing illusions, which made power gentle and obedience liberal, which harmonized the different shades of life, and which, by a bland assimilation, incorporated into pol-

---

[7] In October 1789 Louis XVI, Marie-Antoinette and the young dauphin were forced by a crowd of women demonstrators and the National Guard to return from Versailles to Paris, where they became virtually prisoners in the Tuileries palace.

itics the sentiments which beautify and soften private society, are to be dissolved by this new conquering empire of light and reason. All the decent drapery of life is to be rudely torn off. All the superadded ideas, furnished from the wardrobe of a moral imagination, which the heart owns, and the understanding ratifies, as necessary to cover the defects of our naked, shivering nature, and to raise it to dignity in our own estimation, are to be exploded as a ridiculous, absurd, and antiquated fashion.

On this scheme of things, a king is but a man, a queen is but a woman; a woman is but an animal, and an animal not of the highest order. All homage paid to the sex in general as such, and without distinct views, is to be regarded as romance and folly. Regicide, and parricide, and sacrilege, are but fictions of superstition, corrupting jurisprudence by destroying its simplicity. The murder of a king, or a queen, or a bishop, or a father, are only common homicide; and if the people are by any chance, or in any way, gainers by it, a sort of homicide much the most pardonable, and into which we ought not to make too severe a scrutiny.

On the scheme of this barbarous philosophy, which is the offspring of cold hearts and muddy understandings, and which is as void of solid wisdom as it is destitute of all taste and elegance, laws are to be supported only by their own terrors, and by the concern which each individual may find in them from his own private speculations, or can spare to them from his own private interests. In the groves of *their* academy, at the end of every vista, you see nothing but the gallows. Nothing is left which engages the affections on the part of the commonwealth. On the principles of this mechanic philosophy, our institutions can never be embodied, if I may use the expression, in persons; so as to create in us love, veneration, admiration, or attachment. [. . .]

But power, of some kind or other, will survive the shock in which manners and opinions perish; and it will find other and worse means for its support. The usurpation which, in order to subvert ancient institutions, has destroyed ancient principles, will hold power by arts similar to those by which it has acquired it. When the old feudal and chivalrous spirit of *fealty*, which, by freeing kings from fear, freed both kings and subjects from the precautions of tyranny, shall be extinct in the minds of men, plots and assassinations will be anticipated by preventive murder and preventive confiscation, and that long roll of grim and bloody maxims, which form the political code of all power, not standing on its own honour, and the honour of those who are to obey it. Kings will be tyrants from policy, when subjects are rebels from principle.

Source: E. Burke, *Reflections on the Revolution in France*, Everyman edition, Lonon, Dent, 1955 [1910], pp. 73–5.

Marquis de la Queuille protesting against the oath to the constitution, 1790

Letter by the marquis de la Queuille, former deputy of the nobility of the Auvergne, 28 November 1790, published in the royalist journal, *L'Ami du Roi* (*The King's Friend*), 29 November 1790[8]

The most precious concern for every thinking being is his religion; all that is purely temporal can be sacrificed for the sake of peace, but when it is a question of the eternal truths, every concession becomes a crime.

I therefore declare, in the name of my constituents and on my own behalf, that the decree of 27 November of the Assembly, which has called itself national, is an impious and criminal attempt on the authority and liberty of the Gallican Church, since it seeks to separate France from the union and obedience owed by every Catholic to the pope as Vicar of Jesus Christ.

I wish to live and die in the Catholic, Apostolic and Roman faith, and if the Assembly, which has called itself national, revives the centuries of persecution, I ask God for the grace to be the first martyr either for my faith or for my king.

Signed le marquis de la Queuille, marshal of the king's camps and armies, deputy of the nobility of Auvergne, in the free and general states of France, retired at the end of my period of election.

Paris 28 November 1790.
L'Ami du Roi, No. CLXXXII, 29 November 1790.

Source: J. Gilchrist and W. J. Murray, *The Press in the French Revolution*, London, Cheshire Ginn, 1971, pp. 103–4.

---

[8] In July 1790 the Assembly introduced the Civil Constitution of the Clergy, which almost halved the number of French bishops, provided for a salaried clergy appointed by popular election and marginalised the role of the pope. On 27 November 1790 the Assembly required the clergy to swear an oath to the constitution, including the Civil Constitution of the Clergy. Nearly all bishops and almost half the ordinary clergy refused.

Jean-Paul Marat on 'a general insurrection and popular executions', 1790

Article in Marat's journal *L'Ami du peuple (The People's Friend)*, 18 December 1790

. . . No, it is not on the frontiers, but in the capital that we must rain down our blows. Stop wasting time thinking up means of defence; there is only one means of defence for you. That which I have recommended so many times: *a general insurrection and popular executions*. Begin then by making sure of the king, the dauphin and the royal family: put them under a strong guard and let their heads answer for events. Follow this up by cutting off, without hesitation, the general's head, and those of the counter-revolutionary ministers and ex-ministers; those of the mayor and the anti-revolutionary municipal councillors; then put all [. . . the counter-revolutionaries in] the National Assembly, all the known supporters of despotism, on the edge of the sword. I tell you again, this is the only way which remains for you to save the country. Six months ago five or six hundred heads would have been enough to pull you back from the abyss. Today because you have stupidly let your implacable enemies conspire among themselves and gather strength, perhaps we will have to cut off five or six thousand; but even if it need twenty thousand, there is no time for hesitation.

Source: J. Gilchrist and W. J. Murray, *The Press in the French Revolution*, London, Cheshire Ginn, 1971, p. 268.

Emperor Leopold II of Austria on the French Revolution, 1791

Open letter to Empress Catherine II of Russia, with copies to kings of England, Prussia, Spain, Sicily and Sardinia, July 1791, after the unsuccessful attempt in June by the French royal family to escape ('the flight to Varennes')

July 1791

I am sure that Your Majesty will have learned of the unheard-of attempt to arrest the King of France, the Queen, my sister, and the royal family, with as much surprise and indignation as myself, and that your feelings cannot differ from mine about an event which gives rise to fears of consequences still more atrocious, fixes the seal of illegality to the excesses which had already been perpetrated in France, and compromises the honour of all sovereigns and the security of all governments.

Determined to carry out my duty in regard to these considerations, both as head of the Germanic body and its assembly, and as sovereign of the Austrian dominions, I propose to the Kings of Spain, England, Prussia, Naples and Sardinia, as well as to the Empress of Russia, that they should join together with myself in advising, co-ordinating and taking measures aimed at restoring the liberty and honour of the Most Christian King and his family, and to set limits to the dangerous excesses of the French Revolution.

The most urgent task seems to me to be that we should all join in conveying immediately, through our ministers in France, a common declaration, or similar simultaneous declarations, such as may bring the heads of the violent party to their senses and prevent any desperate decisions, while leaving them the way open to an honourable retreat and to the peaceful establishment of a state of affairs in France which should at least preserve the dignity of the crown and the conditions essential for general tranquillity.

> *Source*: A. Lentin (ed.), *Enlightened Absolutism (1760–1790). A Documentary Sourcebook*, Newcastle-upon-Tyne, Avero Publications, 1985, p. 275.

Emperor Leopold II of Austria and King Frederick-William II of Prussia, *The Declaration of Pillnitz*, 1791

Joint public declaration by Emperor Leopold II of Austria and King Frederick-William II of Prussia, at Pillnitz, 27 August 1791

His Majesty the Emperor and His Majesty the King of Prussia, having heard the wishes and representations of the Count of Provence and the

Count of Artois,[9] jointly declare that they regard the present situation of His Majesty the King of France as an object of common interest to all the sovereigns of Europe.

They trust that this interest cannot fail to be recognised by the Powers whose aid is sought, and that therefore the latter will not refuse, together with their aforementioned Majesties, to employ the most effective measures, relative to their forces, to enable the King of France to consolidate, in perfect freedom, the bases of a monarchical government, in accord both with the rights of sovereigns and with the welfare of the French nation. This being so and under these circumstances, their aforesaid Majesties, the Emperor and the King of Prussia, are resolved to act promptly and by mutual accord with the forces necessary to achieve the proposed common aim. Meanwhile they will give appropriate orders to their troops, so that they may be ready to take action.

Source: A. Lentin (ed.), *Enlightened Absolutism (1760–1790). A Documentary Sourcebook*, Newcastle-upon-Tyne, Avero Publications, 1985, p. 276.

Hébert on Louis XVI after the flight to Varennes, 1791

Article in Hébert's journal *Le Père Duchesne (Old Man Duchesne)*, autumn 1791

You my king. You are no longer my king, no longer my king! You are nothing but a cowardly deserter; a king should be the father of the people, not its executioner. Now that the nation has resumed its rights it will not be so bloody stupid as to take back a coward like you. You, king? You are not even a citizen. You will be lucky to avoid leaving your head on a scaffold for having sought the slaughter of so many men. Ah, I don't doubt that once again you are going to pretend to be honest and that, supported by those scoundrels on the constitutional committee, you are going to promise miracles. They still want to stick the crown on the head of a stag; but no, damn it, that will not happen! From one end of France to the other, there is only an outcry against you, your debauched Messalina, and your whole bastard race.[10]

[9] The younger brothers of Louis XVI.
[10] Marie-Antoinette was rumoured to have cuckolded the king.

No more Capet,[11] this is what every citizen is shouting, and, besides, even if it were possible that they might want to pardon you all your crimes, what trust could now be placed in your remains? You vile perjurer, a man who has broken his oath again and again. We will stuff you into Charenton and your whore into the Hôpital.[12] When you are finally walled up, both of you, and above all when you no longer have a Civil List, I'll be stuffed with an axe if you get away.

Le Père Duchesne, No. 61.

Source: J. Gilchrist and W. J. Murray, *The Press in the French Revolution*, London, Cheshire Ginn, 1971, pp. 132–3.

Hébert calls for the execution of Louis XVI, 1792

Article in Hébert's journal, *Le Père Duchesne*, late 1792

Just think, damn it! how surrounded we are with false brothers. All the conspirators were not at Orléans and the Abbey;[13] their accomplices are still in our midst. These worthy men, [. . .] still dwell in Paris. They are concealed by another mask; but at heart they breathe only blood and slaughter. There is not one good citizen who has not at his heels one of these bad angels, who poisons him with his advice, while waiting his chance to plunge his dagger into his heart [. . .] Yes, damn it! the traitor Louis, shut up like an owl in the Temple tower, would not be so complacent there, if he did not have a strong following in Paris. Already, damn it, they have tried more than one surprise attack to release him. The courtesans, who sneak themselves in everywhere, have more than once got into that famous tower, by greasing the paw of some of his keepers. It is fortunate that we have some sturdy chaps at the Commune, who have their eyes everywhere, and who know all that is going on. Without our agents, damn it, it would have been long since that the brood of howling-toms would have made off for Coblenz.[14] It must not

---

[11] Capet was Louis's surname.
[12] Paris lunatic asylums.
[13] Scenes of the 'September massacres' of priests and other suspected counter-revolutionaries, 1792.
[14] Headquarters of the counter-revolutionary armies.

happen that the greatest scoundrel that has ever been should remain unpunished. It is good that the sovereign people become used to judging kings. Oh! the great day! and how I would have hugged myself for joy if our victorious armies had cleaned up all the crowned brigands, if the Mandarin of Prussia and the little Austrian twerp,[15] chained like wild beasts, had been dragged back to Paris by Dumouriez![16] What a splendid sight to see three guillotines placed in a row with the horny head of paunchy Capet, and those of Frederick and Francis, held in the trap and ready to fall at the one time!

Le Père Duchesne.

Source: J. Gilchrist and W. J. Murray, *The Press in the French Revolution*, London, Cheshire Ginn, 1971, p. 153.

Legislative Assembly, *Decree on the Death Penalty*, 1792

Decree of the Legislative Assembly introducing the guillotine, 20 March 1792

The National Assembly, considering that uncertainty concerning the method of enforcement of Title I, article 3 of the Penal Code[17] delays the punishment of several criminals condemned to death; that it is most urgent to terminate unfavorable conditions which might have unfortunate consequences; that humanity requires that the death penalty be as painless as possible, decrees that Title I, article 3 of the Penal Code be carried out according to the manner indicated and the method approved in the statement signed by the permanent secretary of the Academy of Surgery and annexed to the present decree; and, accordingly, authorizes the Executive Power to make the necessary expenditures in order to achieve this method of execution, in such manner that it may be uniform throughout the entire kingdom.

---

[15] King Frederick-William II of Prussia and Emperor Francis II of Austria.

[16] Commanded French armies in victories over Prussia at Valmy and Austria at Jemappes, 1792.

[17] Article 3 reads: 'Every person condemned [to death] shall be decapitated'.

Motivated opinion on the method of decapitation, 7 March, 1792

"The Committee on Legislation has done me the honor of consulting me concerning two letters written by the National Assembly with regard to the execution of Title I, article 3 of the Penal Code, providing that *every one condemned* to the penalty of death *shall be decapitated*. In these letters the Minister of Justice and the directory of the Department of Paris', on the basis of representations made to them, consider it urgently necessary to determine exactly the manner of procedure in the execution of the law, lest, through defective means or by lack of experience and skill, capital punishment become horrible for the victim and the spectators [. . .]

"I consider the representations just and the fears well founded. Experience and reason alike indicate that the method hitherto used in decapitating criminals exposes them to a capital punishment more frightful than mere deprivation of life, which is the formal aim of the law; in order to achieve it, the execution must be made instantly and by a single blow; examples give proof of the difficulty of succeeding therein.

"The decapitation of M. de Lally must here be recalled;[18] he was on his knees, his eyes bandaged; the executioner struck him on the nape of the neck; the blow did not sever the head [. . .]; the body [. . .] was turned over; and it was only with three or four blows of the sword that the head was finally separated from the body. This *butchery* was viewed with horror [. . .]

"No one is ignorant of the fact that cutting instruments have little or no effect when they strike perpendicularly; by examining them under a microscope it may be seen that they are only more or less fine saws, which must be operated by sliding over the body which is to be divided. One would not succeed in decapitating by a single blow with an axe or knife, the edge of which was in a straight line; but with a convex blade, as on old battle-axes, the blow struck acts perpendicularly only at the middle part of the circle; but the instrument, in penetrating the continuity of the parts it divides, has an oblique sliding action on the sides, and effectively achieves its end.

"In considering the structure of the neck, the center of which is the vertebral column composed of several bones, the connection of which forms overlappings so that there is no joint, it is impossible to be assured of a prompt and perfect separation by trusting to an agent whose skill is influenced by moral and physical factors; for certainty one must depend on invariable mechanical means, the force and effect of which may like-

---

[18] Thomas, Baron de Lally, governor of the French possessions in India, capitulated to the British and was executed for treason in 1766. His case was taken up posthumously by Voltaire.

wise be determined. [. . .] The body of the criminal is laid face down between two posts connected at the top by a crosspiece, from which the convex axe is dropped on the neck by means of a release. The back of the instrument must be strong and heavy enough to act effectively, like a pile driver; it is known that its force increases in proportion to the height from which it falls.

"It would be easy to construct a similar machine, the performance of which would be unfailing. Decapitation would be performed instantly, according to the spirit and aim of the new law. It would be easy to test it on corpses, and even on live sheep. It could be determined whether it was necessary to fasten the victim's head with a crosspiece encircling the neck at the base of the skull; the prongs or extensions of such crosspiece could be held by pegs under the scaffold. This apparatus, if found necessary, would cause no feeling and would scarcely be perceived."

Signed: LOUIS,
*Perpetual Secretary of
the Academy of Surgery*

Source: J. H. Stewart, *A Documentary Survey of the French Revolution*, New York, Macmillan, 1951, pp. 343–6.

National Assembly, *France Calls on the People of Belgium to Revolt*, 1792

Proclamation to the people of Belgium, April 1792

Our armies are at your frontiers, to make war on tyrants and bring liberty to citizens. They expect the peoples of your rich lands to conquer with them and for them. They are off to seek out the despots' troops, to avenge the wrongs done to the French nation. Whose side are you on? They will also avenge the blood shed by you, your rights that have been usurped, and the unworthy slavery in which a proud and brave people groans.

Let the Lion of Belgium awake! The hour of liberty is sounded, the hour of the tyrants' ruin draws near.

Every peaceful citizen who requests protection, safety and liberty, will receive it from the soldiers of a generous nation. Every soldier willing to shed for liberty the blood which he shed for the sake of the ambition of courts, will be received with honour by companions-in-arms who will be proud to fight with him.

Citizens, do you want liberty? If so, your fair lands will be protected from the destructive scourge of war; your ancient laws will revive; you alone will be able to change them; and all your actions will find powerful support.

Soldiers, do you wish to go on fighting, like slaves, for tyrants, or to march, as free men, against tyrants' slaves? Come and serve beneath our banners! Let us march together, to bring victory and liberty to the banks of the Rhine! The French army, a citizen army, has seen its former courage swell again. It calls upon its enemies, it defies them, it seeks them out; but still more does it seek out and call for friends and brothers.

Peoples of Belgium! We swear to make you free. Will you be passive spectators of our efforts for your liberty? Let the union of two nations be a powerful example for all tyrants and the comfort and hope of all oppressed peoples.

Source: A. Lentin (ed.), *Enlightened Absolutism (1760–1790). A Documentary Sourcebook*, Newcastle-upon-Tyne, Avero Publications, 1985, p. 279.

National Assembly, *Decree on the* Levée en masse, 23 August 1793

i   From this time, until the enemies of France have been expelled from the territory of the Republic, all Frenchmen are in a state of permanent requisition for the army. The young men will go to fight; married men will forge arms and transport food and supplies; women will make tents and uniforms and work in hospitals; children will find old rags for bandages; old men will appear in public places to excite the courage of warriors, the hatred of kings, and the unity of the Republic.

ii Public buildings will be converted into barracks, public squares into armament workshops, the soil of cellars will be washed to extract saltpetre.

iii Rifles will be confined exclusively to those who march to fight the enemy; military service in the interior will be performed with sporting guns and side-arms.

iv   Riding horses will be requisitioned for the cavalry corps; draught horses, other than those used in agriculture, will pull artillery and stores.

v   The Committee of Public Safety is charged with the taking of all measures to establish, without delay, an extraordinary factory for arms of all kinds, to cater for the determination and energy of the French people; it is consequently authorised to form as many establishments, factories, workshops and mills as are necessary to carry out the work, as well as requiring, for this purpose, throughout the Republic, craftsmen and workers who can contribute to its success; for this object there is a sum of 30 millions at the disposal of the ministry of war [. . .]

Source: D. G. Wright, *Revolution and Terror in France 1789–1795*, London, Longman, 1976, pp. 115–16.

Robespierre on revolutionary government, June 1793

There must be one will.

It must be either republican or royalist.

For it to be republican, there must be republican ministers, republican newspapers, republican deputies, a republican government.

Whilst the body politic suffers from revolutionary sickness and a divided will, the foreign war is [necessarily] a mortal illness.

The internal dangers come from the bourgeois; to defeat the bourgeois, it is necessary to rally the people. Everything was ready to place the people under the yoke of the bourgeoisie and send the defenders of the republic to the scaffold. They have triumphed at Marseilles, at Bordeaux and at Lyon;[19] they would have triumphed at Paris but for the present insurrection. The present insurrection must continue until the measures necessary to save the republic have been taken. The people must make an alliance with the Convention and the Convention must make use of the people.

The insurrection must spread by degrees along the same lines; the *sans-culottes* must be paid and remain in the towns [rather than being sent to the front].

They must be found arms, incited and enlightened.

[19] Centres of counter-revolutionary activity, 1793.

91

Republican enthusiasm must be exalted by all means possible.

If the [proscribed] deputies are merely sent home, the republicans are lost; the deputies will continue to mislead the departments, and their replacements will be no better.

[General] Custine: to be watched by new and trustworthy commissioners.[20]

Foreign affairs: alliance with the smaller powers; but impossible until we have a single national will.

Source: J. Hardman (ed.), *The French Revolution Sourcebook*, London, Arnold, 1999, p. 163.

Anon., *What is a* sans-culotte?, 1793

A *sans culotte*, you rogues? He is someone who always goes about on foot, who has not got the millions you would all like to have, who has no châteaux, no valets to wait on him, and who lives simply with his wife and children, if he has any, on the fourth or fifth storey. He is useful because he knows how to till a field, to forge iron, to use a saw, to roof a house, to make shoes, and to spill his blood to the last drop for the safety of the Republic. And because he is a worker, you are sure not to meet his person in the Café de Chartres, or in the gaming houses where others plot and wager, nor in the National Theatre, where *L'Ami des Lois* is performed, nor in the Vaudeville Theatre at a performance of *Chaste Susanne*,[21] nor in the literary clubs where for two sous, which are so precious to him, you are offered Gorsas's muck, with the *Chronique* and the *Patriote Français*.[22]

In the evening he goes to the assembly of his Section, not powdered and perfumed and nattily booted, in the hope of being noticed by the citizenesses in the galleries, but ready to support sound proposals with all his might and ready to pulverise those which come from the despised faction of politicians.

---

[20] A former deputy for the nobility at the Estates-General, 1789, the Count de Custine served revolutionary France as a general. Appointed to command the army of the north in May 1793, he was recalled and guillotined in August.

[21] *L'Ami des Lois* (*The Friend of the Laws*) was a fashionable comedy, *Chaste Susanne* an operetta, of 1793.

[22] *La Chronique* and the *Patriote Français* were Girondin newspapers, Gorsas was a Girondin journalist who was to fall victim to the Terror.

Finally, a *sans culotte* always has his sabre well-sharpened, ready to cut off the ears of all opponents of the Revolution; sometimes he carries his pike about with him; but as soon as the drum beats you see him leave for the Vendée, for the Army of the Alps, or for the Army of the North.

Source: D. G. Wright, *Revolution and Terror in France 1789–1795*, London, Longman, 1976, p. 116.

National Assembly, *The Law of Suspects*, 1793

1. Immediately after the publication of this decree, all suspects found on the territory of the Republic and who are still at liberty will be arrested.
2. Suspects are (i) Those who, either by their conduct or their relationships, by their conversation or by their writing, are shown to be partisans of tyranny and federalism and enemies of liberty; (ii) Those who cannot justify, under the provisions of the law of 21 March last, their means of existence and the performance of their civic duties; (iii) Those have been refused certificates of civic responsibility; (iv) Public officials suspended or deprived of their functions by the National Convention or its agents, and not since reinstated, especially those who have been, or ought to be, dismissed by the law of 12 August last; (v) Those former nobles, including husbands, wives, fathers, mothers, sons or daughters, brothers or sisters, and agents of *émigrés*, who have not constantly manifested their loyalty to the Revolution; (vi) Those who have emigrated during the interval between the 1 July 1789 and the publication of the law of 8 April 1792, although they may have returned to France during the period of delay fixed by the law or before.

   The *comités de surveillance* established under the law of 21 March last, or those substituting for them, are empowered by the decrees of the representatives of the people to go to the armies and the departments, according to the particular decrees of the National Convention, and are charged with drawing up, in each local district, a list of suspects, of issuing arrest warrants against them, and of affixing seals to their private papers. The commanders of the public force, to whom these arrest warrants will be conveyed, must carry them out immediately, on pain of dismissal.

Source: D. G. Wright, *Revolution and Terror in France 1789–1795*, London, Longman, 1976, pp. 120–1.

Olympe de Gouges, Letter to her son before execution, 2 November 1793

To Citizen Degouges, general officer in the army of the Rhine.

I die, my dear son, a victim of my idolatry for the fatherland and for the people. Under the specious mask of republicanism, her enemies have brought me remorselessly to the scaffold.

After five months of captivity, I was transferred to a *maison de sante*[23] in which I was as free as I would have been at home. I could have escaped, as both my enemies and executioners know full well, but, convinced that all malevolence combining to ensnare me could not make me take a single step against the Revolution, I myself demanded to go to trial. Could I have believed that unmuzzled tigers would themselves be judges against the laws, against even that assembled public that will soon reproach them with my death?

I was presented with my indictment three days before my death; from the moment this indictment was signed the law gave me the right to see my defenders and whomsoever else I chose to assist my case. All were prevented from seeing me. I was kept as if in solitary confinement, unable to speak even to the gaoler. The law also gave me the right to choose my jurats;[24] I was given the list at midnight and, the following day at 7 o'clock, I was taken to the Tribunal, weak and sick, and lacking the art of speaking to the public; like Jean-Jacques[25] and also on account of his virtues, I was all too aware of my inadequacy. I asked for the *défenseur officieux*[26] that I had chosen. I was told that there wasn't one or that he did not wish to take on my cause; I asked for another to take his place, I was told that I had enough wit to defend myself.

Yes, no doubt I had enough to spare to defend my innocence, which was evident to the eyes of all there present. I do not deny that a *défenseur officieux* could have done much more for me in pointing out all the services and benefits that I have brought the people.

---

[23] maison de sante: lunatic asylum.
[24] *jurats*: members of the jury.
[25] Rousseau.
[26] défenseur officieux: public defender.

Twenty times I made my executioners pale and not knowing how to reply to each sentence that betrayed my innocence and their bad faith, they sentenced me to death, lest the people be led to consider my fate as the greatest example of iniquity the world has ever seen.

Farewell, my son, I shall be no more when you receive this letter. But leave your post, the injustice done to your mother and the crime committed against her are reason enough.

I die, my son, my dear son; I die innocent. All laws have been violated for the most virtuous woman of her century, [two illegible words] the law, always remember the good advice that I have given you.

I leave your wife's watch as well as the receipt for her jewellery at the pawnbrokers, the jar and the keys to the trunk that I sent to Tours.

De Gouges.[27]

Source: O. Blanc, *Last Letters. Prisons and Prisoners of the French Revolution 1793–1794*, trans. Alan Sheridan, London, André Deutsch, 1987, pp. 131–2.

Amable Augustin Clément, Letter addressed to posterity before execution, 27 December 1793

Amable Augustin Clément,[28] born 7 March 1761, died by the sword of the law on 27 December 1793 for having been at the Champ-de-Mars on 17 July 1791 under orders from the municipality of Paris, and condemned out of revenge by Lézerot, who denounced him. That wretched man was under arms and certainly acted no differently from the others, but since traitors are required so that innocence may perish, this man, in order to hide the crime in which he took part, denounced me in order to escape the vengeance of the nation, and committed this base action. But I die without ill feeling towards him, hoping that I am showing him the way and that he will travel along it like the others, for he is as guilty as they, indeed doubly so. But I leave posterity to judge of my innocence.

[27] Olympe de Gouges, author of *The Declaration of the Rights of Woman and Citizen* (1791), victim of the Terror.
[28] As a private soldier in the National Guard, Clément was among those who, on Lafayette's orders, had fired on a crowd of republican demonstrators in the 'massacre of the Champ de Mars' in 1791.

I was born thirty-two years, eight months and twenty days ago, that is a reward for serving my country since 14 July '89.

I hope to bear my sentence with the steadfastness that I have always shown in all matters since the Revolution, unless my strength abandons me. I pray those who will read this sad, last testament to have pity on an unfortunate wretch who is dying for obeying orders, without knowing where he was going. I declare that my commander was as innocent as I, but it will be recognized too late that I did not deserve such a fate.

One of the same batallion, a victim like me, he is called Baron, will accompany me to the scaffold. But it is a theatre of honour when one dies for one's country.

Written on 17 December at half-past seven in the morning.

A. A. Clément, at the Conciergerie.

Source: O. Blanc, *Last Letters. Prisons and Prisoners of the French Revolution 1793–1794*, trans. Alan Sheriden, London, André Deutsch, 1987, pp. 150–1.

Robespierre on 'the principles of revolutionary government', 1793

Speech by Robespierre to the Committee of Public Safety, 25 December 1793

Citizen representatives of the people:
[. . .] The defenders of the Republic are adopting the maxim of Caesar; they believe that *nothing has been done as long as there remains something to do*. Enough dangers remain to occupy all our zeal. To overcome the English and the traitors is an easy enough thing for our Republican soldiers to do; but there exists an undertaking no less important, and more difficult. The eternal intrigues of all the enemies of our liberty must be confounded, and the principles on which we must base public prosperity be made to triumph.

Such are the first tasks you have imposed upon your Committee of Public Safety.

First, we shall discuss the principles of, and the necessity for, revolutionary government; then we shall explain the situation which is threatening to paralyze it at birth.

The theory of revolutionary government is as new as the revolution which brought it into being. There is no point in searching for it in the books of political writers, who did not foresee this revolution, nor in the laws of tyrants, who, content to abuse their power, have little concern for exploring its legitimacy. Consequently, this phrase is merely a subject of terror or a term of abuse for the aristocracy; for tyrants, it is a scandal, and for many people, an enigma. We must explain it to everyone, so at least good citizens may be rallied behind the principles governing public interest.

The purpose of the government is to direct the moral and physical energies of the nation towards the goal for which it was established.

The aim of constitutional government is to maintain the Republic; that of revolutionary government is to establish it.

Revolution is war waged by liberty against its enemies; constitution is the peaceful rule of victorious liberty.

Revolutionary government needs to operate in an extraordinary manner, precisely because it is at war. It is subject to less uniform and less rigorous regulations because the circumstances in which it finds itself are stormy and unstable, and, above all, because it is forced unceasingly to deploy new and swift resources against new and pressing dangers.

Constitutional government is principally concerned with civil liberty, and revolutionary government with public liberty. Under a constitutional régime, it almost suffices to protect individuals against the abuse of power by the state: under a revolutionary régime, it is the state which has to defend itself against all the factions which assail it.

Revolutionary government owes to all good citizens the fullest protection the state can afford; to enemies of the people it owes nothing but death.

These ideas suffice to explain the origin and nature of the laws we call 'revolutionary'. Those who call them 'arbitrary' or 'tyrannical' are stupid or perverse sophists who are attempting to confuse opposites; they wish to have peace and war, health and sickness, subject to the same form of government, or, rather, their only aim is to resurrect tyranny and to destroy the *patrie*. When they invoke the literal application of constitutional principles, it is only because they wish to violate them with impunity. They are cowardly assassins who, in order to massacre the Republic in its cradle without danger to themselves, try to strangle it with vague maxims from which they are well able to disassociate themselves.

The constitutional vessel was not built to remain in the slips for ever; but is it necessary to launch it at the height of the storm, and under the influence of adverse winds? This is what the tyrants and slaves who opposed its construction wanted; but the French people has ordered you to wait for calm to return, and its unanimous will, completely drowning out the clamour of the aristocracy and of federalism, has commanded that you first deliver it from all its enemies.

Source: 'Rapport sur les principes du gouvernement révolution-naire', in Robespierre, *Textes choises*, ed. J. Poperen, Paris, Editions sociales, 1957, pp. 273–5, trans. Patsy Peel.

Robespierre on revolutionary virtue, justice and terror, 1794

Robespierre, speech to the National Convention on 'The principles of public morality', 5 February 1794

What is the goal towards which we are heading? The peaceful enjoyment of liberty and equality, the reign of that eternal justice from which the laws have been engraved not on marble and stone but in the hearts of all men, even in the heart of the slave who forgets them or of the tyrant who denies them.

We want an order of things in which all base and cruel passions will be unknown, and all generous and charitable feelings watched over by the laws; where ambition is the desire to merit glory and to serve the country; where distinctions are born only of equality itself; where the citizen is responsible to the magistrate and the magistrate to the people, and the people to justice; where the country assures the well-being of each individual, and where each individual enjoys with pride the prosperity and glory of the fatherland; where all its members grow by constant exchange of republican sentiments and by the need to merit the esteem of a great people; where the arts are decorations of the liberty that ennobles them; commerce, the source of public prosperity, and not just of the monstrous opulence of a few families.

In our country, we want to substitute morality for egotism, probity for honour, principles for customs, duties for proprieties, the rule of reason for the tyranny of fashion, contempt of vice for contempt of misfortune, pride for insolence, greatness of soul for vanity, love of glory for love of money, good folk for good company, merit for intrigue, genius for wit, truth for brilliance, the charm of happiness for the boredom of sensuousness, the greatness of man for the pettiness of the great; a people magnanimous, powerful, happy, for a people amiable, frivolous and wretched, that is to say, all the virtues and all the miracles of the republic for all the vices and all the absurdities of the monarchy [. . .] Now what is the fundamental principle of democratic or popular government, that is to say, the essential force that maintains and inspires it? It is virtue: I am speaking of public virtue, which brought about so many wonders in Greece and Rome, and which must produce even more astounding ones in republican France: of that virtue that is none other than love of the fatherland and of its laws. [. . .]

If the mainspring of popular government in time of peace is virtue, the mainspring of popular government in time of revolution is at the same time virtue and terror; virtue, without which terror is intolerable; terror, without which virtue is powerless. Terror is nothing other than justice, prompt, stern and inflexible; it is therefore an emanation of virtue; it is not so much a particular principle as a consequence of the general principle of democracy applied to the most urgent needs of our country. It has been said that terror is the mainspring of despotic government. Would ours then resemble a despotism? Yes, just as the sword that shines in the hand of the heroes of liberty resembles that with which the satellites of tyranny are armed. If the despot rules his brutalised subjects by terror, he is right as a despot. Tame the enemies of liberty by terror, and you will be right as the founders of the Republic. The government of the Revolution is the despotism of liberty against tyranny.

La Gazette nationale (or *Le Moniteur universel*), No. 139,
19 Pluviôse, Year II (7 February 1794);
3rd series, vol. 6, pp. 402 and 404.

Source: J. Gilchrist and W. J. Murray, *The Press in the French Revolution*, London, Cheshire Ginn, 1971, pp. 297–8.

Rouget de Lisle, The 'Marseillaise', 1792[29]

Allons, enfants de la patrie,	Come, o ye children of the fatherland,
Le jour de gloire est arrivé!	The day of glory has arrived!
Contre nous de la tyrannie	Against us the standard of tyrants,
L'étendard sanglant est levé!	Yes, the bloodstained standard is raised!
	(the line is repeated)

Entendez-vous dans les campagnes	Now listen, all over the land
Mugir ces féroces soldats?	To the roar of the enemy soldiers,
Ils viennent jusque dans nos bras	Rampaging into our midst,
Egorger nos fils, nos compagnes.	To slaughter sons and wives.

CHORUS

Aux armes, citoyens,	To arms, citizens!
Formez vos bataillons!	Form your batallions!
Marchons! Marchons!	Let's march! Let's march!
Qu'un sang impur	Let impure blood
Abreuve nos sillons!	Water our furrows!

Que veut cette horde d'esclaves	What means this slavish horde before us
De traîtres, de rois conjurés?	Of traitors, and of conspiring kings?
Pour qui ces ignobles entraves,	For whom are these ignoble fetters,
Ces fers dès longtemps préparés?	Those chains so long since prepared?
	(the line is repeated)

Français! Pour vous, ah! Quel outrage!	An outrage for all men of France!
Quels transports il doit exciter!	What feelings must it not provoke!
C'est nous qu'on ose méditer	It is us they dare to contemplate
De rendre à l'antique esclavage!	To make slaves as in the days of old!

CHORUS (AS BEFORE)

Source: text in *Grand Larousse Encyclopédique*, Paris, Larousse, volume 7, 1963, trans. A. Lentin.

---

[29] The 'Marseillaise', originally the 'battle-hymn of the army of the Rhine', was composed by Rouget de Lisle in April 1792 immediately after France declared war on Austria. It acquired its name when a battalion of volunteers from Marseilles reached Paris in July 1792. It became the anthem of the Revolution, and the national anthem by a decree of the Convention in 1795.

PART II

The Napoleonic phenomenon

Documentary extracts
on Napoleon

The following seventeen documents, the core of which are arranged in chronological order, have been selected to illustrate salient aspects of the controversial rule of Napoleon (1799–1815). Twelve are by Napoleon himself. The document by Richard Whately and those by Napoleon dictated to Count Las Cases and Dr Barry O'Meara written in the aftermath of his fall, raise central issues of historical truth and interpretation. In 'Napoleon on historical truth', Napoleon, in sceptical mood, questions the reliability of historical evidence and emphasises the subjectivity of the historian. Yet in most of the retrospective documents dictated from exile on St Helena, he expresses confidence in the *facts* of his achievement and the durability of his fame. The rest of the documents are valuable evidence of Napoleon's reactions to particular issues *at the time*, including his strict press censorship, and his suppression of opposition to his rule in France and Germany. His *Imperial Catechism* shows how he sought to harness the Catholic Church in France to his own purposes. The final four documents by Napoleon represent Napoleon's final refashioning of his career and its significance, the particular 'image' of his achievement and the place in history that he wished to impress on posterity. The final document contains the main criticisms of Napoleon by his most forthright liberal opponent, Mme de Staël.

Richard Whately on Napoleon, 1819

Richard Whately,[1] *Historic Doubts relative to Napoleon Buonaparte*, 1819

This obscure Corsican adventurer, a man, according to some, of extraordinary talents and courage, according to others, of very moderate abilities, and a rank coward, advanced rapidly in the French army, obtained a high command, gained a series of important victories, and, elated by success, embarked in an expedition against Egypt, which was planned and conducted, according to some, with the most consummate skill, according to others, with the utmost wildness and folly: he was unsuccessful, however; and leaving the army of Egypt in a very distressed situation, he returned to France, and found the nation, or at least the army, so favourably disposed towards him, that he was enabled, with the utmost ease, to overthrow the existing government, and obtain for himself the supreme power, at first under the modest appellation of Consul,[2] but afterwards with the more sounding title of Emperor.[3]

While in possession of this power, he overthrew the most powerful coalitions of the other European states against him, and though driven from the sea by the British fleets, overran nearly the whole continent, triumphant: finishing a war, not unfrequently in a single campaign, he entered the capitals of most of the hostile potentates, deposed and created kings at his pleasure, and appeared the virtual sovereign of the chief part of the continent, from the frontiers of Spain to those of Russia. Even those countries we find him invading with prodigious armies, defeating their forces, penetrating to their capitals, and threatening their total subjugation: but at Moscow his progress is stopped: a winter of unusual severity, co-operating with the efforts of the Russians, totally destroys his enormous host;[4] and the German sovereigns throw off the yoke, and combine to oppose him. He raises another vast army, which is also ruined at Leipsic,[5] and again another, with which [. . .] he for some time maintains himself in France, but is finally defeated, deposed, and ban-

---

[1] In his *Historic Doubts relative to Napoleon Buonaparte*, Richard Whately (1787–1863), fellow of Oriel College, Oxford, and clergyman, sought to undermine the sceptical approach to religion of the philosopher David Hume (1711–76) by adopting Hume's own methodology and querying the evidence for Napoleon's existence.

[2] 1799.

[3] 1804.

[4] 1812.

[5] 1813.

ished to the island of Elba, of which the sovereignty is conferred on him:[6] thence he returns, in about nine months, at the head of six hundred men, to attempt the deposition of King Lewis,[7] who had been peaceably recalled; the French nation declare in his favour, and he is reinstated without a struggle. He raises another great army to oppose the allied powers, which is totally defeated at Waterloo; he is a second time deposed, surrenders to the British, and is placed in confinement at the island of St. Helena.[8] Such is the outline of the eventful history presented to us; in the detail of which, however, there is almost every conceivable variety of statement; while the motives and conduct of the chief actor are involved in still greater doubt, and the subject of still more eager controversy.

In the midst of these controversies, the preliminary question, concerning the *existence* of this extraordinary personage, seems never to have occurred to any one as a matter of doubt; and to show even the smallest hesitation in admitting it, would probably be regarded as an excess of scepticism; on the ground that this point has always been taken for granted by the disputants on all sides, being indeed implied by the very nature of their disputes.

Source: R. Whately, *Historic Doubts relative to Napoleon Buonaparte*, 2nd edition, London, 1821, pp. 476–7.

Napoleon on historical truth, 1816

Memoirs dictated to Count Emmanuel Las Cases, St Helena, 20 November 1816

It must be admitted that the *true truths* are very difficult to ascertain in history. Fortunately they have more curiosity interest than real importance. There are so many truths! [. . .]

Historical fact, which is so often invoked, to which everyone so readily appeals, is often a mere word: it cannot be ascertained when events actually occur, in the heat of contrary passions; and if, later on, there is a consensus, this is only because there is no one left to contradict. But if

[6] 1814.
[7] Louis XVIII.
[8] 1815.

this is so, what is this historical truth in nearly every case? An agreed-upon fiction, as has been most ingeniously said.

In all such things there are two very distinct essential elements—material fact and moral intent. Material facts, one should think, ought to be incontrovertible; and yet, go and see if any two accounts agree. There are facts that remain in eternal litigation. As for moral intent, how is one to find his way, supposing even that the narrators are in good faith? And what if they are prompted by bad faith, self-interest, and bias? Suppose I have given an order: who can read the bottom of my thought, my true intention? And yet everybody will take hold of that order, measure it by his own yardstick, make it bend to conform to his plans, his individual way of thinking [. . .] And everybody will be so confident of his own version! The lesser mortals will hear of it from privileged mouths, and they will be so confident in turn! Then the flood of memoirs, diaries, anecdotes, drawing-room reminiscences! And yet, my friend, that is history!

Source: J. Christopher Herold (ed. and trans.), *The Mind of Napoleon. A Selection from His Written and Spoken Words*, New York, Columbia University Press, 1955, pp. 50–1.

Napoleon on political opposition, 1803

Napoleon, conversation with his brother Joseph, 1803

The First Consul (in his bathtub): An opposition, as in England, is that it? I haven't been able to understand yet what good there is in an opposition. Whatever it may be, its only result is to diminish the prestige of authority in the eyes of the people.

Joseph Bonaparte: It's easy to see that you don't like it; you have taken good care of it.

The First Consul: Let another govern in my place, and if he doesn't, like me, make an effort to silence the talkers, he'll see what will happen to him. As for me, let me tell you that in order to govern well one needs absolute unity of power. I won't shout this from the roof tops, since I mustn't frighten a lot of people who would raise loud cries of despotism, if they were allowed to talk, and who would write about it, if they were allowed to write. But I have begun to put good order into all this.

Source: J. Christopher Herold (ed. and trans.), *The Mind of Napoleon. A Selection from His Written and Spoken Words*, New York, Columbia University Press, 1955, pp. 84–5.

Napoleon on press censorship, 1805

Napoleon, letter to Fouché, Minister of Police, 22 April 1805

I want you to write to the editors of the *Journal des Débats*, the *Publiciste*, and the *Gazette de France*—these, I think, are the newspapers that are most widely read—in order to declare to them that [. . .] the revolutionary times are over and that there is but one single party in France; that I shall never tolerate the newspapers to say or do anything against my interests; that they may publish a few little articles with just a little poison in them, but that one fine morning somebody will shut their mouths.

Source: J. Christopher Herold (ed. and trans.), *The Mind of Napoleon. A Selection from His Written and Spoken Words*, New York, Columbia University Press, 1955, p. 132.

Napoleon's *Imperial Catechism*, 1806

Catechism drawn up by Napoleon for the Catholic Church in France

Q. What are the duties of Christians with respect to the princes who govern them, and what are in particular our duties toward Napoleon I, our Emperor?

A. [. . .] love, respect, obedience, fidelity, military service, tributes ordered for the preservation and defense of the Empire and of his throne; we also owe him fervent prayers for his safety and for the spiritual and temporal prosperity of the State.

Q. Why do we have these duties towards our Emperor?

A. First, by bountifully bestowing talents on our Emperor both in peace and war, God has established him as our sovereign and has made him the minister of His power and His image on earth. To honor and serve our Emperor is therefore to honor and serve God himself. Secondly, because our Lord Jesus Christ [. . .] has taught us what we owe to our sovereign [. . .]; He has ordered us to give to Caesar what belongs to Caesar.

Q. Are there not special motives which must attach us more strongly to Napoleon, our Emperor?

A. Yes; for he is the one whom God has given us in difficult times to re-establish the public worship of the holy religion of our fathers and to be the protector of it. He has re-established and maintained public order by his profound and active wisdom; he defends the State with his powerful arm; he has become the Lord's anointed through the consecration which he received from the pontifical sovereign, head of the universal Church.

Q. What must one think of those who may fail in their duty toward our Emperor?

A. According to the apostle Paul, they would resist the established order to God himself and would be worthy of eternal damnation.

Q. Do the duties toward our Emperor bind us equally towards his successors?

A. Yes, undoubtedly; for we read in the Holy Scripture that God, Lord of heaven and earth, [. . .] gives empires not only to one person in particular, but also to his family.

Source: R. B. Holtman, *The Napoleonic Revolution*, Philadelphia, J. B. Lippincott Company, 1967, pp. 130–1.

Napoleon on suppression of anti-French sentiment in Prussia, 1807

Letter from Napoleon to Marshal Berthier, Minister of War, 1807

Send a special courier to Marshal Soult to acquaint him with the event that has occurred at Königsberg,[9] where two actors, who appeared on the stage in the roles of French officers, have been hissed. You will inform Marshal Soult that I have demanded satisfaction from the King of

---

[9] Marshal Soult received the surrender of Königsberg, June 1807.

Prussia for this insult and that I have requested him to have the chief guilty parties shot.

Source: J. Christopher Herold (ed. and trans.), *The Mind of Napoleon. A Selection from His Written and Spoken Words*, New York, Columbia University Press, 1955, p. 172.

Napoleon on his principles of government in the French empire, 1807

Letter from Napoleon to his brother Jérôme, King of Westphalia, 1807

Fontainebleau, 15 November 1807
To Jérôme Bonaparte, King of Westphalia

My Dear Brother, You will find enclosed the constitution of your kingdom. This constitution contains the conditions on which I renounce all my rights of conquest and all the claims I have acquired over your kingdom. You must observe it faithfully. The happiness of your people is important to me, not only because of the influence it can have on both your reputation and mine, but also from the point of view of the whole European system. Refuse to listen to those who tell you that your subjects, accustomed to servitude, will greet the benefits you offer to them with ingratitude. They are more enlightened in the Kingdom of Westphalia than some would have you believe; and your throne will only become truly established with the confidence and affection of the people. What the peoples of Germany impatiently desire is that men of talent, who lack noble rank, will have an equal claim to your favour and to government employment; they also demand that all kinds of servitude and intermediate links between the sovereign and the lowest class of the people be entirely abolished. The benefits of the *Code Napoléon*, public trials, the introduction of juries, will be the distinctive features of your rule [. . .] It is necessary for your subjects to enjoy a degree of liberty, equality and prosperity hitherto unknown among the peoples of Germany; and that your liberal government produces, one way or another, changes which will be most salutary for the Confederation of the Rhine and for the strength of your monarchy. Such a method of government will prove a more powerful barrier separating you from Prussia than the

Elbe, the fortresses and the protection of France. What people would wish to return to the arbitrary government of Prussia when they have tasted the benefits of wise and liberal administration? The peoples of Germany, as well as those of France, Italy and Spain, desire equality and demand liberal ideas. I have been managing the affairs of Europe long enough to be convinced that the burden imposed by the privileged classes is contrary to the wishes of general opinion. Be a constitutional king.

Source: D. G. Wright, *Napoleon and Europe*, London, Longman, 1984, pp. 106–7.

Napoleon on an attempt to assassinate him, 1809

Letter from Napoleon to Fouché, Minister of Police, 1809

Schönbrunn,[10] October 12 1809

Today, during parade, a young man of 17, the son of a Lutheran minister at Erfurt, tried to approach me. He was arrested by the officers: suspicion was excited by his appearance of anxiety: he was searched, and was found to be in possession of a dagger. I had him brought before me, and the wretched young fellow, who seemed to be quite well educated, told me that he intended to assassinate me in order to rid Austria of the presence of the French. I found no traces of religious or political fanaticism in him. He didn't seem to understand that Brutus was a murderer. The fit of exaltation into which he had worked himself prevented my discovering any more. He will be questioned when he is cold and hungry, but possibly nothing will come of it. He will be tried by a military court.[11]

Source: J. M. Thompson, *Letters of Napoleon*, Oxford, Basil Blackwell, 1934, p. 255.

---

[10] The imperial palace at Vienna.

[11] Friedrich Staps, the would-be assassin, was condemned to death on 15 October and executed on 16 October.

General Rapp on the attempt to assassinate Napoleon, 1809

Memoirs of General Rapp,[12] published 1823

[. . .]

I went to apprise the Emperor of this strange event. He told me to have the young man brought to his closet. I transmitted his orders and went back. He was with Bernadotte, Berthier, Savary and Duroc.[13] Two gendarmes came in with Staps, his hands tied behind his back. He was composed. Napoleon's presence had not the slightest effect on him. He bowed, however, in a respectful way. The Emperor asked him whether he could speak French. He replied confidently: 'Very little.' Napoleon instructed me to put the following questions in his name:

'Where do you come from?'

'Naumbourg.'

'What is your father?'

'A Protestant clergyman.'

'How old are you?'

'Eighteen.'

'What were you going to do with your knife?'

'Kill you.'

'You are mad, young man—you are an *illuminé*?'[14]

'I am not mad. I don't know what an *illuminé* is.'

'Then you are sick?'

'I am not sick, I am in good health.'

'Why did you mean to kill me?'

'Because you are the bane of my country.'

'Have I done you any harm?'

'Me and all Germans.'

'Who sent you? Who is egging you to this crime?'

'No one. It was the deep-seated conviction that by killing you I should do the greatest service to my country and Europe which placed a weapon in my hand.'

---

[12] General Count Rapp, aide-de-camp to Napoleon.

[13] Bernadotte and Berthier were marshals, Duroc and Savary were generals. Savary became Minister of Police in 1810.

[14] Religious or political fanatic.

'Is this the first time you have seen me?'
'I saw you at Erfurt, at the time of the interview.'[15]
'Did you not mean to kill me at that time?'
'No, I thought you would not make war on Germany again. I was one of your greatest admirers.'

[. . .]

Source: Jean Savant, *Napoleon in his Time*, trans. Katherine John, London, Putnam, 1958, pp. 225–6.

Fouché on theatre censorship in Germany, 1811

Letter from Fouché, Minister of Police, to superintendent of police at Hamburg, 1811

May I recommend you to take all necessary measures to stop the production, throughout the new departments recently annexed to the Empire, of certain dramatic works by Werner, Kotzebue, Goethe and Schiller, the moral effect of which is clearly to disturb the social order by undermining the respect due to lawful authority. Many of these plays contain, besides, insolent diatribes against the Government of France and the French nation. I expressly warn you about the following plays: *The Robbers, Marie Stuart*, and *William Tell*, by Schiller, *Faust*, by Goethe.[16]

Source: F. W. J. Hemmings, *Culture and Society in France 1789–1848*, Leicester, Leicester University Press, 1987, p. 110.

---

[15] The meeting of Napoleon and Alexander I of Russia, autumn 1808.

[16] The plays by Schiller were written in 1777, 1800 and 1804 respectively. Part I of Goethe's *Faust* was published in 1808.

Fouché on Napoleon before his Russian campaign, 1812

Fouché, Count of Otranto, *Memoirs*, published 1824

[. . .] 'Since my marriage[17] people have thought the lion was dozing. They'll see whether he's dozing. Spain will fall as soon as I have destroyed the English influence at St Petersburg. I needed eight hundred thousand men, and I have them. I am dragging all Europe with me, and nowadays Europe is only an old, rotten whore whom I shall treat as I please with eight hundred thousand men. Didn't you once tell me that for you the mark of genius was to think nothing impossible? Well, in six or eight months you will see what can be done by the most immense schemes combined with the vigour that can set things to work. I go more by the opinion of the army and the people than by yours, gentlemen; you are too rich, and are only trembling for me because you're in terror of a crash. Don't worry. Look on the Russian war as a war of common sense, for the real interests, tranquillity and security of all. Besides, can I help it if an excess of power is sweeping me on to the dictatorship of the world? Had you not a hand in it, you and plenty of others who are now finding fault with me, and would like to turn me into a King Log?[18] My destiny is not fulfilled. I mean to finish what is only roughed out. We need a European code, a European court of appeal, the same currency, the same weights and measures, the same laws. I must make all the nations of Europe into the same nation, and Paris into the capital of the world. That, my lord duke, is the one ending that will do for me.' [. . .] I withdrew aghast. [. . .]

Source: Jean Savant, *Napoleon in his Time*, trans. Katherine John, London, Putnam, 1958, pp. 269–70.

---

[17] Napoleon refers to his marriage in 1810 to Marie-Louise, daughter of the Austrian emperor, Francis.

[18] An inactive monarch. The reference is to classical mythology. Jupiter made a log king of the frogs.

Napoleon on reprisals in Germany, 1813

Napoleon, unsigned decree, 1813

The Prince of Eckmühl[19] is appointed governor general of the department forming the 32nd military area.[20] He is invested with all the extraordinary powers made necessary by the situation [...] He is authorized to take hostages; to draw by lot every tenth inhabitant of such communes as have misbehaved and to order them shot; to burn down any rebellious commune that puts up armed resistance; to pass sentence by *ad hoc* courts-martial on all individuals taken with arms in hand and charged with having provoked or abetted the rebellion; and, finally, to declare all troublemakers outside our protection and outside the law, to be killed with impunity.

Source: J. Christopher Herold (ed. and trans.), *The Mind of Napoleon. A Selection from His Written and Spoken Words*, New York, Columbia University Press, 1955, p. 172.

Napoleon on his achievements, 1816

Memoirs dictated to Count Las Cases, St Helena, 1 May 1816

I have closed the gaping abyss of anarchy, and I have unscrambled chaos. I have cleansed the Revolution, ennobled the common people, and restored the authority of kings. I have stirred all men to competition, I have rewarded merit wherever I found it, I have pushed back the boundaries of greatness. All this, you must admit, is something. Is there any point on which I could be attacked and on which a historian could not take up my defense? My intentions, perhaps? He has evidence enough to clear me. My despotism? He can prove that dictatorship was absolutely necessary. Will it be said that I restricted freedom? He will be able to prove that licence, anarchy, and general disorder were still on our doorstep. Shall I be accused of having loved war too much? He will show that I was always on the defensive. That I wanted to set up a universal

---

[19] Marshal Davout.
[20] The Rhineland.

monarchy? He will explain that it was merely the fortuitous result of circumstances and that I was led to it step by step by our very enemies. My ambition? Ah, no doubt he will find that I had ambition, a great deal of it—but the grandest and noblest, perhaps, that ever was: the ambition of establishing and consecrating at last the kingdom of reason and the full exercise, the complete enjoyment, of all human capabilities! And in this respect the historian will perhaps find himself forced to regret that such an ambition has not been fulfilled, has not been satisfied.

Source: J. Christopher Herold (ed. and trans.), *The Mind of Napoleon. A Selection from His Written and Spoken Words*, New York, Columbia University Press, 1955, pp. 272–3.

Napoleon on his achievements, 1817

Conversation with Dr Barry O'Meara, St Helena, 3 March 1817

[. . .]

In spite of all the libels, I have no fear whatever about my fame. Posterity will do me justice. The truth will be known and the good that I have done, with the faults I have committed, will be compared. Had I succeeded I should have died with the reputation of the greatest man that ever existed. As it is, although I have failed, I shall be considered as an extraordinary man: my elevation was unparalleled because unaccompanied by any crime. I have fought fifty pitched battles, almost all of which I have gained. I have framed and carried into effect a code of laws that will bear my name to the most distant posterity. From nothing I raised myself to be the most powerful monarch in the world. Europe was at my feet. My ambition was great, I admit, but it was of a cold nature and caused by events, and the opinion of great bodies. I have always been of the opinion that the sovereignty lay in the people. In fact the imperial government was a kind of republic.

I certainly wished to make France the most powerful nation in the world but no further. I did not aim at universal dominion. [. . .]

Source: F. Markham, *The Bonapartes*, London, Weidenfeld and Nicolson, 1975, p. 173.

Napoleon on his plans for Europe, 1816

Memoirs dictated to Count Las Cases, St Helena, 24 August 1816

A European code: a court of European appeal, with full powers to redress all wrong decisions, as one's redress at home those of our tribunals. Money of the same value but with different coins the same weight, the same measures, the same laws, etc.

Europe would soon in that manner have really been but the same people, and every one who travelled would have everywhere found himself in one common country. [. . .] I would have associated my son with the empire: my dictatorship would have terminated, and his constitutional reign commenced.

At Amiens[21] I sincerely thought the fate of France and Europe and my own destiny were permanently fixed: I hoped that war was at an end. However, the English Cabinet again kindled the flame. England is alone responsible for all the miseries by which Europe has since been assailed. For my part, I intended to have devoted myself wholly to the internal interests of France: and I am confident I should have wrought miracles. I should have lost nothing in the scale of glory and I should have gained much in the scale of happiness. I should then have achieved the moral conquest of Europe, which I was afterwards on the point of accomplishing by force of arms. Of how much glory was I thus deprived.

One of my great plans was the rejoining, the concentration of those same geographical nations which have been disunited and parcelled out by revolution and policy. There are dispersed in Europe, upwards of thirty million of French, fifteen million of Spaniards, fifteen million of Italians, and thirty million of Germans; and it was my intention to incorporate these people each into one nation [. . .]

At all events this concentration will be brought about, sooner or later by the very force of events. The impulse is given; and I think that since my fall, and the destruction of my system, no grand equilibrium can possibly be established in Europe, except by the concentration and confederation of the principal nations. The sovereign who in the first great conflict, shall sincerely embrace the cause of the people, will find himself at the head of all Europe, and may attempt whatever he pleases.

Source: F. Markham, *The Bonapartes*, London, Weidenfeld and Nicolson, 1975, pp. 174–5.

[21] Peace with Britain was concluded at Amiens, March 1802, but lasted only 14 months.

Napoleon on his fate, 1816

Memoirs dictated to Count Las Cases, St Helena

(a) 24 August 1816

Liberal opinions will rule the universe. They will become the faith, the religion, the morality of all nations; and in spite of all that may be advanced to the contrary, this memorable aim will be inseparably connected with my name; for after all it cannot be denied that I kindled the torch and consecrated the principle, and now persecution renders me the Messiah.

(b) 21 October 1816

I am destined to be their [his detractors'] prey, but I have no fear of becoming their victim. They will be biting into granite [. . .] The memory I leave behind consists of facts that mere words cannot destroy [. . .] I shall survive—and whenever they want to strike a lofty attitude, they will praise me.

(c) 2 November 1816

It is a fact that my destiny is the inverse of other men's. Ordinarily, a man is lowered by his downfall; my downfall raises me to infinite heights. Every day strips me of my tyrant's skin, of my murderousness and ferocity.

(d) 18–19 November 1816

I believe that nature has intended me for great reverses. My soul is made of marble; lightning has found no grip on it and had to slide off it.

(e) Napoleon, letter to Sir Hudson Lowe, Governor of St Helena, 25 July 1817

You have miscalculated the heights to which misfortune, the injustice and persecution of your government, and your own conduct have raised the Emperor. His head wears more than an imperial crown—it wears a crown of thorns.

It is not in your power, or in that of the like of you, to obscure the radiance of that crown.

Source: J. Christopher Herold (ed. and trans.), *The Mind of Napoleon. A Selection from His Written and Spoken Words*, New York, Columbia University Press, 1955, pp. 273–4 (documents (b) to (d)), p. 49 (document (e)); F. Markham, *The Bonapartes*, London, Weidenfeld and Nicolson, 1975, p. 173 (document (a)).

Mme de Staël on Napoleon, 1818

De Staël, *Reflections on the Main Events of the French Revolution*, 1818

(a) Bonaparte's advance to absolute power

The numerous newspapers existing in France were soon subjected to the most rigorous and at the same time the most effective censorship [. . .] All the periodicals repeated the same thing every day, and it was never permitted to contradict them [. . .] Newspapers publish the news which every class of person is avid to learn, and the invention of printing, far from being, as has been said, the guarantee of freedom, becomes the most fearful weapon of despotism if the newspapers which form the sole reading of three quarters of the nation fall under the exclusive control of the authorities [. . .]

Even when Bonaparte commanded a million armed men, he still attached no less importance to the art of influencing public opinion through the newspapers. He himself often dictated newspaper articles [. . .]

(b) Bonaparte as emperor. The counter-revolution brought about by him

When at the end of the last century Bonaparte placed himself at the head of the French people, the entire nation wanted a free and constitutional government [. . .] But Bonaparte conceived the idea of making the counter-revolution work to his advantage by leaving nothing new in the state, as it were, except himself. He re-established the throne, the clergy and the nobility: a monarchy, as Mr Pitt[22] said, without legitimacy and without limits, a clergy which merely preached despotism, a nobility

---

[22] Prime Minister 1783–1801, 1804–6.

consisting of old and new families but which exercised no ruling function in the State and served only to set off absolute power [. . .]

(c) Bonaparte and the Duke d'Enghien

At the moment when Bonaparte wished to have himself named emperor, he thought it necessary, on the one hand, to reassure the revolutionaries about the possibility of a Bourbon restoration, and on the other, to prove to the royalists that by attaching themselves to him, they were breaking irrevocably with the former dynasty. To fulfil this double aim he committed the murder of a prince of the blood, the Duke d'Enghien.[23] He crossed the Rubicon of crime, and from that day his downfall was written in the book of destiny [. . .]

(d) On Napoleon's conduct towards the continent of Europe

There were no doubt many reasonable reforms to be made in the constitutions of Germany; all enlightened men were aware of it and for a long time too they showed themselves favourable to the cause of France, because they hoped it would bring an improvement of their own lot. But, leaving aside the just indignation which any people must feel at the sight of foreign troops on its territory, Bonaparte did nothing in Germany except with the aim of establishing his power there and that of his family. Was such a nation made to serve as a foundation to his egoism? Spain too was bound to react with horror against the perfidious methods which Bonaparte employed to enslave her. What, then, did he offer to the states which he sought to subjugate? Was it freedom, power, riches? No, it was he, always he, with whom they had to divert themselves in exchange for all the goods of this world. [. . .] We think we may affirm that the detailed benefits introduced by Bonaparte – the great roads necessary to his projects, the monuments consecrated to his glory, [. . .] the reform of jurisprudence, of public education, the encouragement of the sciences, all these benefits, I repeat, could not compensate for the debasing yoke which bore down on individuals. What superior man have we seen develop under his reign? [. . .] He did not win for France the friendship of a single nation. He made marriages, rounded off territories and joined them together, he carved up the geographical maps, [. . .] but where did he implant those political principles which are the bastion, the treasure and the glory of England?[24]

[23] The Duke d'Enghien was a member of the royal house of Bourbon-Condé. In 1804, on Napoleon's orders, he was kidnapped in neutral Baden, taken to France, summarily tried and executed by firing squad.

[24] Mme de Staël refers to the liberal principles of representative government and constitutional monarchy.

(e) A statement by Bonaparte in the Moniteur

It was not enough that Bonaparte's every act was stamped with an ever-bolder despotism. It had to reveal in person the secret of his rule, despising humankind enough to do so. He inserted in the *Moniteur*[25] of July 1810 these very words, addressed to the second son of his brother Louis Bonaparte, at that time destined to govern the Grand Duchy of Berg.[26] *Never forget*, he told him, *that, whatever position my policy and the interest of my empire may place you in, your first duty is to me, your second is to France. All your other duties, even those to the peoples whom I may entrust to you, come afterwards.* This is no libel, this is no biased opinion. It is Bonaparte himself, who has denounced himself more harshly than posterity would ever have dared to do. Louis XIV was accused of having said privately: *I am the State*, and enlightened historians have rightly singled out this selfish language in order to condemn his character. [. . .] Bonaparte, [. . .] a man elected by the people, sought to set up his gigantic *Me* in the place of humankind! How could the friends of liberty take him for one instant to be the representative of their cause? Several have said: 'He is the child of the Revolution'. Yes, no doubt, but a child-parricide [. . .]

(f) On the fall of Bonaparte

Bonaparte, who for ten years had roused the world against the freest country [Britain], [. . .] placed himself in her hands. He, who for ten years had outraged her every day, appealed to her generosity. Finally he, who spoke of the laws only with contempt, who so lightly gave orders for arbitrary imprisonment, invoked the liberty of the English, and sought to place himself under its protection:[27] Oh, if he had only granted France that liberty, neither he nor the French would find themselves at the mercy of the victors.

Whether Napoleon lives or dies, whether he returns to the continent of Europe or not, we have but one motive in mentioning him again: the ardent wish that the friends of liberty in France may entirely distance their cause from his, and take care not to confuse the principles of the Revolution with those of the Imperial regime. As I believe I have shown, no counter-revolution has been as fatal to freedom as that which he brought about [. . .] He paid court to priests, nobles and kings in the

---

[25] The *Moniteur* was the official newspaper and mouthpiece of Napoleon's regime.

[26] The Grand Duchy of Berg (capital Düsseldorf) established by Napoleon in 1806 in the Confederation of the Rhine was a client-state under his brother-in-law Marshal Murat.

[27] After his defeat at Waterloo, Napoleon appealed to the Prince Regent for asylum in Britain.

hope of being accepted as a legitimate monarch [. . .] If the principles of liberty are failing in Europe, it is because he has uprooted them from the minds of the peoples; everywhere he has raised up despotism, founded on the hatred which, thanks to him, the nations feel for the French; he has demoralised the human spirit by making his hack-writers produce, throughout fifteen years, every mode of thought that could undermine reason and stifle intelligence. To establish freedom, you need people of talent in every field; Bonaparte sought men of merit only among the military, and no civilian was ever able to make his reputation under his reign.

At the beginning of the Revolution, France was honoured by a host of illustrious names; and one of the main characteristics of an enlightened age is to have many outstanding men, while finding with difficulty one man superior to all the rest. In this respect Bonaparte rose superior to the age: not because he was superior in intelligence, but on the contrary because there was something barbarous and medieval about him; he brought with him from Corsica another age, other modes of conduct, a type of character different from anything we had in France. This very novelty assisted his ascendancy over people's minds [. . .]

His genius and his character may be interpreted in different ways. There is something enigmatic in that man which retains our curiosity. Everyone paints him in different colours, and may well be right, depending on his point of view. Whoever sought to summarize his character in a few words would produce a false impression. For a complete picture one must follow different paths. He is a labyrinth, but a labyrinth with a common thread: egoism. Those who knew him personally may discern in him a certain goodness, which the world certainly did not experience. The devotion of a few really generous friends speaks most in his favour. Time will elucidate the various sides of his character; and those who like to admire an extraordinary man are entitled to find him such. However, the only thing that he brought to France, the only thing he could bring – was misery.

Source: Mme de Staël, *Considérations sur la Révolution Française*, ed. J. Godechot, Paris, Tallendier, 1983, pp. 368, 369, 395, 396, 402, 420, 503–4, trans. A. Lentin.

Documents relating to a painting competition, 1807

In 1807, a competition was staged by the Napoleonic regime for a painting commemorating the recent battle of Eylau, which had been fought in Poland on 7–8 February. A dossier of three documents was issued by Dominique-Vivant Denon (1747–1825), the director of the Louvre Museum (then known as the Musée Napoléon), who was responsible for the regime's official art patronage. Two of these documents are reproduced here. The first of them is Denon's letter of 2 April 1807 announcing the competition and inviting artists to submit their sketches, which was published in the *Journal de Paris, Moniteur* and *Journal de l'Empire* over the next few days. The second document, which accompanied the letter and also appeared in the newspapers, is an account of the subject, outlining both the setting of the scene and the precise action to be depicted. The third document (not reproduced here) was a commentary that accompanied a now lost sketch of the site, which was available for artists to consult in Denon's offices at the Louvre (as specified in his letter). Twenty-six artists entered the competition; their sketches were put on public display in the Louvre from 18 May and the judging took place on 13 June. The winner was Antoine-Jean Gros (1771–1835), to whom the authorities may have intended to award the commission all along. An earlier painting by Gros celebrating Napoleon, *Bonaparte visiting the Plague-Stricken of Jaffa* (1803), is cited as a precedent in Denon's letter. His winning sketch was worked up into a full-scale painting, which was exhibited in the Paris Salon of 1808. With its heaped bodies of the dead and dying in the foreground, Gros's *Napoleon visiting the Field of the Battle of Eylau* is not a propaganda work in any simple or straightforward understanding of the term and can be seen to have played a crucial role in inaugurating Romanticism in French painting.

Dominique-Vivant Denon,
Director of the Musée Napoléon,
letter for the benefit of the competitors

From the Grande Armée 7 March 1807

The battle of Eylau is one of those events with which history is sparing, even in our time; for this reason it becomes the patrimony of the arts, especially of painting which alone can convey the harshness of the site and the climate and the rigour of the season during which this memorable battle took place.

In the absence of any attempt to depict the subject, the Director General of the Musée Napoléon has considered it his duty to propose it publicly to history painters.

Since all battles resemble each other, he has thought it preferable to choose the moment on the day after that of Eylau and when the Emperor visited the battlefield in order to bring assistance and consolation without discrimination to all the honourable victims of the fighting.

The painter of the hospital of Jaffa could quite naturally have been entrusted with the task of executing this painting, given that he has already so well depicted a subject of this kind; but the Director General believed it would be an injustice to the entire body of painters if he had not given all of them the opportunity to try their hand at so great a theme. He therefore asked His Majesty for permission to invite them all to produce a sketch of the subject which will be judged by the fourth class of the Institute.[1] The sketches must be deposited at the secretariat of this class within the space of a month from the publication of the present announcement. The picture will be the same size as that of the hospital of Jaffa and the prize will be 16 000 francs. It will also be executed as a fine tapestry by the Gobelins factory. The two sketches that the class of the Institute judges to merit the position of first and second runner-up will each be honoured with a gold medal and 600 francs.

The Director General includes here a description made on the field of the battle of Eylau at the moment on the day after the battle when the Emperor reviewed the troops which had fought in it.

---

[1] The Institut National was established in 1795 as the official body responsible for learning and the arts in place of the various Royal Academies abolished during the French Revolution. The Fourth Class was the Class of Fine Arts; its membership consisted of painters, sculptors, architects, engravers and musicians.

To give a correct idea of the positions the Director General has deposited in his offices in the Musée Napoléon a sketch of the battlefield. Any artist who wants to enter the competition can consult it by addressing himself to the General Secretary who will provide him with a detailed note of the site and the costumes. The groups of figures in the sketch, however accurate they may be, should not constrain the artists in devising their compositions. Everything that is movable in the foreground is left absolutely up to the painter, who may make his own choice of the situations set out in the description.

Denon

Dominique-Vivant Denon, Descriptive account for the competition of 1807, intended for the artists

The EMPEROR visits the field of the battle of Preuss-Eylau, 9 February 1807

The French army, victorious on the 8 February at Preuss-Eylau, had bivouacked during the night on the field of that memorable battle which had been precipitately abandoned during the same night by the routed Russian army.

On the 9th, at daybreak, the vanguard of the French army pursued the enemy in all directions, and found the roads of Koenisberg covered with abandoned Russian dead, dying and wounded, together with cannon, cases and baggage.

Towards midday, the EMPEROR mounted his horse. He was accompanied by Princes Murat and Berthier, by Marshals Soult, Davoust and Bessières; by the grand-equerry de Caulincourt; by the general aides-de-camp Mouton, Gardanne and Lebrun and by several other officers of his household, together with a squad of chasseurs of the guard and by princes and officers of the Polish guard of honour. He reviewed several divisions of the troops led by Marshals Soult, Augereau and Davoust, which remained on the battlefield, and visited one by one all of the positions that had been occupied, the previous day, by the various French and Russian units. The countryside was entirely covered with thick snow over which were scattered dead bodies, wounded men and the remnants of arms of all kind; traces of blood contrasted with the whiteness of the snow; the places in which cavalry charges had taken place stood out on account of the numbers of dead, dying and abandoned horses; French detachments and Russian prisoners traversed this vast field of carnage in all directions, and removed the wounded in order to take them to the hospitals set up in the town. Long lines of Russian corpses, wounded soldiers, remnants of arms and abandoned haversacks outlined in a bloody fashion the place of each battalion and squadron. The dead were heaped on top of the dying in the midst of broken or burnt cases and dismantled cannon.

The EMPEROR stopped at every pace in front of the wounded, asking them questions in their own language, ensuring that they were comforted and tended before his eyes. The unfortunate victims of the combats had their wounds dressed in front of him; the chasseurs of the guard transported them on their horses; the officers of his household carried out his benevolent orders. Rather than the death that they had been led to expect by the absurd prejudice they had absorbed, the wretched Russians found a generous conqueror. Astonished, they prostrated themselves in front of him or held out their weak arms in gestures of gratitude. The consoling look of the great man seemed to alleviate the horrors of death, and to spread a gentler light over this scene of carnage.

A young Lithuanian hussar, whose knee had been blown off by a bullet, had maintained his courage undiminished in the midst of his expiring comrades. He raised himself up at the sight of the EMPEROR: 'Caesar,' he said to him, 'you desire that I live; well, then! Only let me be healed, and I will serve you faithfully as I have served Alexander.'[2]

Source: Pascal Griener, 'L'Art de persuader par l'image sous le Premier Empire. A Propos d'un concours officiel pour la représentation de Napoléon sur le champ de bataille d'Eylau', *L'Ecrit-Voir*, 1984, 4, pp. 9, 20. Translated for this volume by Emma Barker.

[2] Alexander I, tsar of Russia.

PART III

Slavery, religion and reform

Slave writings

The following extracts are from the writings of Ottobah Cugoano, Robert Wedderburn and Mary Prince. The first four extracts are from Cugoano's *Thoughts and Sentiments on the Evil of Slavery* (1787), and they include both Cugoano's autobiographical memories and his various arguments against slavery. The next four extracts are from four different pieces of writing by Robert Wedderburn. They include Wedderburn's description of his conversion to Christianity, several extracts from Wedderburn's political magazine *The Axe Laid to the Root* (1817), his defence against blasphemy (ghost-written by George Cannon), and an extract from his autobiographical pamphlet *The Horrors of Slavery* (1824). The final extract is the full text of *The History of Mary Prince* (1831).

Quobna Ottobah Cugoano, *Thoughts and Sentiments on the Evil of Slavery*, 1787

Extract 1

One law, and one manner shall be for you, and for the stranger that sojourneth with you; and therefore, all things whatsoever ye would that men should do to you, do ye even so to them.

NUMB[ERS] XV. 16., MATTHEW VII. 12.

AS SEVERAL LEARNED GENTLEMEN of distinguished abilities, as well as eminent for their great humanity, liberality and candour, have written various essays against that infamous traffic of the African Slave Trade, carried on with the West-India planters and merchants, to the great shame and disgrace of all Christian nations wherever it is admitted in any of their territories, or place or situation amongst them; it cannot be amiss that I should thankfully acknowledge these truly worthy and humane gentlemen with the warmest sense of gratitude, for their beneficent and laudable endeavours towards a total suppression of that infamous and iniquitous traffic of stealing, kid-napping, buying, selling, and cruelly enslaving men!

Those who have endeavoured to restore to their fellow-creatures the common rights of nature, of which especially the unfortunate Black People have been so unjustly deprived, cannot fail in meeting with the applause of all good men, and the approbation of that which will for ever redound to their honor; they have the warrant of that which is divine: *Open thy mouth, judge righteously, plead the cause of the poor and needy; for the liberal deviseth liberal things, and by liberal things shall stand.* And they can say with the pious Job, *Did not I weep for him that was in trouble; was not my soul grieved for the poor?*

The kind exertions of many benevolent and humane gentlemen, against the iniquitous traffic of slavery and oppression, has been attended with much good to many, and must redound with great honor to themselves, to humanity and their country; their laudable endeavours have been productive of the most beneficent effects in preventing that savage barbarity from taking place in free countries at home. In this, as well as in many other respects, there is one class of people (whose virtues of probity and humanity are well known) who are worthy of universal approbation and imitation, because, like men of honor and humanity, they have jointly agreed to carry on no slavery and savage barbarity among them; and, since the last war, some mitigation of slavery has been obtained in some respective districts of America, though not in proportion to their own vaunted claims of freedom; but it is to be hoped, that they will yet go on to make a further and greater reformation. However, notwithstanding all that has been done and written against it, that brutish barbarity, and unparalleled injustice, is still carried on to a very great extent in the colonies, and with an avidity as insidious, cruel and oppressive as ever. The longer that men continue in the practice of evil and wickedness, they grow the more abandoned; for nothing in history can equal the barbarity and cruelty of the tortures and murders committed under various pretences in modern slavery, except the annals of the Inquisition and the bloody edicts of Popish massacres.

It is therefore manifest, that something else ought yet to be done; and what is required, is evidently the incumbent duty of all men of enlightened understanding, and of every man that has any claim or affinity to the name of Christian, that the base treatment which the African Slaves undergo, ought to be abolished; and it is moreover evident, that the whole, or any part of that iniquitous traffic of slavery, can no where, or in any degree, be admitted, but among those who must eventually resign their own claim to any degree of sensibility and humanity, for that of barbarians and ruffians.

But it would be needless to arrange an history of all the base treatment which the African Slaves are subjected to, in order to shew the exceeding wickedness and evil of that insidious traffic, as the whole may easily appear in every part, and at every view, to be wholly and totally inimical to every idea of justice, equity, reason and humanity. What I intend to advance against that evil, criminal and wicked traffic of enslaving men, are only some Thoughts and Sentiments which occur to me, as being obvious from the Scriptures of Divine Truth, or such arguments as are chiefly deduced from thence, with other such observations as I have been able to collect. Some of these observations may lead into a larger field of consideration, than that of the African Slave Trade alone; but those causes from wherever they originate, and become the production of slavery, the evil effects produced by it, must shew that its origin and source is of a wicked and criminal nature.

No necessity, or any situation of men, however poor, pitiful and wretched they may be, can warrant them to rob others, or oblige them to become thieves, because they are poor, miserable and wretched: But the robbers of men, the kid-nappers, ensnarers and slave-holders, who take away the common rights and privileges of others to support and enrich themselves, are universally those pitiful and detestable wretches; for the ensnarings of others, and taking away their liberty by slavery and oppression, is the worst kind of robbery, as most opposite to every precept and injunction of the Divine Law, and contrary to that command which enjoins that *all men should love their neighbours as themselves,* and *that they should do unto others, as they would that men should do to them.* As to any other laws that slave-holders may make among themselves, as respecting slaves, they can be of no better kind, nor give them any better character, than what is implied in the common report—that there may be some honesty among thieves. This may seem a harsh comparison, but the parallel is so coincident that, I must say, I can find no other way of expressing my Thoughts and Sentiments, without making use of some harsh words and comparisons against the carriers on of such abandoned wickedness. But, in this little undertaking, I must humbly hope the impartial reader will excuse such defects as may arise from want of better education; and as to the resentment of those who can lay their cruel lash upon the backs of thousands, for a thousand times less crimes than writing against their enormous wickedness and brutal avarice, is what I may be sure to meet with.

However, it cannot but be very discouraging to a man of my complexion in such an attempt as this, to meet with the evil aspersions of some men, who say, "That an African is not entitled to any competent degree of knowledge, or capable of imbibing any sentiments of probity;

and that nature designed him for some inferior link in the chain, fitted only to be a slave." But when I meet with those who make no scruple to deal with the human species, as with the beasts of the earth, I must think them not only brutish, but wicked and base; and that their aspersions are insidious and false: And if such men can boast of greater degrees of knowledge, than any African is entitled to, I shall let them enjoy all the advantages of it unenvied, as I fear it consists only in greater share of infidelity, and that of a blacker kind than only skin deep. And if their complexion be not what I may suppose, it is at least the nearest in resemblance to an infernal hue. A good man will neither speak nor do as a bad man will; but if a man is bad, it makes no difference whether he be a black or a white devil.

By some of such complexion, as whether black or white it matters not, I was early snatched away from my native country, with about eighteen or twenty more boys and girls, as we were playing in a field. We lived but a few days journey from the coast where we were kid-napped, and as we were decoyed and drove along, we were soon conducted to a factory, and from thence, in the fashionable way of traffic, consigned to Grenada. Perhaps it may not be amiss to give a few remarks, as some account of myself, in this transposition of captivity.

I was born in the city of Agimaque, on the coast of Fantyn; my father was a companion to the chief in that part of the country of Fantee, and when the old king died I was left in his house with his family; soon after I was sent for by his nephew, Ambro Accasa, who succeeded the old king in the chiefdom of that part of Fantee known by the name of Agimaque and Assinee. I lived with his children, enjoying peace and tranquillity, about twenty moons, which, according to their way of reckoning time, is two years. I was sent for to visit an uncle, who lived at a considerable distance from Agimaque. The first day after we set out we arrived at Assinee, and the third day at my uncle's habitation, where I lived about three months, and was then thinking of returning to my father and young companion at Agimaque; but by this time I had got well acquainted with some of the children of my uncle's hundreds of relations, and we were some days too venturesome in going into the woods to gather fruit and catch birds, and such amusements as pleased us. One day I refused to go with the rest, being rather apprehensive that something might happen to us; till one of my play-fellows said to me, because you belong to the great men, you are afraid to venture your carcase, or else of the *bounsam*, which is the devil. This enraged me so much, that I set a resolution to join the rest, and we went into the woods as usual; but we had not been above two hours before our troubles began, when several great ruffians came upon us suddenly, and said we had committed a fault against their lord, and we must go and answer for it ourselves before him.

Some of us attempted in vain to run away, but pistols and cutlasses were soon introduced, threatening, that if we offered to stir we should all lie dead on the spot. One of them pretended to be more friendly than the rest, and said, that he would speak to their lord to get us clear, and desired that we should follow him; we were then immediately divided into different parties, and drove after him. We were soon led out of the way which we knew, and towards the evening, as we came in sight of a town, they told us that this great man of theirs lived there, but pretended it was too late to go and see him that night. Next morning there came three other men, whose language differed from ours, and spoke to some of those who watched us all the night, but he that pretended to be our friend with the great man, and some others, were gone away. We asked our keepers what these men had been saying to them, and they answered, that they had been asking them, and us together, to go and feast with them that day, and that we must put off seeing the great man till after; little thinking that our doom was so nigh, or that these villains meant to feast on us as their prey. We went with them again about half a day's journey, and came to a great multitude of people, having different music playing; and all the day after we got there, we were very merry with the music, dancing and singing. Towards the evening, we were again persuaded that we could not get back to where the great man lived till next day; and when bedtime came, we were separated into different houses with different people. When the next morning came, I asked for the men that brought me there, and for the rest of my companions; and I was told that they were gone to the sea side to bring home some rum, guns and powder, and that some of my companions were gone with them, and that some were gone to the fields to do something or other. This gave me strong suspicion that there was some treachery in the case, and I began to think that my hopes of returning home again were all over. I soon became very uneasy, not knowing what to do, and refused to eat or drink for whole days together, till the man of the house told me that he would do all in his power to get me back to my uncle; then I eat a little fruit with him, and had some thoughts that I should be sought after, as I would be then missing at home about five or six days. I enquired every day if the men had come back, and for the rest of my companions, but could get no answer of any satisfaction. I was kept about six days at this man's house, and in the evening there was another man came and talked with him a good while, and I heard the one say to the other he must go, and the other said the sooner the better; that man came out and told me that he knew my relations at Agimaque, and that we must set out to-morrow morning, and he would convey me there. Accordingly we set out next day, and travelled till dark, when we came to a place where we had some supper and slept. He carried a large bag with some gold dust, which he said he had to buy some goods at the sea side to take with him to Agimaque. Next day we travelled on, and in the evening came to a town, where I saw several white people, which made me afraid that they would eat me, according to our notion as children in the inland parts of the country. This made me rest very uneasy all the night, and next morning I had some victuals brought, desiring me to eat and make haste, as my guide and kid-napper told me that he had to go to the castle with some company that were going there, as he had told me before, to get some goods. After I was ordered out, the horrors I soon saw and felt, cannot be well described; I saw many of my miserable countrymen chained two and two, some hand-cuffed, and some with their hands tied behind. We were conducted along by a guard, and when we arrived at the castle, I asked my guide what I was brought there for, he told me to learn the ways of the *browsow*, that is the white faced people. I saw him take a gun, a piece of cloth, and some lead for me, and then he told me that he must now leave me there, and went off. This made me cry bitterly, but I was soon conducted to a prison, for three days, where I heard the groans and cries of many, and saw some of my fellow-captives. But when a vessel arrived to conduct us away to the ship, it was a most horrible scene; there was nothing to be heard but rattling of chains, smacking of whips, and the groans and cries of our fellow-men. Some would not stir from the ground, when they were lashed and beat in the most horrible manner. I have forgot the name of this infernal fort; but we were taken in the ship that came for us, to another that was ready to sail from Cape Coast. When we were put into the ship, we saw several black merchants coming on board, but we were all drove into our holes, and not suffered to speak to any of them. In this situation we continued several days in sight of our native land; but I could find no good person to give any information of my situation to Accasa at Agimaque. And when we found ourselves at last taken away, death was more preferable than life, and a plan was concerted amongst us, that we might burn and blow up the ship, and to perish all together in the flames; but we were betrayed by one of our own countrywomen, who slept with some of the head men of the ship, for it was common for the dirty filthy sailors to take the African women and lie upon their bodies; but the men were chained and pent up in holes. It was the women and boys which were to burn the ship, with the approbation and groans of the rest; though that was prevented, the discovery was likewise a cruel bloody scene.

But it would be needless to give a description of all the horrible scenes which we saw, and the base treatment which we met with in this dreadful captive situation, as the similar cases of thousands, which suffer by this infernal traffic, are well known. Let it suffice to say, that I was thus lost to my dear indulgent parents and relations, and they to me. All my help was cries and tears, and these could not avail; nor suffered long, till one succeeding woe, and dread, swelled up another. Brought from a state of innocence and freedom, and, in a barbarous and cruel manner, conveyed to a state of horror and slavery: this abandoned situation may be easier conceived than described. From the time that I was kid-napped and conducted to a factory, and from thence in the brutish, base, but fashionable way of traffic, consigned to Grenada, the grievous thoughts which I then felt, still pant in my heart; though my fears and tears have long since subsided. And yet it is still grievous to think that thousands more have suffered in similar and greater distress, under the hands of barbarous robbers, and merciless taskmasters; and that many even now are suffering in all the extreme bitterness of grief and woe, that no language can describe. The cries of some, and the sight of their misery, may be seen and heard afar; but the deep sounding groans of thousands, and the great sadness of their misery and woe, under the heavy load of oppressions and calamities inflicted upon them, are such as can only be distinctly known to the ears of Jehovah Sabaoth.

This Lord of Hosts, in his good Providence, and in great mercy to me, made a way for my deliverance from Grenada.—Being in this dreadful captivity and horrible slavery, without any hope of deliverance, for about eight or nine months, beholding the most dreadful scenes of misery and cruelty, and seeing my miserable companions often cruelly lashed, and as it were cut to pieces, for the most trifling faults; this made me often tremble and weep, but I escaped better than many of them. For eating a piece of sugarcane, some were cruelly lashed, or struck over the face to knock their teeth out. Some of the stouter ones, I suppose often reproved, and grown hardened and stupid with many cruel beatings and lashings, or perhaps faint and pressed with hunger and hard labour, were often committing trespasses of this kind, and when detected, they met with exemplary punishment. Some told me they had their teeth pulled out to deter others, and to prevent them from eating any cane in future. Thus seeing my miserable companions and countrymen in this pitiful, distressed and horrible situation, with all the brutish baseness and barbarity attending it, could not but fill my little mind with horror and indignation. But I must own, to the shame of my own countrymen, that I was first kid-napped and betrayed by some of my own complexion, who were the first cause of my exile and slavery; but if there were no buyers there would be no sellers. So far as I can remember, some of the Africans in my country keep slaves, which they take in war, or for debt; but those which they keep are well fed, and good care taken of them, and treated well; and, as to their cloathing, they differ according to the custom of the country. But I may safely say, that all the poverty and misery that any of the inhabitants of Africa meet with among themselves, is far inferior to those inhospitable regions of misery which they meet with in the West-Indies, where their hard-hearted overseers have neither regard to the laws of God, nor the life of their fellow-men.

Thanks be to God, I was delivered from Grenada, and that horrid brutal slavery.—A gentleman coming to England, took me for his servant, and brought me away, where I soon found my situation become more agreeable. After coming to England, and seeing others write and read, I had a strong desire to learn, and getting what assistance I could, I applied myself to learn reading and writing, which soon became my recreation, pleasure, and delight; and when my master perceived that I could write some, he sent me to a proper school for that purpose to learn. Since, I have endeavoured to improve my mind in reading, and have sought to get all the intelligence I could, in my situation of life, towards the state of my brethren and countrymen in complexion, and of the miserable situation of those who are barbarously sold into captivity, and unlawfully held in slavery.

But, among other observations, one great duty I owe to Almighty God, (the thankful acknowledgement I would not omit for any consideration) that, although I have been brought away from my native country, in that torrent of robbery and wickedness, thanks be to God for his good providence towards me; I have both obtained liberty, and acquired the great advantages of some little learning, in being able to read and write, and, what is still infinitely of greater advantage, I trust, to know something of HIM *who is that God whose providence rules over all, and who is the only Potent One that rules in the nations over the children of men. It is unto Him, who is the Prince of the Kings of the earth, that I would give all thanks.* And, in some manner, I may say with Joseph, as he did with respect to the evil intention of his brethren, when they sold him into Egypt, that whatever evil intentions and bad motives those insidious robbers had in carrying me away from my native country and friends, I trust, was what the Lord intended for my good. In this respect, I am highly indebted to many of the good people of England for learning and principles unknown to the people of my native country. But, above all, what have I obtained from the Lord God of Hosts, the God of the Christians! in that divine revelation of the only true God, and the Saviour of men, what a treasure of wisdom and blessings are involved? How wonderful

136

is the divine goodness displayed in those invaluable books the Old and New Testaments, that inestimable compilation of books, the Bible? And, O what a treasure to have, and one of the greatest advantages to be able to read therein, and a divine blessing to understand!

But, to return to my subject, I begin with the Cursory Remarker.[1] This man stiles himself a friend to the West-India colonies and their inhabitants, like Demetrius, the silversmith, a man of some considerable abilities, seeing their craft in danger, a craft, however, not so innocent and justifiable as the making of shrines for Diana, though that was base and wicked enough to enslave the minds of men with superstition and idolatry; but his craft, and the gain of those craftsmen, consists in the enslaving both soul and body to the cruel idolatry, and most abominable service and slavery, to the idol of cursed avarice: And as he finds some discoveries of their wicked traffic held up in a light where truth and facts are so clearly seen, as none but the most desperate villain would dare to obstruct or oppose, he therefore sallies forth with all the desperation of an Utopian assailant, to tell lies by a virulent contradiction of facts, and with false aspersions endeavour to calumniate the worthy and judicious essayist of that discovery, a man, whose character is irreproachable. By thus artfully supposing, if he could bring the reputation of the author, who has discovered so much of their iniquitous traffic, into dispute, his work would fall and be less regarded. However, this virulent craftsman has done no great merit to his cause and the credit of that infamous craft; at the appearance of truth, his understanding has got the better of his avarice and infidelity, so far, as to draw the following concession: "I shall not be so far misunderstood, by the candid and judicious part of mankind, as to be ranked among the advocates of slavery, as I most sincerely join Mr. Ramsay, and every other man of sensibility, in hoping the blessings of freedom will, in due time, be equally diffused over the whole globe."

By this, it would seem that he was a little ashamed of his craftsmen, and would not like to be ranked or appear amongst them. But as long as there are any hopes of gain to be made by that insidious craft, he can join with them well enough, and endeavour to justify them in that most abandoned traffic of buying, selling, and enslaving men. He finds fault with a plan for punishing robbers, thieves and vagabonds, who distress their neighbours by their thrift, robbery and plunder, without regarding any

---

[1] James Tobin (d. 1817) was a West Indian plantation owner who attacked the abolitionist James Ramsay's *An Essay on the Treatment and Conversion of African Slaves in the British Sugar Colonies* (London, 1784). The title of Tobin's attack on Ramsay was *Cursory Remarks upon the Reverend Mr. Ramsay's Essay* . . . (London, 1785); hence Cugoano's reference to him as the 'Cursory Remarker'.

laws human or divine, except the rules of their own fraternity, and in that case, according to the proverb, there may be some honor among thieves; but these are the only people in the world that ought to suffer some punishment, imprisonment or slavery; their external complexion, whether black or white, should be no excuse for them to do evil. Being aware of this, perhaps he was afraid that some of his friends, the great and opulent banditti of slaveholders in the western part of the world, might be found guilty of more atrocious and complicated crimes, than even those of the highwaymen, the robberies and the petty larcenies committed in England. Therefore, to make the best of this sad dilemma, he brings in a ludicrous invective comparison that it would be "an event which would undoubtedly furnish a new and pleasant compartment to that well known and most delectable print, call'd, *The world turn'd up side down*, in which the cook is roasted by the pig, the man saddled by the horse," &c. If he means that the complicated banditties of pirates, thieves, robbers, oppressors and enslavers of men, are those cooks and men that would be roasted and saddled, it certainly would be no unpleasant sight to see them well roasted, saddled and bridled too; and no matter by whom, whether he terms them pigs, horses or asses. But there is not much likelihood of this silly monkeyish comparison as yet being verified, in bringing the opulent pirates and thieves to condign punishment, so that he could very well bring it in to turn it off with a grin. However, to make use of his words, it would be a most delectable sight, when thieves and robbers get the upper side of the world, to see them turned down; and I should not interrupt his mirth, to see him laugh at his own invective monkeyish comparison as long as he pleases.

But again, when he draws a comparison of the many hardships that the poor in Great-Britain and Ireland labour under, as well as many of those in other countries; that their various distresses are worse than the West India slaves—It may be true, in part, that some of them suffer greater hardships than many of the slaves; but, bad as it is, the poorest in England would not change their situation for that of slaves. And there may be some masters, under various circumstances, worse off than their servants; but they would not change their own situation for theirs: Nor as little would a rich man wish to change his situation of affluence, for that of a beggar: and so, likewise, no freeman, however poor and distressing his situation may be, would resign his liberty for that of a slave, in the situation of a horse or a dog. The case of the poor, whatever their hardships may be, in free countries, is widely different from that of the West-India slaves. For the slaves, like animals, are bought and sold, and dealt with as their capricious owners may think fit, even in torturing and tearing them to pieces, and wearing them out with hard labour, hunger and oppression; and should the death of a slave ensue by some other more violent way than that which is commonly the death of thousands, and tens of thousands in the end, the haughty tyrant, in that case, has only to pay a small fine for the murder and death of his slave. The brute creation in general may fare better than man, and some dogs may refuse the crumbs that the distressed poor would be glad of; but the nature and situation of man is far superior to that of beasts; and, in like manner, whatever circumstances poor freemen may be in, their situation is much superior, beyond any proportion, to that of the hardships and cruelty of modern slavery. But where can the situation of any freeman be so bad as that of a slave; or, could such be found, or even worse, as he would have it, what would the comparison amount to? Would it plead for his craft of slavery and oppression? Or, rather, would it not cry aloud for some redress, and what every well regulated society of men ought to hear and consider, that none should suffer want or be oppressed among them? And this seems to be pointed out by the circumstances which he describes; that it is the great duty, and ought to be the highest ambition of all governors, to order and establish such policy, and in such a wise manner, that every thing should be so managed, as to be conducive to the moral, temporal and eternal welfare of every individual from the lowest degree to the highest; and the consequence of this would be, the harmony, happiness and good prosperity of the whole community.

But this crafty author has also, in defence of his own or his employer's craft in the British West-India slavery, given sundry comparisons and descriptions of the treatment of slaves in the French islands and settlements in the West-Indies and America. And, contrary to what is the true case, he would have it supposed that the treatment of the slaves in the former, is milder than the latter; but even in this, unwarily for his own craft of slavery, all that he has advanced, can only add matter for its confutation, and serve to heighten the ardour and wish of every generous mind, that the whole should be abolished. An equal degree of enormity found in one place, cannot justify crimes of as great or greater enormity committed in another. The various depredations committed by robbers and plunderers, on different parts of the globe, may not be all equally alike bad, but their evil and malignancy, in every appearance and shape, can only hold up to view the just observation, that

Virtue herself hath such peculiar mein,
Vice, to be hated, needs but to be seen.

The farther and wider that the discovery and knowledge of such an enormous evil, as the base and villainous treatment and slavery which the poor unfortunate Black People meet with, is spread and made known, the cry for justice, even virtue lifting up her voice, must rise the louder and higher, for the scale of equity and justice to be lifted up in their defence. And doth not wisdom cry, and understanding put forth her voice? But who will regard the voice and hearken to the cry? Not the sneaking advocates for slavery, though a little ashamed of their craft; like the monstrous crocodile weeping over their prey with fine concessions (while gorging their own rapacious appetite) to hope for universal freedom taking place over the globe. Not those inebriated with avarice and infidelity, who hold in defiance every regard due to the divine law, and who endeavour all they can to destroy and take away the natural and common rights and privileges of men. Not the insolent and crafty author for slavery and oppression, who would have us to believe, that the benign command of God in appointing the seventh day for a sabbath of rest for the good purposes of our present and eternal welfare, is not to be regarded. He will exclaim against the teachers of obedience to it; and tells us, that the poor, and the oppressed, and the heavy burdened slave, should not lay down his load that day, but appropriate these hours of sacred rest to labour in some bit of useful ground. His own words are, "to dedicate the unappropriated hours of Sunday to the cultivation of this useful spot, he is brought up to believe would be the worst of sins, and that the sabbath is a day of absolute and universal rest is a truth he hears frequently inculcated by the curate of the parish," &c. But after bringing it about in this round-about way and manner, whatever the curate has to say of it as a truth, he would have us by no means to regard. This may serve as a specimen of his crafty and detestable production, where infidelity, false aspersions, virulent calumnies, and lying contradictions abound throughout. I shall only refer him to that description which he meant for another, as most applicable and best suited for himself; and so long as he does not renounce his craft, as well as to be somewhat ashamed of his craftsmen and their insensibility, he may thus stand as described by himself: "A man of warm imagination (but strange infatuated unfeeling sensibility) to paint things not as they really are, but as his rooted prejudices represent them, and even to shut his eyes against the convictions afforded him by his own senses."

But such is the insensibility of men, when their own craft of gain is advanced by the slavery and oppression of others, that after all the laudable exertions of the truly virtuous and humane, towards extending the beneficence of liberty and freedom to the much degraded and unfortunate Africans, which is the common right and privilege of all men, in every thing that is just, lawful and consistent, we find the principles of justice and equity, not only opposed, and every duty in religion and humanity left unregarded; but that unlawful traffic of dealing with our fellow-creatures, as with the beasts of the earth, still carried on with as great assiduity as ever; and that the insidious piracy of procuring and holding slaves is countenanced and supported by the government of sundry Christian nations. This seems to be the fashionable way of getting riches, but very dishonourable; in doing this, the slave-holders are meaner and baser than the African slaves, for while they subject and reduce them to a degree with brutes, they seduce themselves to a degree with devils.

"Some pretend that the Africans, in general, are a set of poor, ignorant, dispersed, unsociable people; and that they think it no crime to sell one another, and even their own wives and children; therefore they bring them away to a situation where many of them may arrive to a better state than ever they could obtain in their own native country." This specious pretence is without any shadow of justice and truth, and, if the argument was even true, it could afford no just and warrantable matter for any society of men to hold slaves. But the argument is false; there can be no ignorance, dispersion, or unsociableness so found among them, which can be made better by bringing them away to a state of a degree equal to that of a cow or a horse.

But let their ignorance in some things (in which the Europeans have greatly the advantage of them) be what it will, it is not the intention of those who bring them away to make them better by it; nor is the design of slave-holders of any other intention, but that they may serve them as a kind of engines and beasts of burden; that their own ease and profit may be advanced, by a set of poor helpless men and women, whom they despise and rank with brutes, and keep them in perpetual slavery, both themselves and children, and merciful death is the only release from their toil. By the benevolence of some, a few may get their liberty, and by their own industry and ingenuity, may acquire some learning, mechanical trades, or useful business; and some may be brought away by different gentlemen to free countries, where they get their liberty, but no thanks to slave-holders for it. But amongst those who get their liberty, like all other ignorant men, are generally more corrupt in their morals, than they possibly could have been amongst their own people in Africa; for, being mostly amongst the wicked and apostate Christians, they sooner learn their oaths and blasphemies, and their evil ways, than any thing else. Some few, indeed, may eventually arrive at some knowledge of the Christian religion, and the great advantages of it. Such was the case of Ukawsaw Groniosaw,[2] an African prince, who lived in England. He

---

[2] James Albert Ukawsaw Gronniosaw (*c.* 1710 – *c.* 1772), author of *A Narrative of the Most Remarkable Particulars in the Life of James Albert Ukawsaw Gronniosaw, an African Prince, as related by Himself* (Bath, 1772). Cugoano appears to have read or at least heard of this early slave narrative.

was a long time in a state of great poverty and distress, and must have died at one time for want, if a good and charitable attorney had not supported him. He was long after in a very poor state, but he would not have given his faith in the Christian religion, in exchange for all the kingdoms of Africa, if they could have been given to him, in place of his poverty, for it. And such was A. Morrant[3] in America. When a boy, he could stroll away into a desart, and prefer the society of wild beasts to the absurd Christianity of his mother's house. He was conducted to the king of the Cherokees, who, in a miraculous manner, was induced by him to embrace the Christian faith. This Morrant was in the British service last war, and his royal convert, the king of the Cherokee Indians, accompanied General Clinton at the siege of Charles Town.

Source: Quobna Ottobah Cugoano, *Thoughts and Sentiments on the Evil of Slavery and Other Writings*, ed. V. Carretta, Harmondsworth, Penguin, 1999 [1787], pp. 9–24.

Extract 2

[. . .] It may be said with confidence as a certain general fact, that all their foreign settlements and colonies were founded on murders and devastations, and that they have continued their depredations in cruel slavery and oppression to this day: for where such predominant wickedness as the African slave-trade, and the West Indian slavery, is admitted, tolerated and supported by them, and carried on in their colonies, the nations and people who are the supporters and encouragers thereof must be not only guilty themselves of that shameful and abandoned evil and wickedness, so very disgraceful to human nature, but even partakers in those crimes of the most vile combinations of various pirates, kidnappers, robbers and thieves, the ruffians and stealers of men, that ever made their appearance in the world.

Soon after Columbus had discovered America, that great navigator was himself greatly embarrassed and treated unjustly, and his best designs counteracted by the wicked baseness of those whom he led to that discovery. The infernal conduct of his Spanish competitors, whose leading motives were covetousness, avarice and fanaticism, soon made their appearance, and became cruel and dreadful. At Hispaniola the base

---

[3] John Marrant (1755–91), author of *A Narrative of the Lord's Wonderful Dealings with John Marrant, a Black* (London, 1785). Cugoano appears to have read Marrant's narrative, which is a variation on his own conversion narrative in that it is located in North America.

perfidy and bloody treachery of the Spaniards, led on by the perfidious Ovando, in seizing the peaceable Queen Anacoana and her attendants, burning her palace, putting all to destruction, and the innocent Queen and her people to a cruel death, is truly horrible and lamentable. And led on by the treacherous Cortes, the fate of the great Montezuma was dreadful and shocking; how that American monarch was treated, betrayed and destroyed, and his vast extensive empire of the Mexicans brought to ruin and devastation, no man of sensibility and feeling can read the history without pity and resentment. And looking over another page of that history, sensibility would kindle into horror and indignation, to see the base treacherous bastard Pizarra at the head of the Spanish banditti of miscreant depredators, leading them on, and overturning one of the most extensive empires in the world. To recite a little of this as a specimen of the rest: It seems Pizarra, with his company of depredators, had artfully penetrated into the Peruvian empire, and pretended an embassy of peace from a great monarch, and demanded an audience of the noble Atahualpa, the great Inca or Lord of that empire, that the terms of their embassy might be explained, and the reason of their coming into the territories of that monarch. Atahualpa fearing the menaces of those terrible invaders, and thinking to appease them by complying with their request, relied on Pizzara's feigned pretensions of friendship; accordingly the day was appointed, and Atahualpa made his appearance with the greatest decency and splendor he could, to meet such superior beings as the Americans conceived their invaders to be, with four hundred men in an uniform dress, as harbingers to clear the way before him, and himself sitting on a throne or couch, adorned with plumes of various colours, and almost covered with plates of gold and silver, enriched with precious stones, and was carried on the shoulders of his principal attendants. As he approached near the Spanish quarters the arch fanatic Father Vincent Valverde, chaplain to the expedition, advanced with a crucifix in one hand and a breviary in the other, and began with a long discourse, pretending to explain some of the general doctrines of Christianity, together with the fabulous notion of St. Peter's viceregency, and the transmission of his apostolic power continued in the succession of the Popes; and that the then Pope, Alexander, by donation, had invested their master as the sole Monarch of all the New World. In consequence of this, Atahualpa was instantly required to embrace the Christian religion, acknowledge the jurisdiction of the Pope, and submit to the Great Monarch of Castile; but if he should refuse an immediate compliance with these requisitions, they were to declare war against him, and that he might expect the dreadful effects of their vengeance. This strange harangue, unfolding deep mysteries, and alluding to such unknown facts, of which no power of eloquence could translate, and convey, at once, a distinct idea to an American, that its general tenor was altogether incomprehensible to Atahualpa. Some parts in it, as more obvious that the rest, filled him with astonishment and indignation. His reply, however, was temperate, and as suitable as could be well expected. He observed that he was Lord of the domains over which he reigned by hereditary succession; and, said, that he could not conceive how a foreign priest should pretend to dispose of territories which did not belong to him, and that if such a preposterous grant had been made, he, who was the rightful possessor, refused to confirm it; that he had no inclination to renounce the religious institutions established by his ancestors; nor would he forsake the service of the Sun, the immortal divinity whom he and his people revered, in order to worship the God of the Spaniards, who was subject to death; and that with respect to other matters, he had never heard of them before, and did not then understand their meaning. And he desired to know where Valverde had learned things so extraordinary. In this book, replied the fanatic Monk, reaching out his breviary. The Inca opened it eagerly, and turning over the leaves, lifted it to his ear: This, says he, is silent; it tells me nothing; and threw it with disdain to the ground. The enraged father of ruffians, turning towards his countrymen, the assassinators, cried out, To arms, Christians, to arms; the word of God is insulted; avenge this profanation on these impious dogs.

At this the Christian desperadoes impatient in delay, as soon as the signal of assault was given their martial music began to play, and their attack was rapid, rushing suddenly upon the Peruvians, and with their hell-invented enginery of thunder, fire and smoke, they soon put them to flight and destruction. The Inca, though his nobles crouded around him with officious zeal, and fell in numbers at his feet, while they vied with one another in sacrificing their own lives that they might cover the sacred person of their Sovereign, was soon penetrated to by the assassinators, dragged from his throne, and carried to the Spanish quarters. The fate of the Monarch increased the precipitate flight of his followers; the plains being covered with upwards of thirty thousand men, were pursued by the ferocious Spaniards towards every quarter, who, with deliberate and unrelenting barbarity, continued to slaughter the wretched fugitives till the close of the day, that never had once offered at any resistance. Pizarra had contrived this daring and perfidious plan on purpose to get hold of the Inca, notwithstanding his assumed character of an ambassador from a powerful monarch to court an alliance with that prince, and in violation of all the repeated offers of his own friendship. The noble Inca thus found himself betrayed and shut up in the Spanish quarters, though scarce aware at first of the vast carnage and destruction of his people; but

soon conceiving the destructive consequences that attended his confinement, and by beholding the vast treasures of spoil that the Spaniards had
so eagerly gathered up, he learned something of their covetous disposition: and he offered as a ransom what astonished the Spaniards, even
after all they now knew concerning the opulence of his kingdom: the
apartment in which he was confined was twenty-two feet in length and
sixteen in breadth, he undertook to fill it with vessels of gold as high as
he could reach. This tempting proposal was eagerly agreed to by Pizarra,
and a line was drawn upon the walls of the chamber to mark the stipu-
lated height to which the treasure was to rise. The gold was accordingly
collected from various parts with the greatest expedition by the Inca's
obedient and loving subjects, who thought nothing too much for his
ransom and life; but, after all, poor Atahualpa was cruelly murdered,
and his body burnt by a military inquisition, and his extensive and
rich dominions devoted to destruction and ruin by these merciless
depredators.

The history of those dreadfully perfidious methods of forming settlements, and acquiring riches and territory, would make humanity tremble, and even recoil, at the enjoyment of such acquisitions and become
reverted into rage and indignation at such horrible injustice and barbarous cruelty, "It is said by the Peruvians, that their Incas, or Monarchs,
had uniformly extended their power with attention to the good of their
subjects, that they might diffuse the blessings of civilization, and the
knowledge of the arts which they possessed, among the people that
embraced their protection; and during a succession of twelve monarchs,
not one had deviated from this beneficent character." Their sensibility of
such nobleness of character would give them the most poignant dislike
to their new terrible invaders that had desolated and laid waste their
country. The character of their monarchs would seem to vie with as great
virtues as any King in Europe can boast of. Had the Peruvians been visited by men of honesty, knowledge, and enlightened understanding, to
teach them, by patient instruction and the blessing of God, they might
have been induced to embrace the doctrines and faith of Christianity, and
to abandon their errors of superstition and idolatry. Had Christians, that
deserve the name thereof, been sent among them, the many useful things
that they would have taught them, together with their own pious example, would have captivated their hearts; and the knowledge of the truth
would have made it a very desirous thing for the Americans to have those
who taught them to settle among them. Had that been the case the Americans, in various parts, would have been as eager to have the Europeans
come there as they would have been to go, so that the Europeans might
have found settlements enough, in a friendly alliance with the inhabi-

tants, without destroying and enslaving them. And had that been the case it might be supposed, that Europe and America, long before now, would both, with a growing luxuriancy, have been flourishing with affluence and peace, and their long extended and fruitful branches, loaden with benefits to each other, reaching over the ocean, might have been more extensive, and greater advantages have been expected, for the good of both than what has yet appeared. But, alas! at that time there [were] no Christians to send, (and very few now), these were obliged to hide themselves in the obscure places of the earth; that was, according to Sir Isaac Newton, to mix in obscurity among the meanest of the people, having no power and authority; and it seems at that time there was no power among Christians on earth to have sent such as would have been useful to the Americans; and if there had they would have sent after the depredators, and rescued the innocent.

But as I said before, it is surely to the great shame and scandal of Christianity among all the Heathen nations, that those robbers, plunderers, destroyers and enslavers of men should call themselves Christians, and exercise their power under any Christian government and authority. I would have my African countrymen to know and understand, that the destroyers and enslavers of men can be no Christians; for Christianity is the system of benignity and love, and all its votaries are devoted to honesty, justice, humanity, meekness, peace and good-will to all men. But whatever title or claim some may assume to call themselves by it, without possessing any of its virtues, can only manifest them to be the more abominable liars, and the greatest enemies unto it, and as belonging to the synagogue of Satan, and not the adherers to Christ. For the enslavers and oppressors of men, among those that have obtained the name of Christians, they are still acting as its greatest enemies, and contrary to all its genuine principles; they should therefore be called by its opposite, the Antichrist. Such are fitly belonging to that most dissolute sorceress of all religion in the world: "With whom the kings of the earth have lived deliciously; and the inhabitants of the earth have been made drunk with the wine of her abominations; and the merchants of the earth are waxed rich through the abundance of her delicacies, by their traffic in various things, and in slaves and souls of men!" It was not enough for the malignant destroyer of the world to set up his hydra-headed kingdom of evil and wickedness among the kingdom of men; but also to cause an image to be made unto him, by something imported in the only true religion that ever was given to men; and that image of iniquity is described as arising up out of the earth, having two horns like a lamb, which, by its votaries and adherents, has been long established and supported. One of its umbrageous horns of apostacy and delusion is founded, in a more

particular respect, on a grand perversion of the Old Testament dispensations, which has extended itself over all the Mahometan nations in the
East; and the other horn of apostacy, bearing an allusion and professional respect to that of the new, has extended itself over all the Christian nations in the West. That grand umbrageous shadow and image of
evil and wickedness, has spread its malignant influence over all the
nations of the earth, and has, by its power of delusion, given countenance and support to all the power of evil and wickedness done among
men; and all the adherents and supporters of that delusion, and all the
carriers on of wickedness, are fitly called Antichrist. But all the nations
have drunk of the wine of that iniquity, and become drunk with the wine
of the wrath of her fornication, whose name, by every mark and feature,
is the Antichrist; and every dealer in slaves, and those that hold them in
slavery, whatever else they may call themselves, or whatever else they
may profess. And likewise, those nations whose governments support
that evil and wicked traffic of slavery, however remote the situation
where it is carried on may be, are, in that respect, as much Antichristian
as any thing in the world can be. No man will ever rob another unless he
be a villain: nor will any nation or people ever enslave and oppress
others, unless themselves be base and wicked men, and who act and do
contrary and against every duty in Christianity.

The learned and ingenious author of Britannia Libera,[4] as chiefly
alluding to Great-Britain alone, gives some account of that great evil and
wickedness carried on by the Christian nations, respecting the direful
effects of the great devastations committed in foreign parts, whereby it
would appear that the ancient and native inhabitants have been
drenched in blood and oppression by their merciless visitors (which have
formed colonies and settlements among them) the avaricious depredators, plunderers and destroyers of nations. As some estimate of it, "to
destroy eleven million, and distress many more in America, to starve and
oppress twelve million in Asia, and the great number destroyed, is not
the way to promote the dignity, strength and safety of empire, but to
draw down the Divine vengeance on the offenders, for depriving so
many of their fellow-creatures of life, or the common blessings of the
earth: whereas by observing the humane principles of preservation with
felicitation, the proper principles of all rulers, their empire might have
received all reasonable benefit, with the encrease of future glory." But
should it be asked, what advantages Great-Britain has gained by all its

---

[4] *Britannia Libera, or a Defence of the Free State of Man in England* (1772) was written by
William Bollan (*c.* 1710–76), and provides ambiguous support for Cugoano's view that
slavery was inimical to British values of freedom.

extensive territories abroad, the devastations committed, and the abominable slavery and oppression carried on in its colonies? It may be answered according to the old proverb,

> It seldom is the grand-child's lot,
> To share of wealth unjustly got.

This seems to be verified too much in their present situation: for however wide they have extended their territories abroad, they have sunk into a world of debt at home, which must ever remain an impending burden upon the inhabitants. And it is not likely, by any plan as yet adopted, to be ever paid, or any part of it, without a long continued heavy annual load of taxes. Perhaps, great as it is some other plan, more equitable for the good of the whole community, if it was wanted to be done, and without any additional taxes, might be so made use of to pay it all off in twenty or thirty years time, and in such manner as whatever emergencies might happen, as never to need to borrow any money at interest. The national debt casts a sluggish deadness over the whole realm, greatly stops ingenuity and improvements, promotes idleness and wickedness, clogs all the wheels of commerce, and drains the money out of the nation. If a foreigner buys stock, in the course of years that the interest amounts to the principal, he gets it all back; and in an equitable time the same sum ever after, and in course must take that money to foreign parts. And those who hold stock at home, are a kind of idle drones, as a burden to the rest of the community: whereas if there were no funds, those who have money would be obliged to occupy it in some improvements themselves, or lend it to other manufacturers or merchants, and by that means useful employments, ingenuity and commerce would flourish. But all stock-jobbing, lotteries, and useless business, has a tendency to slavery and oppression; for as the greater any idle part of the community is, there must be the greater labour and hardships resting upon the industrious part who support the rest; as all men are allotted in some degree to eat their bread with the sweat of their brow; *but it is evil with any people when the rich grind the face of the poor.* Lotteries must be nearly as bad a way of getting money for the good of a nation, as it is for an individual when he is poor, and obliged to pawn his goods to increase his poverty, already poor. On the reverse, if a nation was to keep a bank to lend money to merchants and others, that nation might flourish, and its support to those in need might be attended with advantage to the whole; but that nation which is obliged to borrow money from others, must be in a poor and wretched situation, and the inhabitants, who have to bear the load of its taxes, must be greatly burdened, and perhaps many of those employed in its service (as soldiers and others) poorly paid. It was

148

otherwise with *the people of Israel of old*; it was the promise and blessing of God to them, *That they should lend unto many nations, but
should not borrow.*

But when a nation or people do wickedly, and commit cruelties and
devastations upon others, and enslave them, it cannot be expected that
they should be attended with the blessings of God, neither to eschew evil.
They often become infatuated to do evil unawares; and those employed
under their service sometimes lead them into debt, error and wickedness,
in order to enrich themselves by their plunder, in committing the most
barbarous cruelties, under pretences of war, wherein they were the first
aggressors, and which is generally the case in all unnatural and destructive disputes of war. In this business money is wanted, the national debt
becomes increased, and new loans and other sums must be added to the
funds. The plunderers abroad send home their cash as fast as they can,
and by one means and another the sums wanted to borrow, are soon
made up. At last when the wars subside, or other business calls them
home, laden with the spoils of the East or elsewhere, they have then the
grand part of their business to negotiate, in buying up bank stock, and
lodging their plunder and ill-got wealth in the British or other funds.
Thus the nation is loaded with more debt, and with an annual addition
of more interest to pay, to the further advantage of those who often occasioned it by their villainy; who, if they had their deserts, like the Popish
inquisitors, are almost the only people in the world who deserve to be
hung on the rack.

But so it happens in general, that men of activity and affluence, by
whatever way they are possessed of riches, or have acquired a greatness
of such property, they are always preferred to take the lead in matters of
government, so that the greatest depredators, warriors, contracting com-
panies of merchants, and rich slave-holders, always endeavour to push
themselves on to get power and interest in their favour; that whatever
crimes any of them commit they are seldom brought to a just punishment. Unless that something of this kind had been the case, 'tis impossible to conceive how such an enormous evil as the slave-trade could have
been established and carried on under any Christian government: and
from hence that motly system of government, which hath so sprung up
and established itself, may be accounted for, and as being an evident and
universal depravity of one of the finest constitutions in the world; and it
may be feared if these unconstitutional laws, reaching from Great-
Britain to her colonies, be long continued in and supported, to the carrying on that horrible and wicked traffic of slavery, must at last mark out
the whole of the British constitution with ruin and destruction; and that
the most generous and tenacious people in the world for liberty, may also

at last be reduced to slaves. And an Ethiopian may venture to assert, that so long as slavery is continued in any part of the British dominions, that more than one-half of the legislature are the virtual supporters and encouragers of a traffic which ought to be abolished, as it cannot be carried on but by some of the most abandoned and profligate men upon earth.

> *Source*: Quobna Ottobah Cugoano, *Thoughts and Sentiments on the Evil of Slavery and Other Writings*, ed. V. Carretta, Harmondsworth, Penguin, 1999 [1787], pp. 62–71.

Extract 3

[. . .]

The vast carnage and murders committed by the British instigators of slavery, is attended with a very shocking, peculiar, and almost unheard of conception, according to the notion of the perpetrators of it; they either consider them as their own property, that they may do with as they please, in life or death; or that the taking away the life of a black man is of no more account than taking away the life of a beast. A very melancholy instance of this happened about the year 1780, as recorded in the courts of law; a master of a vessel bound to the Western Colonies, selected 132 of the most sickly of the black slaves, and ordered them to be thrown overboard into the sea, in order to recover their value from the insurers, as he had perceived that he was too late to get a good market for them in the West-Indies. On the trial, by the counsel for the owners of the vessel against the underwriters, their argument was, that the slaves were to be considered the same as horses; and their plea for throwing them into the sea was nothing better than that it might be more necessary to throw them overboard to lighten their vessel than goods of greater value, or something to that effect. These poor creatures, it seems, were tied two and two together when they were thrown into the sea, lest some of them might swim a little for the last gasp of air, and, with the animation of their approaching exit, breath[e] their souls away to the gracious Father of spirits. Some of the last parcel, when they saw the fate of their companions, made their escape from tying by jumping overboard, and one was saved by means of a rope from some in the ship. The owners of the vessel, I suppose, (inhuman connivers of robbery, slavery, murder and fraud) were rather a little defeated in this, by bringing their villainy to light in a court of law; but the inhuman monster of a captain was kept out of the way of justice from getting hold of him. Though such perpetrators of murder and fraud should have been sought after from the British Dan in the East-Indies, to her Beershebah in the West.[5]

But our lives are accounted of no value, we are hunted after as the prey in the desert, and doomed to destruction as the beasts that perish. And for this, should we appear to the inhabitants of Europe, would they dare to say that they have not wronged us, and grievously injured us, and that the blood of millions do not cry out against them? And if we appeal to the inhabitants of Great-Britain, can they justify the deeds of their conduct towards us? And is it not strange to think, that they who ought to be considered as the most learned and civilized people in the world, that they should carry on a traffic of the most barbarous cruelty and injustice, and that many, even among them, are become so dissolute, as to think slavery, robbery and murder no crimes? But we will answer to this, that no man can, with impunity, steal, kidnap, buy or sell another man, without being guilty of the most atrocious villainy. And we will aver, that every slave-holder that claims any property in slaves, or holds them in an involuntary servitude, are the most obnoxious and dissolute robbers among men; and that they have no more right, nor any better title to any one of them, than the most profligate and notorious robbers and thieves in the world, has to the goods which they have robbed and stole from the right owners and lawful possessor thereof. But should the slave-holders say that they buy them; their title and claim is no better then that of the most notorious conniver, who buys goods from other robbers, knowing them to be stole, and accordingly gives an inferior price for them. According to the laws of England, when such connivers are discovered, and the property of others unlawfully found in their possession; the right owners thereof can oblige the connivers to restore back their property, and to punish them for their trespass. But the slave-holders, universally, are those connivers, they do not only rob men of some of their property, but they keep men from every property belonging to them, and compel them to their involuntary service and drudgery; and those whom they buy from other robbers, and keep in their possession, are greatly injured by them when compared to any species of goods whatsoever; and accordingly they give but a very inferior price for men, as all their vast estates in the West-Indies is not sufficient to buy one of them, if the rightful possessor was to sell himself to them in the manner that they claim possession of him. Therefore let the inhabitants of any civilized nation determine, whether, if they were to be treated in the same manner that the Africans are, by various pirates, kidnappers, and slave-holders, and

---

[5] Dan was the most northern city, and Beersheba the most southern city in the Holy Land, and the phrase therefore meant from one end of (Britain's) political realm to the other.

their wives, and their sons and daughters were to be robbed from them, or themselves violently taken away to a perpetual and intolerable slavery; or whether they would not think those robbers, who only took away their property, less injurious to them than the other. If they determine it so, as reason must tell every man, that himself is of more value than his property; then the executors of the laws of civilization ought to tremble at the inconsistency of passing judgment upon those whose crimes, in many cases, are less than what the whole legislature must be guilty of, when those of a far greater is encouraged and supported by it wherever slavery is tolerated by law, and, consequently, that slavery can no where be tolerated with any consistency to civilization and the laws of justice among men; but if it can maintain its ground, to have any place at all, it must be among a society of barbarians and thieves, and where the laws of their society is, for every one to catch what he can. Then, when theft and robbery become no crimes, the man-stealer and the conniving slaveholder might possibly get free.

But the several nations of Europe that have joined in that iniquitous traffic of buying, selling and enslaving men, must in course have left their own laws of civilization to adopt those of barbarians and robbers, and that they may say to one another, *When thou sawest a thief, then thou consentest with him, and hast been partaker with all the workers of iniquity*. But whereas every man, as a rational creature, is responsible for his actions, and he becomes not only guilty in doing evil himself, but in letting others rob and oppress their fellow-creatures with impunity, or in not delivering the oppressed when he has it in his power to help them. And likewise that nation which may be supposed to maintain a very considerable degree of civilization[,] justice and equity within its own jurisdiction, is not in that case innocent, while it beholds another nation or people carrying on persecution, oppression and slavery, unless it remonstrates against that wickedness of the other nation, and makes use of every effort in its power to help the oppressed, and to rescue the innocent. For so it ought to be the universal rule of duty to all men that fear God and keep his commandments, to do good to all men wherever they can; and when they find any wronged and injured by others, they should endeavour to deliver the ensnared whatever their grievances may be; and should this sometimes lead them into war they might expect the protection and blessing of heaven. How far other motives may appear eligible for men to oppose one another with hostile force, it is not my business to enquire. But I should suppose the hardy veterans who engage merely about the purposes of envying one another concerning any different advantages of commerce, or for enlarging their territories and dominions, or for the end of getting riches by their conquest; that if they fall in the combat, they must generally die, as the fool dieth, vaunting in vain glory; and many of them be like to those who go out in darkness, never to see light; and should they come off alive, what more does their honour and fame amount to, but only to be like that antediluvian conqueror, *who had slain a man to his own wounding, and a young man to his hurt.* But those mighty men of renown in the days of old, because of their apostacy from God, and rebellion and wickedness to men, were at last all swallowed up by an universal deluge for their iniquity and crimes.

But again let me observe, that whatever civilization the inhabitants of Great-Britain may enjoy among themselves, they have seldom maintained their own innocence in that great duty as a Christian nation towards others; and I may say, with respect to their African neighbours, or to any other wheresoever they may go by the way of commerce, they have not regarded them at all. And when they saw others robbing the Africans, and carrying them into captivity and slavery, they have neither helped them, nor opposed their oppressors in the least. But instead thereof they have joined in combination against them with the rest of other profligate nations and people, to buy, enslave and make merchandize of them, because they found them helpless and fit to suit their own purpose, and are become the head carriers on of that iniquitous traffic. But the greater that any reformation and civilization is obtained by any nation, if they do not maintain righteousness, but carry on any course of wickedness and oppression, it makes them appear only the more inconsistent, and their tyranny and oppression the more conspicuous. Wherefore because of the great wickedness, cruelty and injustice done to the Africans, those who are greatest in the transgression give an evident and undubious warrant to all other nations beholding their tyranny and injustice to others, if those nations have any regard to their own innocence and virtue, and wish to maintain righteousness, and to remain clear of the oppression and blood of all men; it is their duty to chastize and suppress such unjust and tyrannical oppressors and enslavers of men. And should none of these be found among the enlightened and civilized nations, who maintain their own innocence and righteousness, with regard to their duty unto all men; and that there may be none to chastize the tyrannical oppressors of others; then it may be feared, as it has often been, that fierce nations of various insects, and other annoyances, may be sent as a judgment to punish the wicked nations of men. For by some way or other every criminal nation, and all their confederates, who sin and rebel against God, and against his laws of nature and nations, will each meet with some awful retribution at last, unless they repent of their iniquity. And the greater advantages of light, learning, knowledge and civilization that any people enjoy, if they do not maintain righteousness, but do wickedly, they will meet with the more severe rebuke when the visitations of God's judgment cometh upon them. And the prophecy which was given to Moses, is still as much in force against the enlightened nations now for their wickedness, in going after the abominations of heathens and barbarians, for none else would attempt to enslave and make merchandize of men, as it was when denounced against the Israelitish nation of old, when they departed, or should depart, from the laws and statutes of the Most High. *The Lord shall bring a nation against thee, from far, from the ends of the earth, as swift as the eagle flieth, a nation whose tongue thou shalt not understand,* &c. See Deut[eronomy] xxviii.

But lest any of these things should happen to the generous and respectful Britons, who are not altogether lost to virtue and consideration; let me say unto you, in the language of a wise and eminent Queen,[6] as she did when her people were sold as a prey to their enemies: That it is not all your enemies [(]for they can be reckoned nothing else), the covetous instigators and carriers on of slavery and wickedness, that can in any way countervail the damage to yourselves, to your king, and to your country; nor will all the infamous profits of the poor Africans avail you any thing if it brings down the avenging hand of God upon you. We are not saying that we have not sinned, and that we are not deserving of the righteous judgments of God against us. But the enemies that have risen up against us are cruel, oppressive and unjust; and their haughtiness of insolence, wickedness and iniquity is like to that of Haman the son of Hammedatha,[7] and who dare suppose, or even presume to think, that the inhuman ruffians and ensnarers of men, the vile negociators and merchandizers of the human species, and the offensive combinations of slave-holders in the West have done no evil? And should we be passive, as the suffering martyrs dying in the flames, whose blood crieth for vengeance on their persecutors and murderers; so the iniquity of our oppressors, enslavers and murderers rise up against them. For we have been hunted after as the wild beasts of the earth, and sold to the enemies of mankind as their prey; and should any of us have endeavoured to get away from them, as a man would naturally fly from an enemy that waylaid him; we have been pursued after, and, by haughty mandates and laws of iniquity, overtaken, and murdered and slain, and the blood of millions cries out against them. And together with these that have been cruelly spoiled and slain, the very grievous afflictions that we have long

---

[6] The Queen Cugoano refers to here is the Biblical queen Esther, who outwitted Haman, the son of Hammedatha, and thus saved the Jewish people.
[7] See fn. 6.

suffered under, has been long crying for vengeance on our oppressors; and the great distress and wretchedness of human woe and misery, which we are yet lying under, is still rising up before that High and Sovereign Hand of Justice, where men, by all their oppression and cruelty, can no way prevent; their evil treatment of others may serve to increase the blow, but not to evade the stroke of His power, nor withhold the bringing down that arm of vengeance on themselves, and upon all their connivers and confederators, and the particular instigators of such wilful murders and inhuman barbarity. The life of a black man is of as much regard in the sight of God, as the life of any other man; though we have been sold as a carnage to the market, and as a prey to profligate wicked men, to torture and lash us as they please, and as their caprice may think fit, to murder us at discretion.

And should any of the best of them plead, as they generally will do, and tell of their humanity and charity to those whom they have captured and enslaved, their tribute of thanks is but small; for what is it, but a little restored to the wretched and miserable whom they have robbed of their all; and only to be dealt with, like the spoil of those taken in the field of battle, where the wretched fugitives must submit to what they please. For as we have been robbed of our natural right as men, and treated as beasts, those who have injured us, are like to them who have robbed the widow, the orphans, the poor and the needy of their right, and whose children are rioting on the spoils of those who are begging at their doors for bread. And should they say, that their fathers were thieves and connivers with ensnarers of men, and that they have been brought up to the iniquitous practice of slavery and oppression of their fellow-creatures, and they cannot live without carrying it on, and making their gain by the unlawful merchandize and cruel slavery of men, what is that to us, and where will it justify them? And some will be saying, that the Black people, who are free in the West Indies, are more miserable than the slaves;—and well they may; for while they can get their work and drudgery done for nothing, it is not likely that they will employ those whom they must pay for their labour. But whatever necessity the enslavers of men may plead for their iniquitous practice of slavery, and the various advantages which they get by it, can only evidence their own injustice and dishonesty. A man that is truly honest, fears nothing so much as the very imputation of injustice; but those men who dare not face the consequence of [not] acting uprightly in every case are detestable cowards, unworthy the name of men; for it is manifest that such men are more afraid of temporal inconveniencies than they are of God: *And I say unto you, my friends, be not afraid of them that kill the body, and after that have no more they can do; but I will forewarn you whom you shall*

fear: Fear him, who, after he hath killed, hath power to cast into hell.
Luke xii. 4, 5.

But why should total abolition, and an universal emancipation of slaves, and the enfranchisement of all the Black People employed in the culture of the Colonies, taking place as it ought to do, and without any hesitation, or delay for a moment, even though it might have some seeming appearance of loss either to government or to individuals, be feared at all? Their labour, as freemen, would be as useful in the sugar colonies as any other class of men that could be found; and should it even take place in such a manner that some individuals, at first, would suffer loss as a just reward for their wickedness in slave-dealing, what is that to the happiness and good of doing justice to others; and, I must say, to the great danger, otherwise, that must eventually hang over the whole community? It is certain, that the produce of the labour of slaves, together with all the advantages of the West-India traffic, bring in an immense revenue to government; but let that amount be what it will, there might be as much or more expected from the labour of an equal increase of free people, and without the implication of any guilt attending it, and which, otherwise, must be a greater burden to bear, and more ruinous consequences to be feared from it, than if the whole national debt was to sink at once, and to rest upon the heads of all that might suffer by it. Whereas, if a generous encouragement were to be given to a free people, peaceable among themselves, intelligent and industrious, who by art and labour would improve the most barren situations, and make the most of that which is fruitful; the free and voluntary labour of many, would soon yield to any government, many greater advantages than any thing that slavery can produce. And this should be expected, wherever a Christian government is extended, and the true religion is embraced, that the blessings of liberty should be extended likewise, and that it should diffuse its influences first to fertilize the mind, and then the effects of its benignity would extend, and arise with exuberant blessings and advantages from all its operations. Was this to be the case, every thing would increase and prosper at home and abroad, and ten thousand times greater and greater advantages would arise to the state, and more permanent and solid benefit to individuals from the service of freemen, than ever they can reap, or in any possible way enjoy, by the labour of slaves.

Source: Quobna Ottobah Cugoano, *Thoughts and Sentiments on the Evil of Slavery and Other Writings*, ed. V. Carretta, Harmondsworth, Penguin, 1999 [1787], pp. 85–92.

Extract 4

[. . .] I would hereby presume to offer the following considerations, as some outlines of a general reformation which ought to be established and carried on. And first, I would propose, that there ought to be days of mourning and fasting appointed, to make enquiry into that great and pre-eminent evil for many years past carried on against the Heathen nations, and the horrible iniquity of making merchandize of us, and cruelly enslaving the poor Africans; and that you might seek grace and repentance, and find mercy and forgiveness before God Omnipotent; and that he may give you wisdom and understanding to devise what ought to be done.

Secondly, I would propose that a total abolition of slavery should be made and proclaimed; and that an universal emancipation of slaves should begin from the date thereof, and be carried on in the following manner: That a proclamation should be caused to be made, setting forth the Antichristian unlawfulness of the slavery and commerce of the human species; and that it should be sent to all the courts and nations in Europe, to require their advice and assistance, and as they may find it unlawful to carry it on, let them whosoever will join to prohibit it. And if such a proclamation be found advisable to the British legislature, let them publish it, and cause it to be published, throughout all the British empire, to hinder and prohibit all men under their government to traffic either in buying or selling men; and, to prevent it, a penalty might be made against it of one thousand pounds, for any man either to buy or sell another man. And that it should require all slave-holders, upon the immediate information thereof, to mitigate the labour of their slaves to that of a lawful servitude, without tortures or oppression; and that they should not hinder, but cause and procure some suitable means of instruction for them in the knowledge of the Christian religion. And agreeable to the late *royal Proclamation, for the Encouragement of Piety and Virtue, and for the preventing and punishing of Vice, Profaneness and Immorality*; that by no means, under any pretence whatsoever, either for themselves or their masters, the slaves under their subjection should not be suffered to work on the Sabbath days, unless it be such works as necessity and mercy may require. But that those days, as well as some other hours selected for the purpose, should be appropriated for the time of their instruction; and that if any of their owners should not provide such suitable instructors for them, that those slaves should be taken away from them and given to others who would maintain and instruct them for their labour. And that it should be made known to the slaves, that those who had been above seven years in the islands or elsewhere, if they had obtained any competent degree of knowledge of the Christian religion, and the laws of civilization, and had behaved themselves honestly and decently, that they should immediately become free; and that their owners should give them reasonable wages and maintenance for their labour, and not cause them to go away unless they could find some suitable employment elsewhere. And accordingly, from the date of their arrival to seven years, as they arrive at some suitable progress in knowledge, and behaved themselves honestly, that they should be getting free in the course of that time, and at the end of seven years to let every honest man and woman become free; for in the course of that time, they would have sufficiently paid their owners by their labour, both for their first purpose, and for the expences attending their education. By being thus instructed in the course of seven years, they would become tractable and obedient, useful labourers, dutiful servants and good subjects; and Christian men might have the honor and happiness to see many of them vieing with themselves to praise the God of their salvation. And it might be another necessary duty for Christians, in the course of that time, to make enquiry concerning some of their friends and relations in Africa; and if they found any intelligent persons amongst them, to give them as good education as they could, and find out a way of recourse to their friends; that as soon as they had made any progress in useful learning and the knowledge of the Christian religion, they might be sent back to Africa, to be made useful there as soon, and as many of them as could be made fit for instructing others. The rest would become useful residentors in the colonies; where there might be employment enough given to all free people, with suitable wages according to their usefulness, in the improvement of land; and the more encouragement that could be given to agriculture, and every other branch of useful industry, would thereby encrease the number of the inhabitants; without which any country, however blessed by nature, must continue poor.

And, thirdly, I would propose, that a fleet of some ships of war should be immediately sent to the coast of Africa, and particularly where the slave trade is carried on, with faithful men to direct that none should be brought from the coast of Africa without their own consent and the approbation of their friends, and to intercept all merchant ships that were bringing them away, until such a scrutiny was made, whatever nation they belonged to. And, I would suppose, if Great-Britain was to do any thing of this kind, that it would meet with the general approbation and assistance of other Christian nations; but whether it did or not, it could be very lawfully done at all the British forts and settlements on the coast of Africa; and particular remonstrances could be given to all the rest, to warn them of the consequences of such an evil and enormous wicked traffic as is now carried on. The Dutch have some crocodile set-tlers at the Cape, that should be called to a particular account for their murders and inhuman barbarities. But all the present governors of the British forts and factories should be dismissed, and faithful and good men appointed in their room; and those forts and factories, which at present are a den of thieves, might be turned into shepherd's tents, and have good shepherds sent to call the flocks to feed beside them. Then would doors of hospitality in abundance be opened in Africa to supply the weary travellers, and that immense abundance which they are enriched with, might be diffused afar; but the character of the inhabi-tants on the west coast of Africa, and the rich produce of their country, have been too long misrepresented by avaricious plunderers and mer-chants who deal in slaves; and if that country was not annually ravished and laid waste, there might be a very considerable and profitable trade carried on with the Africans. And, should the noble Britons, who have often supported their own liberties with their lives and fortunes, extend their philanthropy to abolish the slavery and oppression of the Africans, they might have settlements and many kingdoms united in a friendly alliance with themselves, which might be made greatly to their own advantage, as well as they might have the happiness of being useful to promoting the prosperity and felicity of others, who have been cruelly injured and wrongfully dealt with. Were the Africans to be dealt with in a friendly manner, and kind instruction to be administered unto them, as by degrees they became to love learning, there would be nothing in their power, but what they would wish to render their service in return for the means of improving their understanding; and the present British facto-ries, and other settlements, might be enlarged to a very great extent. And as Great-Britain has been remarkable for ages past, for encouraging arts and sciences, and may now be put in competition with any nation in the known world, if they would take compassion on the inhabitants of the coast of Guinea;[8] and to make use of such means as would be needful to enlighten their minds in the knowledge of Christianity, their virtue, in this respect, would have its own reward. And as the Africans became refined and established in light and knowledge, they would imitate their noble British friends, to improve their lands, and make use of that indus-try as the nature of their country might require, and to supply those that would trade with them, with such productions as the nature of their cli-

---

[8] Guinea was a part of West Africa that was plundered extensively for slaves. It had a promi-nence in the minds of the abolitionists as a result of Anthony Benezet's critical account *Some Historical Account of Guinea, Its Situation, Produce, and the General Disposition of Its Inhab-itants. With an Inquiry into the Rise and Progress of the Slave Trade, Its Nature, and Lamen-table Effects* (London, 1771).

mate would produce; and, in every respect, the fair Britons would have the preference with them to a very great extent; and, in another respect, they would become a kind of first ornament to Great-Britain for her tender and compassionate care of such a set of distressed poor ignorant people. And were the noble Britons, and their august Sovereign, to cause protection and encouragement to be given to those Africans, they might expect in a short time, if need required it, to receive from thence great supplies of men in a lawful way, either for industry or defence; and of other things in abundance, from so great a source, where every thing is luxurious and plenty, if not laid waste by barbarity and gross ignorance. Due encouragement being given to so great, so just, and such a noble undertaking, would soon bring more revenue in a righteous way to the British nation, than ten times its share in all the profits that slavery can produce; and such a laudable example would inspire every generous and enterprizing mind to imitate so great and worthy a nation, for establishing religion, justice, and equity to the Africans, and, in doing this, would be held in the highest esteem by all men, and be admired by all the world.

These three preceding considerations may suffice at present to shew, that some plan might be adopted in such a manner as effectually to relieve the grievances and oppression of the Africans, and to bring great honour and blessings to that nation, and to all men whosoever would endeavour to promote so great good to mankind; and it might render more conspicuous advantages to the noble Britons, as the first doers of it, and greater honour than the finding of America was at first to those that made the discovery: Though several difficulties may seem to arise at first, and the good to be sought after may appear to be remote and unknown, as it was to explore the unknown regions of the Western Ocean; should it be sought after, like the intrepid Columbus, if they do not find kingdoms of wealth by the way, they may be certain of finding treasures of happiness and of peace in the end. But should there be any yet alive deserving the infamy and character of all the harsh things which I have ascribed to the insidious carriers on of the slavery and commerce of the human species, they will certainly object to any thing of this kind being proposed, or ever thought of, as doing so great a good to the base Black Negroes whom they make their prey. To such I must say again, that it would be but a just commutation for what cannot be fully restored, in order to make restoration, as far as could be, for the injuries already done to them. And some may say, that if they have wages to pay to the labourers for manufacturing the West-India productions, that they would not be able to sell them at such a price as would suit the European market, unless all the different nations agreed to raise the price of their commodities in proportion. Whatever bad neighbours men may have to deal with, let the upright shew themselves to be honest men, and that difficulty, which some may fear, would be but small, as there can be no reason for men to do wrong because others do so; but as to what is consumed in Great-Britain, they could raise the price in proportion, and it would be better to sip the West-India sweetness by paying a little more money for it (if it should be found needful) than to drink the blood of iniquity at a cheaper rate. I know several ladies in England who refuse to drink sugar in their tea, because of the cruel injuries done to the Black People employed in the culture of it at the West-Indies. But should it cost the West-Indians more money to have their manufactories carried on by the labour of freemen than with slaves, it would be attended with greater blessings and advantages to them in the end. What the wages should be for the labour of freemen, is a question not so easily determined; yet I should think, that it always should be something more than merely victuals and cloaths; and if a man works by the day, he should have the three hundredth part of what might be estimated as sufficient to keep him in necessary cloaths and provisions for a year, and, added to that, such wages of reward as their usefulness might require. Something of this kind should be observed in free countries, and then the price of provisions would be kept at such a rate as the industrious poor could live, without being oppressed and screwed down to work for nothing, but only barely to live. And were every civilized nation, where they boast of liberty, so ordered by its government, that some general and useful employment were provided for every industrious man and woman, in such a manner that none should stand still and be idle, and have to say that they could not get employment, so long as there are barren lands at home and abroad sufficient to employ thousands and millions of people more than there are. This, in a great measure, would prevent thieves and robbers, and the labour of many would soon enrich a nation. But those employed by the general community should only have their maintenance either given or estimated in money, and half the wages of others, which would make them seek out for something else whenever they could, and half a loaf would be better than no bread. The men that were employed in this manner, would form an useful militia, and the women would be kept from a state of misery and want, and from following a life of dissolute wickedness. Liberty and freedom, where people may starve for want, can do them but little good. We want many rules of civilization, in Africa; but, in many respects, we may boast of some more essential liberties than any of the civilized nations in Europe enjoy; for the poorest amongst us are never in distress for want, unless some general and universal calamity happen to us. But if any nation or society of men were to observe the laws of God, and to keep his commandments, and walk in the way of

161

righteousness, they would not need to fear the heat in sultry hot climates, nor the freezing inclemency of the cold, and the storms and hurricanes would not hurt them at all; they might soon see blessings and plenty in abundance showered down upon their mountains and vallies; and if his beneficence was sought after, who martials out the drops of the dew, and bids the winds to blow, and to carry the clouds on their wings to drop down their moisture and fatness on what spot soever he pleaseth, and who causeth the genial rays of the sun to warm and cherish the productions of the earth in every place according to that temperature which he sees meet; then might the temperate climes of Great-Britain be seen to vie with the rich land of Canaan of old, which is now, because of the wickedness of its inhabitants, in comparison of what it was, as only a barren desert.

Particular thanks is due to every one of that humane society of worthy and respectful gentlemen, whose liberality hath supported many of the Black poor about London. *Those that honor their Maker have mercy on the poor; and many blessings are upon the head of the just; may the fear of the Lord prolong their days, and cause their memory to be blessed, and may their number be encreased to fill their expectation with gladness*; for they have not only commiserated the poor in general, *but even those which are accounted as beasts, and imputed as vile in the sight of others.* The part that the British government has taken, to co-operate with them, has certainly a flattering and laudable appearance of doing some good; and the fitting out ships to supply a company of Black People with clothes and provisions, and to carry them to settle at Sierra Leona, in the West coast of Africa, as a free colony to Great-Britain, in a peaceable alliance with the inhabitants, has every appearance of honour, and the approbation of friends. According to the plan, humanity hath made its appearance in a more honorable way of colonization, than any Christian nation have ever done before, and may be productive of much good, if they continue to encourage and support them. But after all, there is some doubt whether their own flattering expectation in the manner as set forth to them, and the hope of their friends may not be defeated and rendered abortive; and there is some reason to fear, that they never will be settled as intended, in any permanent and peaceable way at Sierra Leona.[9]

---

[9] There was a drive in the 1780s to re-settle displaced free Africans in Britain and the Americas to Sierra Leone, West Africa (what Cugoano refers to as Sierra Leona) in a self-governing, free settlement. Cugoano was critical of the project, as he feared that while the slave trade continued, such relocated Africans would remain vulnerable to recapture. The first settlers arrived in Sierra Leone on 10 May 1787, and after suffering great hardship, were dispersed in December 1789 when a local chieftain destroyed the settlement. Subsequent groups of black settlers managed to survive, and formed the basis of a community that has endured to the present.

This prospect of settling a free colony to Great-Britain in a peaceable alliance with the inhabitants of Africa at Sierra Leona, has neither altogether met with the credulous approbation of the Africans here, nor yet been sought after with any prudent and right plan by the promoters of it. Had a treaty of agreement been first made with the inhabitants of Africa, and the terms and nature of such a settlement fixed upon, and its situation and boundary pointed out; then might the Africans, and others here, have embarked with a good prospect of enjoying happiness and prosperity themselves, and have gone with a hope of being able to render their services, in return, of some advantage to their friends and benefactors of Great-Britain. But as this was not done, and as they were to be hurried away at all events, come of them after what would; and yet, after all, to be delayed in the ships before they were set out from the coast, until many of them have perished with cold, and other disorders, and several of the most intelligent among them are dead, and others that, in all probability, would have been most useful for them were hindered from going, by means of some disagreeable jealousy of those who were appointed as governors, the great prospect of doing good seems all to be blown away. And so it appeared to some of those who are now gone, and at last, hap hazard, were obliged to go; who endeavoured in vain to get away by plunging into the water, that they might, if possible wade ashore, as dreading the prospect of their wretched fate, and as beholding their perilous situation, having every prospect of difficulty and surrounding danger.

What with the death of some of the original promoters and proposers of this charitable undertaking, and the death and deprivation of others that were to share the benefit of it, and by the adverse motives of those employed to be the conductors thereof, we think it will be more than what can be well expected, if we ever hear of any good in proportion to so great, well-designed, laudable and expensive charity. Many more of the Black People still in this country would have, with great gladness, embraced the opportunity, longing to reach their native land; but as the old saying is, A burnt child dreads the fire, some of these unfortunate sons and daughters of Africa have been severally unlawfully dragged away from their native abodes, under various pretences, by the insidious treachery of others, and have been brought into the hands of barbarous robbers and pirates, and, like sheep to the market, have been sold into captivity and slavery, and thereby have been deprived of their natural liberty and property, and every connection that they held dear and valuable, and subjected to the cruel service of the hard-hearted brutes called planters. But some of them, by various services either to the public or to individuals, as more particularly in the course of last war, have gotten their liberty again in this free country. They are thankful for the respite, but afraid of being ensnared again; for the European seafaring people in general, who trade to foreign parts, have such a prejudice against Black People, that they use them more like asses than men, so that a Black Man is scarcely ever safe among them. Much assiduity was made use of to perswade the Black People in general to embrace the opportunity of going with this company of transports; but the wiser sort declined from all thoughts of it, unless they could hear of some better plan taking place for their security and safety. For as it seemed prudent and obvious to many of them taking heed to that sacred enquiry, *Doth a fountain send forth at the same place sweet water and bitter?* They were afraid that their doom would be to drink of the bitter water. For can it be readily conceived that government would establish a free colony for them nearly on the spot, while it supports its forts and garrisons, to ensnare, merchandize, and to carry others into captivity and slavery.

Above fifty years ago, P. Gordon, in his Geography, though he was no advocate against slavery, complains of the barbarities committed against the Heathen nations, and the base usage of the negro slaves subjected to bondage as brutes, and deprived of religion as men. His remark on the religion of the American islands, says: "As for the negroe slaves, their lot has hitherto been, and still is, to serve such Christian masters, who sufficiently declare what zeal they have for their conversion, by unkindly using a serious divine some time ago, for only proposing to endeavour the same." This was above half a century ago, and their unchristian barbarity is still continued. Even in the little time that I was in Grenada, I saw a slave receive twenty-four lashes of a whip for being seen at a church on a Sunday, instead of going to work in the fields; and those whom they put the greatest confidence in, are often served in the same manner. The noble proposals offered for instructing the heathen nations and people in his Geography, has been attended to with great supineness and indifference. The author wishes, that "sincere endeavours might be made to extend the limits of our Saviour's kingdom, with those of our own dominions; and to spread the true religion as far as the British sails have done for traffic." And he adds, "Let our planters duly consider, that to extirpate natives, is rather a supplanting than planting a new colony; and that it is far more honourable to overcome paganism in one, than to destroy a thousand pagans. Each convert is a conquest."

To put an end to the wickedness of slavery and merchandizing of men, and to prevent murder, extirpation and dissolution, is what every righteous nation ought to seek after; and to endeavour to diffuse knowledge and instruction to all the heathen nations wherever they can, is the grand duty of all Christian men. But while the horrible traffic of slavery is admitted and practiced, there can be but little hope of any good proposals meeting with success anywhere; for the abandoned carriers of it on have spread the poison of their iniquity wherever they come, at home and abroad. Were the iniquitous laws in support of it, and the whole of that oppression and injustice abolished, and the righteous laws of Christianity, equity, justice and humanity established in the room thereof, multitudes of nations would flock to the standard of truth, and instead of revolting away, they would count it their greatest happiness to be under the protection and jurisdiction of a righteous government. And in that respect, *in the multitude of the people is the King's honour; but in the want of people, is the destruction of the Prince.*

We would wish to have the grandeur and fame of the British empire to extend far and wide; and the glory and honor of God to be promoted by it, and the interest of Christianity set forth among all the nations wherever its influence and power can extend; but not to be supported by the insidious pirates, depredators, murderers and slave-holders. And as it might diffuse knowledge and instruction to others, that it might receive a tribute of reward from all its territories, forts and garrisons, without being oppressive to any. But contrary to this the wickedness of many of the White People who keep slaves, and contrary to all the laws and duties of Christianity which the Scriptures teach, they have in general endeavoured to keep the Black People in total ignorance as much as they can, which must be a great dishonor to any Christian government, and injurious to the safety and happiness of rulers.

But in order to diffuse any knowledge of Christianity to the unlearned Heathens, those who undertake to do any thing therein ought to be wise and honest men. Their own learning, though the more the better, is not so much required as that they should be men of the same mind and principles of the apostle Paul; men that would hate covetousness, and who would hazard their lives for the cause and gospel of our Lord and Saviour Jesus Christ. "I think it needless to express how commendable such a design would be in itself, and how desirable the promotion thereof should be to all who stile themselves Christians, of what party or profession soever they are." Rational methods might be taken to have the Scriptures translated into many foreign languages; "and a competent number of young students of theology might be educated at home in these foreign languages, to afford a constant supply of able men, who might yearly go abroad, and be sufficiently qualified at their first arrival to undertake the great work for which they were sent." But as a hindrance to this, the many Anti-christian errors which are gone abroad into the world, and all the popish superstition and nonsense, and the various assimilations unto it, with the false philosophy which abounds among Christians, seems to threaten with an universal deluge; but God hath promised to fill the world with a knowledge of himself, and he hath set up his bow, in the rational heavens, as well as in the clouds, as a token that he will stop the proud ways of error and delusion, that hitherto they may come, and no farther. The holy arch of truth is to be seen in the azure paths of the pious and wise, and conspicuously painted in crimson over the martyrs tombs. These, with the golden altars of truth, built up by the reformed churches, and many pious, good and righteous men, are bulwarks that will ever stand against all the sorts of error. Teaching would be exceeding necessary to the pagan nations and ignorant people in every place and situation; but they do not need any unscriptural forms and ceremonies to be taught unto them; they can devise superstitions enough among themselves, and church government too, if ever they need any.

And hence we would agree in this one thing with that erroneous philosopher,[10] who has lately wrote *An Apology for Negro Slavery*, "But if the slave is only to be made acquainted with the form, without the substance; if he is only to be decked out with the external trappings of religion; if he is only to be taught the uncheering principles of gloomy superstition; or, if he is only to be inspired with the intemperate frenzy of enthusiastic fanaticism, it were better that he remained in that dark state, where he could not see good from ill." But these words *intemperate, frenzy, enthusiastic*, and *fanaticism* may be variously applied, and often wrongfully; but, perhaps never better, or more fitly, than to be ascribed as the genuine character of this author's brutish philosophy; and he may subscribe it, and the meaning of these words, with as much affinity to himself, as he bears a relation to a *Hume*, or to his friend *Tobin*. The poor negroes in the West-Indies, have suffered enough by such religion as the philosophers of the North produce; Protestants, as they are called, are the most barbarous slave-holders, and there are none can equal the Scotch floggers and negroe-drivers, and the barbarous Dutch cruelties. Perhaps as the church of Rome begins to sink in its power, its followers may encrease in virtue and humanity; so that many, who are the professed adherents thereof, would even blush and abhor the very mention of the cruelty and bloody deeds that their ancestors have committed; and we find slavery itself more tolerable among them, than it is in the Protestant countries.

But I shall add another observation, which I am sorry to find among Christians, and I think it is a great deficiency among the clergy in general, when covetous and profligate men are admitted among them, who

---

[10] Cugoano is referring to Gordon Turnbull, author of the pro-slavery publications, *An Apology for Negro Slavery* (London, 1784) and *Letters to a Young Planter; or, Observations on the Management of Sugar-plantations* (London, 1785).

either do not know, or dare not speak the truth, but neglect their duty much, or do it with such supineness, that it becomes good for nothing. Sometimes an old woman selling matches, will preach a better, and a more orthodox sermon, than some of the clergy, who are only decked out (as Mr. Turnbul [sic] calls it) with the external trappings of religion. Much of the great wickedness of others lieth at their door, and these words of the Prophet are applicable to them: *And first, saith the Lord, I will recompence their iniquity, and their sin double; because they have defiled my land, they have filled mine inheritance with the carcases of their detestable and abominable things.* Such are the errors of men. Church, signifies an assembly of people; but a building of wood, brick or stone, where the people meet together, is generally called so; and should the people be frightened away by the many abominable dead carcases which they meet with, they should follow the multitudes to the fields, to the vallies, to the mountains, to the islands, to the rivers, and to the ships, and compel them to come in, that the house of the Lord may be filled. But when we find some of the covetous connivers with slave-holders, in the West-Indies, so ignorant as to dispute whether a Pagan can be baptized without giving him a Christian name, we cannot expect much from them, or think that they will follow after much good. No name, whether Christian or Pagan, has any thing to do with baptism; if the requisite qualities of knowledge and faith be found in a man, he may be baptized let his name be what it will. And Christianity does not require that we should be deprived of our own personal name, or the name of our ancestors; but it may very fitly add another name unto us, Christian, or one anointed. And it may as well be answered so to that question in the English liturgy, *What is your name?*—A Christian.

"*A Christian is the highest stile of man!*
And is there, who the blessed cross wipes off
As a foul blot, from his dishonor'd brow?
If angels tremble, 'tis at such a sight:
The wretch they quit disponding of their charge,
More struck with grief or wonder who can tell?"

And let me now hope that you will pardon me in all that I have been thus telling you, O ye inhabitants of Great-Britain! to whom I owe the greatest respect; to your king! to yourselves! and to your government! And tho' many things which I have written may seem harsh, it cannot be otherwise evaded when such horrible iniquity is transacted: and tho' to some what I have said may appear as the rattling leaves of autumn, that may soon be blown away and whirled in a vortex where few can hear and know: I must yet say, although it is not for me to determine the manner, that the voice of our complaint implies a vengeance, because of the great iniquity that you have done, and because of the cruel injustice done unto us Africans; and it ought to sound in your ears as the rolling waves around your circum-ambient shores; and if it is not hearkened unto, it may yet arise with a louder voice, as the rolling thunder, and it may encrease in the force of its volubility, not only to shake the leaves of the most stout in heart, but to rend the mountains before them, and to cleave in pieces the rocks under them, and to go on with fury to smite the stoutest oaks in the forest; and even to make that which is strong, and wherein you think that your strength lieth, to become as stubble, and as the fibres of rotten wood, that will do you no good, and your trust in it will become a snare of infatuation to you!

FINIS.

Source: Quobna Ottobah Cugoano, *Thoughts and Sentiments on the Evil of Slavery and Other Writings*, ed. V. Carretta, Harmondsworth, Penguin, 1999 [1787], pp. 98–111.

Robert Wedderburn, *Truth Self-Supported*, 1802

Extract 5

CANDID READER,

Could the AUTHOR present you a Diamond in the rough, you certainly would not refuse it; do not then reject the following essential truths, on account of his unpolished ability to send them forth into the world, with their deserved splendor.

TRUTH SELF-SUPPORTED;

The writer is a West-Indian, son of JAMES WEDDERBURN, Esq. of INVERESK, near *Edinburgh*, and came over to England in the year 1778. Providence casting his lot in a family professing religion, he had a desire to become a Christian; but, hearing so many jarring sentiments and opinions concerning the truth, staggered his mind, and he knew not which to embrace—yet, persuaded it was essential to his happiness, both here and hereafter, to become a Christian, being confident it was the religion of the Bible, which he had no doubt was the revealed Will of God, he had a strong propensity to become one.

A short time after, Providence placed him in another situation of life, amongst a set of abandoned reprobates; he there became a profligate, and so continued for the space of seven years; Conscience frequently smiteing him, and telling him, that the way he pursued was the road to everlasting ruin; to lull and calm these reflections, he frequently promised to reform; but, Sin being such a constant companion, and so sweet to his taste, his efforts and strivings were all in vain.

Passing the Seven-Dials one Lord's day, the author stopped to hear a preacher of Mr. Westley's connection. The words that he spoke, struck his mind with strong conviction of the awful state he was in, both by nature and practice; he noticed, that the minister asserted with confidence, that he would pledge his own soul, that every man, conscious of the enormity of sin, and willing to turn from the evil of his ways, and accept of the mercy offered in the Gospel, the Lord would abundantly pardon; and he was enabled, by the Holy Spirit, to accept with joy, the offered Grace.

In a short time, the author was further enabled to say, 'O!God, my Father and Friend!' and that God's love to him was unmerited—unchangeable—from everlasting to everlasting. At that time, he was perfectly ignorant of the true doctrines contained in the scriptures, and so become a prey to erroneous preachers, who corrupted his judgment before he was able to discern the difference between truth and error; indeed, such was the influence of the errors they taught, that they darkened his understanding.

In this state he was denied the privilege of examining their doctrines; telling him, that if he rejected their dogmas, he was in danger of eternal damnation; but, as they differed so very materially in their tenets, he was confident they could not all be in the right: he then thought it his privilege and duty to admit of no doctrine, however plausible, but what he perceived in his own judgment was clearly and evidently contained in the holy scriptures; not in the least alarmed by the threatenings of the preachers, confident that God had sealed him unto the day of redemption, not only sealed, but removed him by *HIS* power from a legal state of mind, into a state of Gospel Liberty, that is to say, a deliverance from the power or authority of the law, considering himself not to be under the power of the law, but under Grace; therefore, being thus secure, he was enabled with boldness to examine the various doctrines, that he heard advanced at different times.

Persuaded that he is arrived to a state of manhood in religion, and being made wiser than his teachers, he shall now undertake to instruct them, and as they are ready prepared to condemn all doctrines contrary to their own, he does not expect *his* will be very cordially received, yet, he thinks it a duty incumbent upon him to detect error—support and maintain truth, and leave the event to Providence; for he must not fear the face of any man, but speak the word of God with boldness, for, every word of God is pure—he is a shield to those that trust in him, the author will not endeavor to add to his word, nor yet diminish, least HE should reprove him, and then he should be found a liar.

The doctrines contained in the Scriptures, are,

1. Before a man can become a Christian, he must be thoroughly sensible, and believe himself a fallen creature, and partaker of a corrupt nature, in consequence of the transgression of Adam.

2. There is no possibility of escaping future punishment and divine wrath, but by a belief in Jesus Christ, for there is salvation in no other.

By believing in Jesus Christ, the author comprehends ONE ETERNAL GOD AND UNIVERSAL FATHER, in no other sense than as a Creator and Preserver. Jesus Christ the first child of his power.

> *Source*: Robert Wedderburn, *The Horrors of Slavery and Other Writings by Robert Wedderburn*, ed. I. McCalman, Edinburgh, Edinburgh University Press, 1991 [1824], pp. 66–7.

Robert Wedderburn, from issues of *The Axe Laid to the Root*, 1817

Extract 6

The Axe Laid to the Root or A Fatal Blow to Oppressors, Being an Address to the Planters and Negroes of the Island of Jamaica. No. 1 [1817]

TO THE EDITOR

Be it known to the world, that, I Robert Wedderburn, son of James Wedderburn, esq. of Inveresk, near Musselborough, by Rosannah his slave, whom he sold to James Charles Shalto Douglas, esq. in the parish of St. Mary, in the island of Jamaica, while pregnant with the said Wedderburn, who was not held as a slave, (a provision made in the agreement, that the child when born should be free.) This Wedderburn, doth charge all potentates, governors, and governments of every description with felony, who does wickedly violate the sacred rights of man—by force of arms, or otherwise, seizing the persons of men and dragging them from their native country, and selling their stolen persons and generations.— Wedderburn demands, in the name of God, in the name of natural justice, and in the name of humanity, that all slaves be set free; for innocent individuals are entitled to the protection of civil society; and that all stealers, receivers, and oppressors in this base practice be forgiven, as the crime commenced in the days of ignorance, and is now exposed in the enlightened age of reason.

Oh, ye oppressed, use no violence to your oppressors, convince the world you are rational beings, follow not the example of St. Domingo, let not your jubilee, which will take place, be stained with the blood of your oppressors, leave revengeful practices for European kings and ministers.

My advice to you, is, to appoint a day wherein you will all pretend to sleep one hour beyond the appointed time of your rising to labour; let the appointed day be twelve months before it takes place; let it be talked of in your market place, and on the roads. The universality of your sleeping and non-resistance, will strike terror to your oppressors. Go to your labour peaceably after the hour is expired; and repeat it once a year, till you obtain your liberty. Union among you, will strike tremendous terror to the receivers of stolen persons. But do not petition, for it is degrading to human nature to petition your oppressors. Above all, mind and keep possession of the land you now possess as slaves; for without that, freedom is not worth possessing; for if you once give up the possession of your lands, your oppressors will have power to starve you to death, through making laws for their own accommodation; which will force you to commit crimes in order to obtain subsistance; as the landholders in Europe are serving those that are disposessed of lands; for it is a fact, that thousands of families are now in a starving state; the prisons are full: humanity impells the executive power to withdraw the sentence of death on criminals, whilst the landholders, in fact, are surrounded with every necessary of life. Take warnings by the sufferings of the European poor, and never give up your lands you now possess, for it is your right by God and nature, for the 'earth was given to the children of men.'

Oh, ye christians, you are convinced of the crime of stealing human beings; and some have put a stop to it. By law, give up the stolen families in possession, and perfect your repentance. I call on a mighty people, and their sovereign, to burst the chains of oppression, and let the oppressed go free, says 'the Lord;' and so says Wedderburn the deluded Spencean. Oh, ye Africans and relatives now in bondage to the Christians, because you are innocent and poor; receive this the only tribute the offspring of an African can give, for which, I may ere long be lodged in a prison, without even a trial; for it is a crime now in England to speak against oppression.

Dear countrymen and relatives, it is natural to expect you will enquire what is meant be a deluded Spencean; I must inform you it is a title given by ignorant or self-interested men, to the followers of one Thomas Spence,[11] who knew that the earth was given to the children of men, making no difference for colour or character, just or unjust; and that any person calling a piece of land his own private property, was a criminal; and though they may sell it, or will it to their children, it is only transferring of that which was first obtained by force or fraud, this old truth, newly discovered, has completely terrified the landholders in England, and confounded the Attorney General and the Crown Lawyers; and what is more alarming, it is not in the power of the legislature, with all their objections to the doctrines to make a law to prevent the publishing of self evident truths, while a shadow of the British Constitution remains. The landholders, whose interest it is to oppose, is driven to the necessity of falsefying and misrepresenting the motives of the disciples of Spence; but truth once known, will dispel falsehood, as the rising sun excludes darkness.

Your humble servant being a Spencean Philanthropist, is proud to wear the name of a madman; if the landholders please, they may call me a traitor, or one who is possessed with the spirit of Beelzebub. What can the landholders, priests or lawyers say, or do more than they did against Christ; yet his doctrine is on record, which says 'woe unto them that add house to 'house, or field to field.' When you are exorted to hold the land, and never give it up to your oppressors, you are not told to hold it as private property, but as tenants at will to the sovereignty of the people

Beware of the clergy of every description, they are bound by law and interest, in all countries, to preach agreable to the will of the governor under whom they live: as proof of which, they must have a licence, if not of the established church. Lissen to them as far as your reason dictates of a future state, but never suffer them to interfere in your worldly affairs; for they are cunning, and therefore are more capable of vice than you are; for instance, one was hung at Kingston, for coining; one in London, for forgery; one for a rape; one for murder; one was detected throwing the sleave of his surplice over the plate, while he robbed it, even at the time he was administering the Lord's supper, in the Borough; and Bishop Burn, of Kent, who had 800 l. per annum, confessed on his death

---

[11] Thomas Spence (1750–1814) grew up on the Newcastle waterfront, and was, from an early age, committed to radical political movements that opposed the enclosure of common lands, and promoted in its stead common ownership. His publications included *The Rights of Man* (1793), which asserts rights of political and economic equality, *The Marine Republic* (1794), in which a dying man gives his ship to his sons as common property, and *The Giant Killer* (1814), which praises the shared system of land ownership of native Americans. Spence was imprisoned for his political activism on a number of occasions, but he retained a significant following, and 'Spence's Plan' for common land ownership and the redistribution of wealth was widely known, and attracted popular support throughout the period.

bed, he had practised the same offence for 40 years, and all these were college bred men, and of course gentlemen. You know also they buy and sell your persons as well as others, and thereby encouraging that base practice. This is not doing as they would be done by.

Adieu, for the present, my afflicted countrymen and relatives yet in bondage, though the prince, lords, and commons, are convinced it is a crime deserving of death, to steal and hold a man in bondage.

I am a West-Indian, a lover of liberty, and would dishonour human nature if I did not shew myself a friend to the liberty of others.

ROBERT WEDDERBURN.

TO THE EDITOR

As the present state of affairs will not afford matters of importance to fill up your paper, I am encouraged to hope for your indulgance in granting me an opportunity to contend with all our enemies, who may be disposed to enter into a paper war respecting the Spencean doctrine.

It appears to me very necessary, for it is only by rational contention, that truth is to be attained, It is not right to take for granted that the Spenceans are fools, and mad traitors:—it is their opinion they are wise, loyal, and in their senses, and they alone, respecting landed property. While they hold such opinions, they will naturally be disposed to believe it is their duty before God and man, to preach Spenceanism at all times, and in all countries. Persecutions, whether legal or permiscous, has failed to put a stop to opinions in all ages, whether such be true or false; for it holds the human mind in chains which cannot be broken but by argument. It is my intention to conduct myself in a becoming manner to all opposers.

It is necessary that the doctrine should be stated fairly, that the opposers may make their attact as seems most to their own advantage. The Spenceans presume that the earth cannot be justly the private property of individuals, because it was never manufactured by man; therefore whoever first sold it, sold that which was not his own, and of course there cannot be a title deed produced consistent with natural and universal justice. Secondly, that it is inconsistent with justice, that a few should have the power to till or not to till the earth, thereby holding the existence of the whole population in their hands. They can cause a famine, or create abundance; they, the landholders, can say to a great majority of any nation:—I may grow, till, or destroy at my will, as occasion serves my interest; is not Ireland, sufficient to support its inhabitants? Is England able to support its population? The Spenceans say it will, if the land was not held as private property. Furthermore, the Spenceans say, that land monopoly is the cause of unequal laws. The majority are thereby deprived of the power of having a pure government. All reformation attempted by the most virtuous, whether Major Cartwright,[12] or Sir Francis Burdett,[13] or any other virtuous character,—is only an attempt to heal, without extracting the core.

To have a parliament, and every man to vote, is just and right; a nation without it, may be charged with ignorance and cowardice: but without an equal share in the soil, no government can be pure, let its name or form be what it may. The Spenceans recommend a division of rents, in preference to a division of lands:—as Moses's failed, Spence's plan is an improvement upon that system which came from heaven. It admits no mortgages; it needs no jubilee.

It is natural to expect the doctrine will spread, and the army of the rising generation may be composed of Spenceans.

Therefore the landholders, who are our despots, will do well to use arguments in time, and convince the Spenceans; though it has been said that the bayonet is necessary to enforce the law; but that will not be used in a bad cause, when men are better taught. The Spenceans say, the clergy must be wilfully blind, or under a servile fear of man, that will not preach Spenceanism; for it is not contrary to the old and new testament.

Spenceanism admits no with-holding an equal share of the rents from any one, not even from a criminal, much less from persons of different political or religious opinions; birth or death is the alpha and omega right or exclusion.

The opponants, however they may be armed with the powerful means of education, whether laiety or clergy, will find that a simple Spencean, who cannot write his name, will receive his opponant as David did the giant Goliah; and with simple means destroy his gigantic impositions.

Spenceanism cannot be confined in a dungeon, if the Evans[14] are. Hector Campbel, in particular is requested to renew the attact. No private correspondence will be held, while the British government is under the necessity of allowing fortunes to false swearing informers.

[12] Major John Cartwright (1740–1824) was a respected radical reformer, who consistently advocated universal suffrage, and is best remembered as one of the founding figures in the Chartist movement.

[13] Sir Francis Burdett (1770–1844) was an independent MP, who campaigned in the 1790s against government corruption. A moderate himself, he nonetheless continued in the first decades of the nineteenth century to take up a number of radical opposition causes.

[14] The Evans referred to here by Wedderburn is probably his fellow-Spencean, the Welshman Thomas Evans (1766–1833), who was also imprisoned on several occasions for political subversion, and was the author of over twenty pamphlets, including *Christian Policy, the Salvation of the Empire* (1816). Evans shared Wedderburn's view that the early Christians practised a form of communism that should be revived as an antidote to slavery and the expropriation of common lands.

To all who love to hear of the increase of liberty, are these few lines directed

The slaves of Jamaica, are ready now to demand a day of their masters, in addition to the day and a half that was allowed before, being taught by the methodists that it is a crime to labour on the sabbath day; and it is the opinion of many, that they will have it.

This information is by my brother's wife, who is held as a slave by a clergyman of the church of England; whether she obtained this information from the conversation which passed at her master's table, or whether it is her own observation, on what she had heard among her fellow slaves, I will not avow; but this information is confirmed by a letter from a book-keeper to his mother, who informed me, that it is the opinion of her son, that the island of Jamaica will be in the hands of the blacks within twenty years. Prepare for flight, ye planters, for the fate of St. Domingo awaits you. Get ready your blood hounds, the allies which you employed against the Maroons.[15] Recollect the fermentation will be universal. Their weapons are their bill-hooks; their store of provision is every were in abundance; you know they can live upon sugar canes, and a vast variety of herbs and fruits,—yea, even upon the buds of trees. You cannot cut off their supplies. They will be victorious in their flight, slaying all before them; they want no turnpike roads: they will not stand to engage organised troops, like the silly Irish rebels. Their method of fighting is to be found in the scriptures, which they are now learning to read. They will slay man, woman, and child, and not spare the virgin, whose interest is connected with slavery, whether black, white, or tawny. O ye planters, you know this has been done; the cause which produced former bloodshed still remains,—of necessity similar effects must take place. The holy alliance of Europe, cannot prevent it, they have enough to do at home, being compelled to keep a standing army in the time of peace, to enforce the civil law.

My heart glows with revenge, and cannot forgive. Repent ye christians, for flogging my aged grandmother before my face when she was accused of witchcraft by a silly European. O Boswell,[16] ought not your colour and countrymen to be visited with wrath, for flogging my mother before my face, at the time when she was far advanced in pregnancy. What was her crime? did not you give her leave to visit her aged mother; (she did not

---

[15] 'Maroon' or 'mulatto' was the term used to describe people of mixed race. Although they were free, the maroons occupied a precarious social and economic space between the black slaves and free whites, with their allegiances split between the two. Wedderburn would have been defined as a maroon.

[16] James Boswell (1740–95) was the Scottish biographer of Samuel Johnson (*The Life of Johnson* (1791)). Unlike Johnson, Boswell supported slavery, and this together with his Scottish origins connects him in Wedderburn's mind with his own father, James Wedderburn.

acquaint her mistress at her departure,) this was her fault. But it origi-nates in your crime in holding her as a slave—could not you wait till she returned, but travel 15 miles to punish her on that visit. You set a pattern to your slaves to treat your wife with contempt, by taking your negro wenches to your adultrous bed, in preference to your wedded wife. It being a general practice in the island, is no excuse for you,—who was a scholar and professed to be a christian—how can I forgive you? Oh! my father, what do you deserve at my hands? Your crimes will be visited upon your legitimate offspring: for the sins of a wicked father will be vis-ited upon his children, who continues in the practice of their father's crimes. Ought I not to encourage your slaves, O my brother, to demand their freedom even at the danger of your life, if it could not be obtained without. Do not tell me you hold them by legal right. No law can be just which deprives another of his liberty, except for criminal offences: such law-makers according to the rules of equity, are felons of the deepest dye; for they attempt to justify wickedness. The time is fast approaching, when such rulers must act righteously, or be drawn from their seats; for truth and justice must prevail—combined armies cannot stop their progress—religious superstition, the support of tyrants, gives way.

The priesthood who took the lead, are compelled to sculk in the rear, and take shelter under Bell's[17] system of education, to impress on the minds of youth their nonsensical creed; dreading the purity of the Lan-casterian mode.[18] But you my countrymen, can act without education; the equality of your present station in slavery, is your strength. You all feel the injury—you are all capable of making resistance. Your oppressors know—they dread you—they can foresee their downfal when you deter-mine to obtain your liberty, and possess your natural right—that is free-dom. Beware, and offend not your God, like the jews of old, in choosing

---

[17] Andrew Bell (1753–1832) devised a system of mass schooling that was widely adopted in Victorian Britain. Bell developed the system while in Madras, India from 1787 to 1796, where he responded to the lack of teachers and large numbers of pupils by establishing a system of monitors, with older pupils supervising the younger ones. Soon after he returned to Britain, Bell introduced and refined his methods, with the system of monitors supplemented by rote learn-ing and strictly enforced hierarchies of punishment and reward. Bell's system was adopted and promoted by the Anglican Church's National Society for Promoting the Education of the Poor in the Principles of the established Church in 1811.

[18] Joseph Lancaster (1778–1838) developed a method of schooling very similar to that of Bell in England in the 1790s. The 'Lancasterian mode' had substantially the same features as Bell's system – monitors, rote learning, strict and elaborate procedures of punishment – but was taken up by the British and Foreign School Society in 1798 and introduced in its expanding numbers of schools for the poor. Lancaster enjoyed the support of reformers like William Wilberforce, Robert Owen, Jeremy Bentham and James Mill, and for several decades, a debate raged as to whether Bell or Lancaster – and their respective sponsors – had first perfected the monitorial system of mass schooling.

a king; agrandise no man by forms of law. He who preserves your liberty, will of necessity receive universal praise, like Washington, to endless generations, without the aid of hireling priests to celebrate his fame.

Check if possible by law and practice, that avarice in man, which is never satisfied. If you suffer any among you to become emensly rich, he will want homage, and a title; yea, he will dispose of your lives, liberty, and property; and to support his divine right, he will establish a priesthood—he will call in foreign usurpers to assist him to oppress you. Under the protection of foreign bayonets, he will threaten to erect a gallows at every door. France is reduced to this state of humiliation. A black king is capable of wickedness, as well as a white one.

WEDDERBURN.

The Axe Laid to the Root No. 2 [1817]

ADDRESS TO THE SLAVES OF JAMAICA

DEAR COUNTRYMEN,

It is necessary for you to know how you may govern yourselves without a king, without lords, dukes, earls, or the like; these are classes of distinction which tend only to afflict society. I would have you know, with all the proud boasting of Europeans they are yet ignorant of what political liberty is: the Britons boast of the perfection of their free government, and excellent constitution, and yet they are constantly finding fault with their rulers. You would hardly think it possible that tens of thousands of Englishmen, would give their votes to elect a Member, for a cheap dinner, and a day's drunkenness, others for a few pounds, some for promises of future rewards, and yet take a solemn oath that they gave their vote freely, and the person they voted for is the man of their choice. Many of them know, at the same time, that they are telling lies. If all liars and false swearers were struck dead at this period there would be but few voters left: The government of England was founded on principles of liberty, and it is said, its constitution is the work of a wise and brave people, who, considering that all power was derived from them, and was to be subservient to their happiness. After they had formed this constitution, and recovered, by their exertion their liberty, they had not sense to keep it, they placed it into the hands of those they called their three States, then their freedom ceased that is to say, they chose three masters. These three, when they agree, may dispose of their lives and properties. Britons, where is your liberty now? Why, it is in the hands of your governors, you have made them omnipotent, they can do any thing; they can make bastards lawful; they can dissolve marriages, and, at the same time say, whoever God or the Established Priests has joined together, no man shall separate; they can make a child of one year old twenty one by saying so; they can make right wrong, or wrong right; they punish in this country for stealing of children though the thief be rich, and intends the child to inherit his estates; and, at the same time, they make it right that hundreds of thousands of Africans may be stolen, and sold, like cattle, in the market; in truth, they can do, what is impossible for God to do. I have mentioned these things, my countrymen, to warn you against this mode of governing, it being absurd and ridiculous. You might expect, that I should point out a form of government for you, this I leave to your judgment; but my opinion is, the foundation of your government should be this, that every thing should be settled by votes throughout your nation. Should Experience prove the first majority wrong, Necessity will compel you to pole the second time: the public will is easy attained by that mode, and Class yourselves in divisions, chuse a delegate to represent you, one for every 2,000, change them once a year, let ten years elapse before you send the same person again: a continual change will improve and qualify many of you, to understand your laws and customs, and check that tyranny which is natural to man. Have no white delegate in your assembly, never have a man worth more than five hundred a year: all laws framed by your assembly, must be sanctioned by a majority of votes throughout the nation. Put no man to death for any crime, flog no body after fourteen years of age, nor cut off the nose nor ears, as is the practice in Jamaica. Let there be state caps, marked with the different crimes, whether it be murder, false-swearing, etc. Let each criminal, after a trial by jury, wear the cap which describes his crime; murder, for life, others in proportion to their guilt: he who attempts to take a man's life away falsely should be deemed a murderer. Let the cap be secure as a helmet. Let no man be pardoned who breaks your laws, let every individual learn the art of war, yea, even the females, for they are capable of displaying courage. You will have need of all your strength to defend yourself against those men, who are now scheming in Europe against the blacks of St. Domingo. Teach your children these lines, let them be sung on the Sabbath day, in remembrance of your former sufferings, which will show you what you may expect from the hands of European Christians, by what they have practised before.

[. . .]

Let every male and female be provided with instruments of war, at the age of 18. Like the industrious bee, protect your hive, drive out the drones, let no one live amongst you, who contributes not to the welfare of the state; he that will not labour in body or mind, let him not eat, says the apostle: the word of God is, thou shalt get thy bread by the sweat of thy brow. The founders of Christianity have set you a pattern, Paul laboured with his hands. Should the quakers or any other religious sect forbid you using the sword, put them in the front of the battle, as David did Uria: he that will not contend for his liberty is not worthy of it. Have no lawyers amongst you, they cannot be honest in their profession; have no barracks, but keep your arms and ammunition in your own possession. Appoint inspectors to see that all are provided; have no prisons, they are only schools for vice, and depots for the victims of tyranny; appoint a fools-cap to be worn at the age of five, by every one who knows not the alphabet; let the females be the teachers, till the children can read and write; appoint a cap of wisdom, expressing on it the degree of improvement to which the child has attained; this will cause emulation in the youth and parents, to cast away the cap of ignorance; wear the cap of wisdom to the age of fourteen. Let the alphabet be engraven on your trees, and on every public wall, for knowledge is god-like strength, which will regulate your physical force. Bribe no one to serve the public. For glory and immortal fame will perpetuate the remembrance of the hero to endless generations.—That is a sufficient reward.

In some countries the law is spun to an invisible thread, framed in language the vulgar cannot understand. The judges cannot comprehend it, they vary in opinion. The means to obtain justice is so expensive, that justice cannot be obtained by the poor; there are many in England who gain a livelihood by laying legal traps to slay the ignorant poor for reward, and with all, the innumerable laws that are in being, there is not one to punish these legal murderers. They have the interest of the rich at their heart; therefore, I advise you to be aware of the rich, for they hate the poor, says 'Solomon.' Again I say, have no lawyers amongst you, every dispute may be decided in your own villages, by 12 men and 12 women; let them be above fifty; do not despise the judgment of old women, for they are generally clear in their perceptions. Let them be chosen from the adjoining village, should they give a wrong decision, they will only be like the refined Europeans, who, frequently in their courts of law, let the guilty escape, and punish the supporters of justice and truth. Administer no oath amongst you, it is all a deception, honest persons do not need it, a rogue cannot be bound by it. If you discover any amongst you giving false evidence wilfully, let him wear a criminal's cap for life, with this inscription on it—I AM A LIAR.

Pardon no man, for it is an indirect violation of law, and a positive perversion of justice, it is a fludgate to corruption; let your delegates be judges, to try all cases of magnitude in the house of assembly, and for convenience and accuracy, let evidence of the case be taken on the spot, where the crime was committed; a jury in the village ought to take down the evidence, let it be sealed up, and sent to the assembly, there to be decided. This method of proceeding will prevent inconveniency and expence; for thousands have been ruined in the process towards a trial, and afterwards been proved innocent. The system that admits of this wretched practice, of necessity, must afflict the innocent. The lawyers in England drink a health to the glorious uncertainty of the law: they may be compared to tricking gamblers, playing at the game of pricking in the garter. This game will always be carried on while the great manage the law, and the younger son is deprived of a share of his father's estate you must know, that in this country, the eldest son gets the whole, and the others are turned on the public; he that is wild or ungovernable is trained for war, he that is crafty and can out-wit his play-mates and companions is brought up to the law; but, if there should be a third who discovers little or no sense, he will, notwithstanding, be inclined to piety, he is made a parson of; therefore you see the necessity for war, for imperfect laws and church establishment, so that all the sons of the rich may be provided for.

R.W.

The Axe Laid to the Root No. 4 [1817]

TO MISS CAMPBELL

DEAR MISS CAMPBELL,[19]
WHEN I heard of your kindness to my aged mother, it affected my whole frame, and made such an impression on my mind that I was at a loss to know which way to make you amends, but I soon accused myself for such a thought, when I recollected that it was a West Indian that performed the deed, who knows no merit in doing acts of humanity: but, how was I struck with wonder and astonishment, when John, our brother, described to me your manner and action when you went to your drawer and took the record and presented it to him, saying, here, John, take your freedom. What you then performed is beyond the power of princes to imitate. Oh! Miss Campbell, the greatness of the deed has inspired me with a zeal to extend freedom beyond present conception: Yes, the slaves shall be free, for a multiplied combination of ideas, which amount to prophetic inspiration and the greatness of the work that I am

---

[19] Wedderburn records that the Campbell family purchased his mother Rosanna, and treated her kindly. 'Miss Campbell' apparently inherited the sugar estates, and might herself have been a mulatto – Wedderburn hints that she might have been his half-sister. Wedderburn's correspondence here is fictitious, but his editor McCalman assumes that 'Miss Campbell' was probably a real person.

to perform has influenced my mind with an enthusiasm, I cannot support: I must give vent, I have commenced my carear, the press is my engine of destruction. I come not to make peace; my fury shall be felt by princes, bidding defiance to pride and prejudice. Truth is my arrow stained with Africans' blood, rendered poisonous by guilt, while they hold my innocent fellow as a slave, I will kindle wrath in their inmost souls which the eternal God himself, whose throne is founded on the bed of justice, will not be willing to take away until they make a public confession, and give up the stolen Africans now in their possession. An act of Parliament will not afford a cover for their guilty heads, for the makers of unjust laws throughout the earth are in a state of condemnation. Fast bound by eternal truth, I have hold of the God of Israel, like a Jacob, and will not let him go. I will be made a prince by prevailing, though a halter be about my neck. Jacob, I will excell you in proportion to the present improved state of society. Miss Campbell, though a goddess, I have a command for thee to obey: like the Christians of old, you have fallen from the purity of the Maroons, your original, who fought for twenty years against the Christians, who wanted to reduce them again to slavery, after they had fled into the woods from the Spaniards. Yes, the English, in the days of Cromwell, while they were asserting the rights of man at home, were destroying your ancestors then fighting for their liberty; but the Calamantees, as the late Pitt declared, in the House of Commons, led to victory, other tribes less valiant. They were reckoned worth five pounds per head, or each pair of ears; this was the price the Christians bid for your forefathers. The Maroons were not barbarous, nor voracious; this was proved by a bold flag of truce, whose name, I am sorry to say, I cannot recollect; but he was such a character as their present governor, the Duke of Manchester.[20] The Maroons were human beings, and ought not to be hunted down by Britons acting the bloodhound's part. Yes, Miss Campbell, this mediator, I can give him no greater name, he went to the woods without protection excepting that of the generous negro to whom he went. There was not a London assassin with a bloody dagger to give a criminal stab, as was done to Wat Tyler.[21]

[20] The Duke of Manchester Wedderburn refers to here was William Montagu (1768–1843), the fifth Duke of Manchester, and governor of Jamaica from 1808 to 1827. He was responsible for moderate reforms in the treatment of slaves during his tenure, but at the same time treated slave rebellions with great severity.

[21] Wat Tyler was one of the ringleaders of the large-scale peasant rebellion in 1381 that was inspired by demands that church land be redistributed among parishioners, and that serfdom be abolished in England. The rebels occupied London briefly, but were ultimately betrayed and defeated, and Tyler's head was paraded on a pole through London as a warning to other potential rebels.

A treaty was agreed to on the spot, without a written document, which exists to this day, by verbal tradition; but more of this hereafter.

Now, my Dear Miss Campbell, be not alarmed or surprised, though you hold slaves, they must be let free, tho' sanctioned by the laws of England, agreeable to the laws of Spain. Your property is in them you say: the Spaniards had the same wicked supposed right in you, and all your property, by that original base law of slave-holding; besides, you cannot hold them long. I will inform you for your present safety, and for the future good of your offspring, to let the slaves go free immediately, for in their prison house a voice is heard, loose him and let him go.

Chuse ye, as Moses said to the Jews, I have given you time to consider. Have you decided? Yes, I have. My conclusion is this, a mind free from guilt is a heaven on earth. Human nature wants but little, nor that little long. I will trust to the sympathy of nature's universal law, then call your slaves together, let them form the half circle of a new moon, tell them to sit and listen to the voice of truth, say unto them, you who were slaves to the cruel Spaniards stolen from your country, and brought here, but Cromwell, the great, who humbled kings at his feet, and brought one to the scaffold, sent a fleet out, whose admiral dared not return without performing something to please his master. Came here and drove the Spaniards out; the slaves, my people, then fled to the woods for refuge, the invaders called to them to return to bondage, they refused; they contended for twenty years, and upwards; bondage was more terrific than death. At last, a wise and good man appeared from England, and ventured amongst them without a guard, proposed a treaty of peace, agreeable to their own will, which they agreed to. Here, you see my origin, and the cause of my freedom, but I have been tempted to purchase you as slaves, by the example of the white men, who are sanctioned by the English government, being void of shame. I am now instructed by a child of nature, to resign to you your natural right in the soil on which you stand, agreeable to Spence's plan. You are no longer slaves my conscience is free from guilt, but the blood of my ancestors, who fell for freedom's cause will be required at the hands of the white men, who, against knowledge, refuse obedience to nature's law. The unexpected sound, you are no longer slaves, deprived them of speech; some fainted with joy, the rest were amazed, an old man, whose head was white as snow, cried out, Lord help us! Missy, Missy, you sall sit on de same seat wid de Virgin Mary; may God make dee his servant. I will go to toder country in peace. He then dropped, like Palmer, on the stage: by this time, the rest of the slaves recovered from their stupor, four young men with solemn respect, bore the corpse away The slaves seemed all disposed to speak at once.

Oh! Missy, good Missy, good Missy, what me do for you, proceeded from all their tongues. Oh! says Miss Campbell, I have enough to be done by you all, I have afflicted many of you for crimes produced by the slavish system of oppression.

Oh! Elizabeth, who first sanctioned the inhuman traffic, canst thou take away my guilt? No, cried a voice from some invisible being, the people should have resisted inhuman laws when proposed. Princes cannot help you, they have guilt enough, they can hardly answer for their own iniquities. In tophit voices are heard: Behold the man who gave fortunes to swear away the lives of men, to keep them on their blood stained thrones, is now become like one of us. Oh! Lucifer, son of Corruption, who art fallen, is it thou who made the earth to tremble. Miss Campbell being well acquainted with the scriptures, recollected a passage that relieved her mind, which was, confess your sins, one to the other, and be forgiven: she then addressed herself to the negros, in these words; I appeal to the simplicity of your nature; forgive me, I have the written word of God to plead in my behalf: you are commanded to forgive—I confess my guilt—I have given up the wicked claim. The slaves cried out, Oh! What me forgive? You was always good, missy, missy, we will live wid you—we no go away. Miss Campbell then cried, the land is yours, not because Wedderburn, the Spencean says so, for I have read the word of God, and it says, the Lord gave the earth to the children of men. You are the children of men as well as others. I can show no title deeds that are just. Those who sold it to me murdered them who lived on it before. I will manage it myself, as your steward, my brother will assist us, we shall live happy, like the family of the Shariers in the parish of St. Mary's, who have all things common. The Christians of old, attempted this happy mode of living in fellowship or brotherhood, but, after the death of Christ and the apostles, the national priests persuaded their emperor to establish the Christian religion, and they also embraced, in hypocrisy, the Christian faith. They took possession of the Church property, and called it theirs, which remains in their hands to this day; but they have taken care to hedge it about with laws which punish with death all those who dare attempt to take it away. Yea, the bayonet is engaged to enforce the law, should the people discover the trick, and prove turbulent; and the Clergy, for this military security, pervert the doctrines of Christ, which ordered the sword to be put up, it not becoming his followers to shed human blood. The clergy practically declare, that Christ knew not what he said; they being wiser than him persuade the people to draw the sword, contrary to the command of Christ, and slay their brethren. They threatened with eternal damnation all who dare refuse obedience to their command; but they are very kind to persuade you to confess you are guilty, when you are not, but Cashman,[22] Bellingham,[23] Despard,[24] and the political sacrifices in France, were not to be cozened by hypocrites, the holy league with the Pope will not be able to hoodwink the people, though Lewis the 18th is labouring hard, priescraft cannot be grafted on the philosophic tree of liberty. You see Miss Campbell, the necessity of the exortation I give your people, watch your priests, pay them for their labour, never let them meddle with your worldly affairs.

Source: Robert Wedderburn, *The Horrors of Slavery and Other Writings by Robert Wedderburn*, ed. I. McCalman, Edinburgh, Edinburgh University Press, 1991 [1824], pp. 81–7, 89–90, 92–4, 96–100.

Robert Wedderburn, *Defence Against Blasphemy*, 1820

Extract 7

EASTER TERM 1820; TUESDAY THE 9TH OF MAY. THE KING AGAINST ROBERT WEDDERBURN.

The Defendant having been found guilty of uttering a blasphemous libel at the sittings after Hilary Term, appeared pursuant to a notice he had received from the Solicitors to the Treasury, to receive judgment.

THE LORD CHIEF JUSTICE went through the notes he had taken on the Trial, recapitulating minutely the words of the libel as stated in the indictment, and as given in evidence by each of the witnesses William Plush and Matthew Matthewson.

---

[22] John Cashman was an Irish sailor and war hero, who was wounded nine times in the Napoleonic Wars. He was discharged with no back-pay, and was subsequently arrested and hanged to widespread public anger for his peripheral role in the Spa Fields Riot of 2 December 1816.

[23] John Bellingham (1770–1812) nursed a grievance for money owed to him by the government, and was so incensed that on 11 May 1812, he assassinated the Prime Minister, Spencer Perceval in the House of Commons. Though transparently insane, Bellingham was executed at Newgate, but because of the great unpopularity of the government became for a time a folk hero.

[24] Colonel Edward Marcus Despard (1751–1803) was an Irishman, who served the British Army with great distinction in the West Indies, Central America and during the Napoleonic Wars. He too was shabbily treated when discharged from the army, and in 1798 was imprisoned for persistent complaints. He associated closely with the Irish immigrant community in London, and actively supported the United Irish and United English revolutionary underground. In 1802, he was seized by the British government on charges of treason, and was executed despite a public outcry and the pleas for clemency from Lord Horatio Nelson on 21 February 1803.

The Defendant was then asked if he had any affidavits to put in, to which he replied in the negative, but said he had something to say to the court, and proceeded to state:—

That however long the counts of the indictment against him might be; and however strongly they had been sworn to, yet he did not think he had said so much, or at least in the manner precisely as stated by the evidence.

That in consequence of his being thrown into prison, his chapel was shut up and his congregation dispersed, which circumstances had prevented him from seeking from amongst them evidence to contradict or invalidate the testimony on the part of the Crown. As for himself his memory was extremely bad, and it was impossible for him to recollect all he might have said on the occasion. Every observation he made arose spontaneous on the spur of the moment; his sermons or speeches were never the result of previous contrivance, but he did certainly remember to have spoken upon the story of the Witch of Endor.

His impression on this subject arose from the circumstance of seeing his aged grandmother, a poor black slave in the island of Jamaica, several times most cruelly flogged by order of her master, a white man and a *christian*, for being a WITCH; now as he, when a child, had frequently picked her pocket of sixpences and shillings, he was well convinced she could not possess the qualities and powers attributed to witches, or she must have detected his petty depredations. When he came to be a Christian, and read the story of Saul and the Witch of Endor, with these impressions upon his mind, that witches must be bad people, he could never bring himself to believe that such characters could work miracles and raise the dead.

The Defendant was proceeding with similar illustrations to show the origin of his scepticism, respecting Balaam's ass speaking, but the court considered his language was of a nature which they could not tolerate.

He then said, it might save time and prevent him wounding the ears of the court, if the paper was read that he had in his pocket, which was in the nature of a motion in arrest of judgment. He then put in a brief, which was read by one of the officers of the court as follows.

May it please your Lordships. I am well aware that the gentlemen of the bar will smile, at what they will call the vanity and presumption of a humble individual like myself, in attempting to address the court on an occasion like the present. They are welcome to smile, but I will tell them that the most brilliant efforts which the ablest of them could make, were I capable of employing them, would, be equally as useless in *this place*, and on *this subject*, as what I am now going to offer.

However humble I may be as a member of society, and whatever efforts may be made to degrade me and render me contemptible in the eyes of the world, I have nevertheless the pride, and the ambition, to flat-

185

ter myself, that even my simple exertions will one day or other be of no mean importance to the cause I am embarked in, which is that of *Religious Liberty* and the *Universal Right of Conscience.*

If we would obtain the privileges to which we are entitled, neither death nor dungeons must terrify us; we must keep in mind the example of Christ and his apostles, of Penn and the primitive Quakers, who all promulgated *what they considered* was true and beneficial to mankind, without the slightest regard to the evil consequences which such, their bold, independent, and disinterested conduct might bring down upon themselves. What was the result? Christianity in the first instance, and Quakerism in the second, were established by the very opposition that they met with.

VOLTAIRE has justly observed, that 'Martyrs are productive of proselytes;' and the history of every age proves the assertion. The execution of Jesus Christ, a mild and amiable man, between two abandoned characters, excited sympathy in the breasts of the people, and roused a spirit of enquiry as to what were the doctrines for which he was condemned.

The early Quakers were a stern and stubborn set of men, determined both to risk and to suffer persecution in the attainment of their object; and by this means they ultimately secured, and do still enjoy, greater religious liberties than any other sect without the pale of the state religion. Why then may not the numerous *Latitudinarians* of the present day hope, by zeal, industry, courage, and perseverance, to gain that toleration which is granted to others; or I should rather say, those rights to which by the law of nature they are entitled; for the very term *toleration* is a *delusion*; and as our GRAND PATRIARCH, hath well said, 'It is not the *opposite* of INTOLERANCE, but only its *counterfeit*'; and a very shrewd and acute writer of modern times has remarked, that 'The legislature might as well pass an act to tolerate and empower the Almighty to receive the worship of the Jew, the Turk &c. as to pretend to tolerate, or permit to suffer either of those characters to worship their respective gods according to their several and peculiar notions.'

I feel firmly persuaded, that no effort, however humble, will ultimately be lost to the cause of Truth and Liberty; and that even my trifling productions may, perhaps, 'Like bread cast on the waters, be seen after many days.' The progress of TRUTH is *slow*,' says HELVETIUS, 'and may be compared to a stone thrown into a lake; the waters separate at the point in contact, and produce a circle; that circle is surrounded by another, and that by others still larger, and so on, until they break against the shore, and become mingled with the general mass.' It is by these slow degrees that all new truths are propagated, because they must necessarily meet with considerable opposition from the ignorant, the prejudiced, and above all, *from those whose interests would be injured* by the public adoption of these new truths.

Having made these general observations, I shall now proceed to offer some reasons, why judgment should not pass against me; but I must only be considered as doing it in the character of an advocate for religious liberty, and not as one asking for mercy, or fearing, or wishing to avert your sentence, however severe.

In the first place, I most solemnly protest against the authority of this, or any other court upon earth, to interfere with matters of conscience, and contend that they are superior to the controul of any human tribunal. Both the advocate on the part of the crown, and the learned judge who presided during my trial, evaded the main question, by stating, that I was not prosecuted for entertaining this, or that opinion; but for grossly reviling the religion established by law.

With all due deference to such high authorities, I humbly submit, that this is a sophism which will not stand the test of fair examination; because, of what use is the liberty of thinking, or the liberty of conscience, if we are not permitted to give vent to them. The celebrated politician MACHIAVELLI, has said, 'Man has a right to think all things, speak all things, and write all things, but not to impose his opinions.' We have not however, to thank any human being, for acknowledging our right to think; as 'tis neither in their power, nor our own, to controul our thoughts; neither chains, nor dungeons, nor the terrors of being burnt alive, can prevent us from thinking freely; neither ought they to prevent us from speaking freely, writing freely, and publishing freely; if we think we can benefit mankind, by exposing falsehood and error.

JUSTIN MARTYR, one of the earliest and most learned writers of the eastern church, being at Rome during the reign of Antoninus Pius, and finding that the Christians were grievously persecuted in some of the distant provinces, addressed two apologies to that emperor in their behalf, pointing out in a very able manner the impropriety and absurdity of religious persecution. In his second Apology he says, 'Reason informs, and admonishes us, that true philosophers, and men of virtue, have in every age loved and honored the simple Truth, and have turned aside from following the ancients, whenever their opinions have been found erroneous and bad; and that the inquisitive searcher after truth should prefer it to his life, and should not be deterred by the fear of death, or the threats of torture, from speaking and acting according to justice.'

In consequence of these apologies, that *Pagan* emperor wrote to the states of Asia, not only forbidding the Christians to be persecuted, but enjoining, that 'If any one hereafter shall go on to inform against this sort of men, *purely* because they are Christians, let the persons accused be discharged, although they are Christians, and let the informer himself undergo the punishment.'

It is of no use, my lords, to say we are tolerated to worship that *power*, or those *powers*, which the greater portion of mankind agree in *placing* above NATURE, if we are to be checked at every moment, and told we must not do it in this, or that manner; because instruction by preaching forms a part of most religious worship; and it must certainly happen, that when we are all assembled to worship our common Father, we shall be found mutually abusing each other, or, at least, the doctrines of each other.

How can the different priests, or teachers, warn their respective audiences against what *they concieve* to be erroneous, without endeavoring to place that error in the strongest light—to show that it is ridiculous—or absurd—or contradictory—or gross falsehood. Must not the Catholic enlarge upon the heresy of the Protestant; the Protestant upon the idolatry and superstition of the Catholic; the Dissenter upon the lukewarmness and formality of the church of England; the Unitarian upon the droll hypothesis of the Trinity; the Deist upon what he conceives to be the absurdities and inconsistences contained in that book which all the former revere as a divine revelation; and lastly, must not the Atheist (who has the same right with the rest,) when lecturing on his system, necessarily treat the whole as fables and fiction?

How, I ask, can religious liberty exist, if this be not permitted? How could the teacher of Nazareth, and his zealous disciples, have preached upon the purity and simplicity of their monotheistic system, without contrasting it with the absurdities of polytheism? Was it possible to establish a Deistical religion, without proving that the fables of the Grecian and Roman gods, goddesses, and demigods were not only false, but puerile and ridiculous—and was not this *openly reviling that religion which was identified with, and the foundation of all the administration of justice* in those countries.

Eusebius in his life of Constantine the Great, records the following direction given by that emperor: 'Let those that are in error, enjoy the same peace and tranquility as the faithful; and restoration of intercourse may go far to reclaim them to the right way. Let none molest another; but let every one act as his conscience dictates. Let those who have a true opinion of the Deity, believe that such only as regulate their lives by the rule of his laws, lead a holy and upright life; but let those who conform not thereto, erect temples, (if they will,) and consecrate groves to vanity. And let no man in any point, of which he is ever so clearly convinced, offend in any wise, or endanger another; but when a man has discovered a truth, let him therein benefit his neighbour if possible, otherwise pass him by. For a man voluntarily to strive after immortality, is one thing; it is another to be compelled thereto by fear of punishment.'

I cannot help adding one more instance of princely liberality, worthy the imitation of modern potentates. It is from the annals of our own country: when Pope Gregory the First sent the monk Austin, and forty missionaries, to plant the gospel in Great Britain, that prince, *though an idolater*, went out to meet them with the greatest courtesy, sat in the open air to hear their leader preach; and after listening to them attentively, made the following handsome reply, which we have preserved by the venerable *Bede*. 'Your proposals are noble, your promises are inviting, but I cannot resolve upon quitting the religion of my ancestors for one that appears to me supported only by the testimony of persons who are entire strangers to me. However, since as I perceive you have taken a long journey, on purpose to impart to us what you deem most important and valuable, you shall not be sent away without some satisfaction. I will take care that you are treated civilly, and supplied with all things necessary and convenient; and if any of my subjects, convinced by what you shall say to them, desire to embrace your religion, I shall not be against it.'

I shall now proceed to a second ground of argument, why judgment should not pass against me. It has no personal reference to myself; viz. the weak and narrow policy which dictated this prosecution; because those doctrines which would have been confined to my obscure chapel—to my small congregation,—are now by the fostering aid of my prosecutors, published to the whole world. They themselves are the means of widely disseminating that which they pretend to condemn. They have effectually advertized the very thing which they dislike. By preventing me from preaching, they have compelled me to become an author. They have dragged me from obscurity into public notice; and since they have made me a member of the Republic of Letters, I beg leave to recommend to their attention a critical, historical, and admonitory letter, which I have just published, '*Addressed to the Right Reverend Father in God, his Grace the Lord Archbishop of Canterbury, on the alarming Progress of Infidelity; and the means which ought immediately to be resorted to, to check its frightful career.*'

Lord Shaftsbury[25] says, 'It is a hard matter for a government to settle wit,' and the great Lord Chancellor Bacon observes, 'The punishment of wits serves to enhance their authority; and a forbidden writing is thought to be a certain spark or truth, that flies up in the face of them who seek to tread it out.' And I appeal to the experience of all men, whether they have not uniformly perused a condemned libel with greater eagerness, and consequently received a stronger impression from it, than they would have if

[25] The reference is to Anthony Ashley Cooper, the first Earl of Shaftesbury (1621–83), who played a prominent role in the politics of the English Civil War. He is best remembered for switching allegiance from the Crown to Parliament in 1644, and for sponsoring the famous political philosopher, John Locke (1632–1704).

it had not been prohibited. My prosecutors evince great ignorance of human nature, if they think they can tell the world of the existence of a singular doctrine, or a curious book, without at the same time creating in them a strong desire to become acquainted with it. They should keep in mind the *allegory* of our great grandmother Eve, and the tree of knowledge. She was forbidden to taste its fruit, *lest her eyes should be opened*, but her curiosity could not resist the temptation to disobey, though the punishment attached was so great. Will my prosecutors admit that they are suppressing my opinions from the *same motives*, and that their ends are thwarted in a *similar manner*. I know I shall be told again, that 'tis not my doctrines, but my language, for which I am prosecuted. This I contend is contemptible sophistry. If I am a low, vulgar man, and incapable of delivering my sentiments in an elegant and polished manner, am I to be condemned, when I find two pages in the Bible most palpably contradicting each other, for asserting that one of them must be A LIE?—for stating the history of the Witch of Endor to be an idle tale, and old woman's story:— and for attempting to divest the simple Deistical and Republican system of Jesus, of those gaudy appendages, those trumpery additions, with which craft and ignorance combined, have conspired to corrupt its native purity, its original simplicity. If this is not permitted, if any system is to be considered infallible, a bar is put to all human improvement. They must look up the human understanding, (that most glorious ornament wherewith NATURE hath vouchsafed to embellish her creature man,) in the trammels of superstition. They must tell mankind that all other sciences may be improved with credit, honor, and reward, but that no new lights must be thrown on the science of theology, under the penalty of dungeons and death.

Many obstacles are cast in the way of improvement in the science of government, but I may call the game laws,—the right of primogeniture, and several others,—'Relics of feudal barbarism'—'unjust infringements of the law of nature;'—I may ridicule them and revile them, and you have no law to punish me; but if I comment upon what I conceive to be errors, inconsistencies, or contradictions in the Act of Parliament Religion, in a plain and intelligible manner, I am to be thrown into a prison.

That excellent writer GORDON,[26] in a work called *Cato's Letters*, says, 'whoever would overturn the liberties of a nation, must begin by subverting the freedom of speech;' but I have no fear that the REMAIN-

---

[26] Thomas Gordon (d. 1750) together with the Whig politician John Trenchard began in 1720 the publication of *Cato's Letters*, which first appeared in serial form in the journals *London* and the *British Journal*, and were then reprinted in a four-volume edition in 1724. Gordon's anti-Tory political sentiments are expressed in detail in his *A Letter to an Archbishop* (1719), which went through a number of subsequently expanded editions.

ING liberties of this country can be destroyed as long as there are people willing to suffer, and I am proud in reflecting that there are hundreds like myself, who aspire to the crown of martyrdom.

My Lords, some persons in my situation would endeavour to press upon your consideration the jury's recommendation to mercy, and the long imprisonment I experienced before I was bailed out to prepare for my defence. But it is by no means my wish to obtrude these circumstances on the notice of your Lordships, as I am so extremely poor that a prison will be a home to me; and as I am so far advanced in life I shall esteem it an honor to die immured in a Dungeon for advocating THE CAUSE OF TRUTH, OF RELIGIOUS LIBERTY, AND THE UNIVERSAL RIGHT OF CONSCIENCE.

Source: Robert Wedderburn, *The Horrors of Slavery and Other Writings by Robert Wedderburn*, ed. I. McCalman, Edinburgh, Edinburgh University Press, 1991 [1824], pp. 132–9.

Robert Wedderburn, *The Horrors of Slavery*, 1824

Extract 8

TO WILLIAM WILBERFORCE, ESQ. MP

Respected Sir,

An oppressed, insulted, and degraded African—to whom but you can I dedicate the following pages, illustrative of the treatment of my poor countrymen? Your name stands high in the list of the glorious benefactors of the human race; and the slaves of the earth look upon you as a tower of strength in their behalf. When in prison, for conscience-sake, at Dorchester, you visited me, and you gave me—your advice, for which I am still your debtor, and likewise for the two books beautifully bound in calf, from which I have since derived much ghostly consolation. Receive, Sir, my thanks for what you have done; and if, from the following pages, you should be induced to form any motion in parliament, I am ready to prove their contents before the bar of that most Honourable House.

I remain, Sir,

Your most obedient, and

most devoted Servant,

ROBERT WEDDERBURN.

23, Russell Court,
Drury Lane.

LIFE
OF THE
REV. ROBERT WEDDERBURN

The events of my life have been few and uninteresting. To my unfortunate origin I must attribute all my miseries and misfortunes. I am now
upwards of sixty years of age, and therefore I cannot long expect to be
numbered amongst the living. But, before I pass from this vale of tears,
I deem it an act of justice to myself, to my children, and to the memory
of my mother, to say what I am, and who were the authors of my existence; and to shew the world, that, not to my own misconduct is to be
attributed my misfortunes, but to the inhumanity of a MAN, whom I am
compelled to call by the name of FATHER. I am the offspring of a slave,
it is true; but I am a man of free thought and opinion; and though I was
immured for two years in his Majesty's gaol at Dorchester, for daring to
express my sentiments as a free man, I am still the same in mind as I was
before, and imprisonment has but confirmed me that I was right. They
who know me, will confirm this statement.

To begin then with the beginning—I was born in the island of Jamaica,
about the year 1762, on the estate of a Lady Douglas, a distant relation
of the Duke of Queensbury. My mother was a woman of colour, by name
ROSANNA, and at the time of my birth a slave to the above Lady Douglas. My father's name was JAMES WEDDERBURN, Esq. of Inveresk, in
Scotland, an extensive proprietor, of sugar estates in Jamaica, which are
now in the possession of a younger brother of mine, by name, A.
COLVILLE, Esq. of No.35, Leadenhall Street.

I must explain at the outset of this history—what will appear unnatural to some—the reason of my abhorrence and indignation at the conduct of my father. From him I have received no benefit in the world. By
him my mother was made the object of his brutal lust, then insulted,
abused, and abandoned; and, within a few weeks from the present time,
a younger and more fortunate brother of mine, the aforesaid A. Colville,
Esq. has had the insolence to revile her memory in the most abusive language, and to stigmatise her for that which was owing to the deep and
dark iniquity of my father. Can I contain myself at this? or, have I not the
feelings of human nature within my breast? Oppression I can bear with
patience, because it hath always been my lot; but when to this is added
insult and reproach from the authors of my miseries, I am forced to take
up arms in my own defence, and to abide the issue of the conflict.

My father's name, as I said before, was JAMES WEDDERBURN, of
Inveresk, in Scotland, near Musselborough, where, if my information is
correct, the Wedderburn family have been seated for a long time. My

grandfather was a staunch Jacobite, and exerted himself strenuously in the cause of the Pretender, in the rebellion of the year 1745. For his aiding to restore the exiled family to the throne of England, he was tried, condemned, and executed. He was hung by the neck till he was dead; his head was then cut off, and his body was divided into four quarters. When I first came to England, in the year 1779, I remember seeing the remains of a rebel's skull which had been affixed over Temple Bar; but I never yet could fully ascertain whether it was my dear grandfather's skull, or not. Perhaps my dear brother, A. COLVILLE, can lend me some assistance in this affair. For this act of high treason, our family estates were confiscated to the King, and my dear father found himself destitute in the world, or with no resource but his own industry. He adopted the medical profession; and in Jamaica he was Doctor and Man-Midwife, and turned an honest penny by drugging and physicing the poor blacks, where those that were cured, he had the credit for, and for those he killed, the fault was laid to their own obstinacy. In the course of time, by dint of *booing* and *booing*, my father was restored to his father's property, and he became the proprietor of one of the most extensive sugar estates in Jamaica. While my dear and honoured father was poor, he was chaste as any Scotchman, whose poverty made him virtuous; but the moment he became rich, he gave loose to his carnal appetites, and indulged himself without moderation, but as parsimonious as ever. My father's mental powers were none of the brightest, which may account for his libidinous excess. It is a common practice, as has been stated by Mr. Wilberforce in parliament, for the planters to have lewd intercourse with their female slaves; and so inhuman are many of these said planters, that many well-authenticated instances are known, of their selling their slaves while pregnant, and making that a pretence to enhance their value. A father selling his offspring is no disgrace there. A planter letting out his prettiest female slaves for purposes of lust, is by no means uncommon. My father ranged through the whole of his household for his own lewd purposes; for they being his personal property, cost nothing extra; and if any one proved with child—why, it was an acquisition which might one day fetch something in the market, like a horse or pig in Smithfield. In short, amongst his own slaves my father was a perfect parish bull; and his pleasure was the greater, because he at the same time increased his profits.

I now come to speak of the infamous manner with which JAMES WEDDERBURN, Esq. of Inveresk, and father to A. COLVILE, Esq. No. 35, Leadenhall Street, entrapped my poor mother in his power. My mother was a lady's maid, and had received an education which perfectly qualified her to conduct a household in the most agreeable manner. She was the property of Lady Douglas, whom I have before mentioned; and, prior to the time she met my father, was chaste and virtuous. After my father had got his estate, he did not renounce the pestle and mortar, but, in the capacity of Doctor, he visited Lady Douglas. He there met my mother for the first time, and was determined to have possession of her. His character was known; and therefore he was obliged to go *covertly* and *falsely* to work. In Jamaica, slaves that are esteemed by their owners have generally the power of refusal, whether they will be sold to a particular planter, or not; and my father was aware, that if *he* offered to purchase her, he would meet with a refusal. But his brutal lust was not to be stopped by trifles; my father's conscience would stretch to any extent; and he was a firm believer in the doctrine of 'grace abounding to the chief of sinners.' For this purpose, he employed a fellow of the name of Cruikshank, a brother doctor and Scotchman, to strike a bargain with Lady Douglas for my mother; and this scoundrel of a Scotchman bought my mother for the use of my father, in the name of another planter, a most respectable and highly esteemed man. I have often heard my mother express her indignation at this base and treacherous conduct of my father—a treachery the more base, as it was so calm and premeditated. Let my brother COLVILLE deny this if he can; let him bring me into court, and I will prove what I here advance. To this present hour, while I think of the treatment of my mother, my blood boils in my veins; and, had I not some connections for which I was bound to live, I should long ago have taken ample revenge of my father. But it is as well as it is; and I will not leave the world without some testimony to the injustice and inhumanity of my father.

From the time my mother became the property of my father, she assumed the direction and management of his house; for which no woman was better qualified. But her station there was very disgusting. My father's house was full of female slaves, all objects of his lusts; amongst whom he strutted like Solomon in his grand seraglio, or like a bantam cock upon his own dunghill. My good father's slaves did increase and multiply, like Jacob's kine; and he cultivated those talents well which God had granted so amply. My poor mother, from being the housekeeper, was the object of their envy, which was increased by her superiority of education over the common herd of female slaves. While in this situation, she bore my father two children, one of whom, my brother James, a millwright, I believe, is now living in Jamaica, upon the estate. Soon after this, my father introduced a new concubine into his seraglio, one ESTHER TROTTER, a free tawny, whom he placed over my mother, and to whom he gave the direction of his affairs. My brother

COLVILLE asserts, that my mother was of a violent and rebellious temper. I will leave the reader now to judge for himself, whether she had not some reason for her conduct. Hath not a slave feelings? If you starve them, will they not die? If you wrong them, will they not revenge? Insulted on one hand, and degraded on the other, was it likely that my poor mother could practise the Christian virtue of humility, when her Christian master provoked her to wrath? She shortly afterwards became again pregnant; and I have not the least doubt but that from her rebellious and violent temper during that period, that I have inherited the same disposition—the same desire to see justice overtake the oppressors of my countrymen—and the same determination to lose no stone unturned, to accomplish so desirable an object. My mother's state was so unpleasant, that my father at last consented to sell her back to Lady Douglas; but not till the animosity in my father's house had grown to such an extent, that my uncle, Sir JOHN WEDDERBURN, my father's elder brother, had given my mother an asylum in his house, against the brutal treatment of my father. At the time of sale, my mother was five months gone in pregnancy; and one of the stipulations of the bargain was, that the child which she then bore should be FREE from the moment of its birth. I was that child. When about four months old, the ill-treatment my mother had experienced had such an effect upon her, that I was obliged to be weaned, to save her life. Lady Douglas, at my admission into the Christian church, stood my godmother, and, as long as she lived, never deserted me. She died when I was about four years old.

From my mother I was delivered over to the care of my grandmother, who lived at Kingston, and who earned her livelihood by retailing all sorts of goods, hard or soft, smuggled or not, for the merchants of Kingston. My grandmother was the property of one JOSEPH PAYNE, at the east end of Kingston; and her place was to sell his property—cheese, checks, chintz, milk, gingerbread, etc; in doing which, she trafficked on her own account with the goods of other merchants, having an agency of half-a-crown in the pound allowed her for her trouble. No woman was perhaps better known in Kingston than my grandmother, by the name of '*Talkee Amy*,' signifying a chattering old woman. Though a slave, such was the confidence the merchants of Kingston had in her honesty, that she could be trusted to any amount; in fact, she was the regular agent for selling smuggled goods.

I never saw my dear father but once in the island of Jamaica, when I went with my grandmother to know if he meant to do anything for me, his son. Giving her some abusive language, my grandmother called him a mean Scotch rascal, thus to desert his own flesh and blood; and declared, that as she had kept me hitherto, so she would yet, without his paltry assistance. This was the parental treatment I experienced from a Scotch West-India planter and slave-dealer.

When I was about eleven years of age, my poor old grandmother was flogged for a witch by her master, the occasion of which I must relate in this place. Joseph Payne, her master, was an old and avaricious merchant, who was concerned in the smuggling trade. He had a vessel manned by his own slaves, and commanded by a Welchman of the name of Lloyd, which had made several profitable voyages to Honduras for mahogany, which was brought to Jamaica, and from thence forwarded to England. The old miser had some notion, that Lloyd cheated him in the adventure, and therefore resolved to go himself as a check upon him. Through what means I know not, but most likely from information given by Lloyd out of revenge and jealousy, the Spaniards surprised and captured the vessel; and poor old Payne, at seventy years of age, was condemned to carry stones at Fort Homea, in the Bay of Honduras, for a year and a day; and his vessel and his slaves were confiscated to the Spaniards. On his way home he died, and was tossed overboard to make food for fishes. His nephew succeeded to his property; and a malicious woman-slave, to curry favour with him, persuaded him, that the ill-success of old Payne's adventures was owing to my grandmother's having bewitched the vessel. The old miser had liberated five of his slaves before he set out on his unlucky expedition; and my grandmother's new master being a believer in the doctrine of Witchcraft, conceived that my grandmother had bewitched the vessel, out of revenge for her not being liberated also. To punish her, therefore, he tied up the poor old woman of seventy years and flogged her to that degree, that she would have died, but for the interference of a neighbour. Now, what aggravated the affair was, that my grandmother had brought up this young villain from eight years of age, and, till now, he had treated her as a mother. But my grandmother had full satisfaction soon afterwards. The words of our blessed Lord and Saviour Jesus Christ were fulfilled in this instance: 'Do good to them that despitefully use you, and in so doing you shall heap coals of fire upon their heads.' This woman had an only child, which died soon after this affair took place (plainly a judgment of God); and the mother was forced to come and beg pardon of my grandmother for the injury she had done her, and solicit my grandmother to assist her in the burial of her child. My grandmother replied, 'I can forgive you, but I can never forget the flogging;' and the good old woman instantly set about assisting her in her child's funeral, it being as great an object to have a decent burial with the blacks in Jamaica, as with the lower classes in Ireland. This same woman, who had so wickedly calumniated my grandmother, afterwards made public confession of her guilt in the market-place at

Kingston, on purpose to ease her guilty conscience, and to make atonement for the injury she had done. I mention this, to show upon what slight grounds the planters exercise their cow-skin whips, not sparing even an old woman of seventy years of age. But to return—

After the death of Lady Douglas, who was brought to England to be buried, James Charles Sholto Douglas, Esq. my mother's master, promised her her freedom on his return to Jamaica; but his covetous heart would not let him perform his promise. He told my mother to look out for another master to purchase her; and that her price was to be £100. The villain Cruikshank, whom I have mentioned before, offered Douglas £10 more for her; and Douglas was so mean as to require £110 from my mother; otherwise he would have sold her to Cruikshank against her will, for purposes the reader can guess. One Doctor Campbell purchased her; and in consequence of my mother having been a companion of, and borne children to my father, Mrs. Campbell used to upbraid her for not being humble enough to her, who was but a doctor's wife. This ill-treatment had such an effect on my mother, that she resolved to starve herself to death; and, though a cook, abstained from victuals for six days. When her intention was discovered, Doctor Campbell became quite alarmed for his £110, and gave my mother leave to look out for another owner; which she did, and became the property of a Doctor Boswell. The following letter, descriptive of her treatment in this place, appeared in 'BELL'S LIFE IN LONDON,' a Sunday paper, on the 29th February 1824:–

To The Editor of *Bell's Life in London*

February 20th, 1824

SIR,—Your observations on the Meeting of the Receivers of Stolen Men call for my sincere thanks, I being a descendant of a Slave by a base Slave-Holder, the late JAMES WEDDERBURN, Esq. of Inveresk, who sold my mother when she was with child of me, HER THIRD SON BY HIM!!! She was FORCED to submit to him, being *his Slave*, THOUGH HE KNEW SHE DISLIKED HIM! She knew that he was mean, and, when gratified, would not give her her freedom, which is the custom for those, *as a reward*, who have preserved their persons, with Gentlemen (if I may call a Slave-Dealer a Gentleman). I have seen my poor mother stretched on the ground, tied hands and feet, and FLOGGED in the most indecent manner, though PREGNANT AT THE SAME TIME!!! her *fault* being the not acquainting her mistress that her master had *given her leave to go to see her mother in town!* So great was the anger of this Christian Slave-Dealer, that he went fifteen miles to punish her while on the visit! Her master was then one B O S W E L L; his chief companion was C A P T A I N   P A R R, who *chained a female Slave to a stake, and starved her to death!* Had it not been for a British Officer in the Army, who had her dug up and proved it, this fact would not have been known. *The murderer was sentenced to transport himself for one year.* He came to England, and returned in the time—this was *his punishment.* My uncle and aunt were sent to America, and sold by their father's brother, who said that he sent them to be educated. *He had a little shame,* for the law in Jamaica allowed him to sell them, or even had they been his children— *so much for humanity and Christian goodness.* As for these men, who wished that the King would proclaim that there was no intention of emancipation,—Oh, what barbarism!—

R O B E R T   W E D D E R B U R N.
No.27, Crown Street, Soho
I little expected, when I sent this letter, that my dear brother, A. C O L V I L L E, Esq. of No.35, Leadenhall Street, would have dared to reply to it. But he did; and what all my letters and applications to him, and my visit to my father, could not accomplish, was done by the above plain letter. The following is the letter of Andrew, as it appeared in the same paper on the 21st of March last, with the Editor's comments:—
B R O T H E R   O R   N O   B R O T H E R—'T H A T   I S   T H E   Q U E S T I O N?'

---

*A letter from another son of the late slave-dealer,
James Wedderburn, Esq*

Our readers will recollect, that on the 29th ult. we published a letter signed R O B E R T   W E D D E R B U R N, in which the writer expressed his feelings in bitter terms of reproach against the atrocities of the man he called his F A T H E R, practised, as he declared them to have been, upon his unhappy Mother, and who was, as he stated, at once the victim of his Father's lust and subsequent barbarity. When we inserted the Letter alluded to, we merely treated on the horrors of the station generally, to which Slavery reduced our fellow-beings, but without pledging ourselves to the facts of the statements in question, as narrated by the son, against so inhuman a parent. But we are now more than ever inclined to believe them literally true; since we have received the following letter by the hands of *another son*—apparently, however, a greater favourite with his father than R O B E R T—and in which the brutalities stated by the latter to have been practised upon his mother, are not attempted to be denied.

The following letter we publish *verbatim et literatim* as we received it—
a remark or two upon its contents presently:—

To The Editor of *Bell's Life in London*

SIR,—Your Paper of the 29th ult. containing a Letter signed ROBERT
WEDDERBURN, was put into my hands only yesterday, otherwise I
should have felt it to be my duty to take earlier notice of it.

In answer to this most slanderous publication, I have to state, that the
person calling himself Robert Wedderburn is NOT a son of the late Mr.
James Wedderburn, of Inveresk, who never had any child by, or any connection of *that kind* with the mother of this man. The pretence of his using
the name of Wedderburn at all, arises out of the following circumstances:—
The late Mr. James Wedderburn, of Inveresk, had, when he resided in the
parish of Westmoreland, in the Island of Jamaica, a negro woman-*slave*,
whom he employed as a cook; this woman had so violent a temper that she
was continually quarrelling with the other servants, and occasioning a disturbance in the house. He happened to make some observation upon her
troublesome temper, when a gentleman in company said, he would be very
glad to *purchase* her if she was a good cook. The *sale accordingly took
place*, and the woman was removed to the residence of the gentleman, in
the parish of Hanover. Several years afterwards, this woman was delivered
of a mulatto child, and as *she could not tell who was the father*, her master,
in a foolish joke, named the child Wedderburn. About twenty-two or
twenty-three years ago, this man applied to me for money upon the
strength of his name, claiming to be a son of Mr. James Wedderburn, of
Inveresk, which occasioned me to write to my father, when he gave me the
above explanation respecting this person; adding, that a few years after he
had returned to this country, and married, this same person importuned
him with the same story that he now tells; and as he persisted in annoying
him after the above explanation was given to him, that he found it necessary to have him brought before the Sheriff of the county of Edinburgh. But
whether the man was punished, or only discharged upon promising not to
repeat the annoyance, *I do not now recollect.*

'Your conduct, Sir, is most unjustifiable in thus lending yourself to be
the vehicle of such foul slander upon the character of the respected
dead—when the story is so improbable in itself—when upon the slightest enquiry you would have discovered that it referred to a period of
between sixty and seventy years ago, and *therefore* is not applicable to
any argument upon the present condition of the West India Colonies—
and when, upon a little further enquiry, you might easily have obtained
the above contradiction and explanation.

'I have only to add, that in the event of your not inserting this letter in your Paper of Sunday next, or of your repeating or insinuating any further slander upon the character of my father, the late Mr. James Wedderburn, of Inveresk, I have instructed my Solicitor to take immediate measures for obtaining legal redress against you.

'I am, Sir, your humble Servant,

A. COLVILLE.

35, Leadenhall Street, March 17th, 1824.

[. . .]

To The Editor of *Bell's Life in London*

SIR,—I did not expect, when I communicated my statement, as it appeared in your Paper of the 29th ult. that any person would have had the temerity, not to say audacity, to have contradicted my assertion, and thereby occasion me to PROVE the deep depravity of the man to whom I owe my existence. I deem it now an imperative duty to reply to the infamous letter of A. COLVILE, alias WEDDERBURN, and to defend the memory of my unfortunate mother, a woman virtuous in principle, but a Slave, and a sacrifice to the unprincipled lust of my father.—Your Correspondent, *my dear and affectionate brother*, will, doubtless, laugh, when he hears of the VIRTUES of SLAVES, *unless such as will enhance their price*—but I shall leave it to your readers to decide on the *laugh* of a Slave-Dealer after the picture of lust and cruelty and avarice, which I mean to lay before them. *My dear brother's statement* is FALSE, when he says that I was not born till several years after my mother was sold by my father:—but let me tell him, that my mother was pregnant *at* the time of *sale*, and that I was born within four months after it took place. One of the conditions of the sale was, that her offspring, your humble servant, was to be free, from its birth, and I thank my GOD, that through a long life of hardship and adversity, I have ever been free both in mind and body: and have always raised my voice in behalf of my enslaved countrymen! My mother had, previously to my birth, borne two other sons to JAMES WEDDERBURN, Esq. of Inveresk, Slave-Dealer, one of whom, a mill-wright, works now upon the family estate in Jamaica, and has done his whole life-time; and so far was my father from doubting me to be his son, that he recorded my freedom, and that of my brother JAMES, the millwright, himself, in the Government Secretary's Office; where it may be seen to this day. *My dear brother* states that my mother was of a violent temper, which was the reason of my father selling her;— yes, and I glory in her *rebellious* disposition, and which I have inherited from her. My honoured father's house was, in fact, nothing more than a

Seraglio of Black Slaves, miserable objects of an abandoned lust, guided by avarice; and it was from this den of iniquity that she (my mother) was determined to escape. A Lady DOUGLAS, of the parish of St. Mary, was my mother's purchaser, and also stood my godmother. Perhaps, *my dear brother* knows nothing of one ESTHER TROTTER, a free tawny, who bore my father two children, a boy and a girl, and which children my inhuman father *transported to Scotland*, to gratify his malice, because their mother refused to be any longer the object of his lust, and because she claimed support for herself and offspring? Those children *my dear and loving brother* knows under the name of Graham, being brought up in the same house with them at Inveresk. It is true that I did apply to *my dear brother*, A. COLVILE—as he signs himself, but his real name is WEDDERBURN—for some pecuniary assistance; but it was upon the ground of *right*, according to *Deuteronomy*, xxi.10, 17.

'If a man have two wives, one beloved and another hated, and they have borne him children, both the beloved and the hated, and if the first-born son be her's that was hated;

'Then it shall be, when he maketh his sons to inherit that which he hath, that he may not make the son of the beloved first-born before the son of the hated, which is, indeed, the first-born;

'But he shall acknowledge the son of the hated for the first-born, by giving him a double portion of all that he hath, for he is the beginning of his strength, the right of the first-born is his.'

I was at that time, Mr. Editor, in extreme distress; the quartern loaf was then 1s. 10d., I was out of work, and my wife was lying in, which I think was some excuse for applying to an *affectionate brother*, who refused to relieve me. He says that he knew nothing of me before that time; but he will remember seeing me at his father's house five years before—the precise time I forget, but A. COLVILE will recollect it, when I state, that it was the very day on which one of our *dear* father's cows died in calving, and when a butcher was sent for from Musselburgh, *to kill the dead beast*, and take it to market—a perfect specimen of Scotch economy. It was seven years after my arrival in England that I visited my father, who had the inhumanity to threaten to send me to gaol if I troubled him. I never saw my worthy father in Britain but this time, and then he did not abuse my mother, as my dear brother, A. COLVILE, has done; nor did he deny me to be his son, but called me a *lazy fellow*, and said he would do nothing for me. From his cook I had one draught of small beer, and his footman gave me a cracked sixpence—and these are all the obligations I am under to my *worthy* father and *my dear brother*, A. COLVILLE. It is false where my brother says I was taken before the Sheriff of the County—I applied to the Council of the City of Edinburgh for assistance, and they gave me 16d. and a travelling pass; and for my passage up to London I was indebted to the Captain of a Berwick smack.

In conclusion, Mr. Editor, I have to say, that if *my dear brother* means to *show fight* before the Nobs at Westminster, I shall soon give him an opportunity, as I mean to publish my whole history in a cheap pamphlet, and to give the public a specimen of the inhumanity, cruelty, avarice, and diabolical lust of the West-India Slave-Holders; and in the Courts of Justice I will defend and prove my assertions.

I am, Sir, your obedient Servant,

ROBERT WEDDERBURN

23, Russell Court, Drury Lane.

I could expatiate at great length on the inhumanity and cruelty of the West-India planters, were I not fearful that I should become wearisome on so notorious a subject. My brother, ANDREW COLVILE, is a tolerable specimen of them, as may be seen by his letter, his cruelty venting itself in slandering my mother's memory, and his bullying in threatening the Editor with a prosecution. I have now fairly given him the challenge; let him meet it if he dare. My readers can form some idea what Andrew is in a free country, and what he would be in Jamaica, on his sugar estates, amongst his own slaves. Verily, he is 'a chip of the old block.' To make one exception to this family, I must state, that ANDREW COLVILE's elder brother, who is now dead, when he came over to Jamaica, acknowledged his father's tawny children, and, amongst them, my brothers as his brothers. He once invited them all to a dinner, and behaved very free and familiar to them. I was in England at that time. Let my dear brother Andrew deny this, if he can, also.

I should have gone back to Jamaica, had I not been fearful of the planters; for such is their hatred of any one having black blood in his veins, and who dares to think and act as a free man, that they would most certainly have trumped up some charge against me, and hung me. With them I should have had no mercy. In a future part of my history I shall give some particulars of the treatment of the blacks in the West Indies, and the prospect of a general rebellion and massacre there, from my own experience. In the mean time, I bid my readers farewell.

R. WEDDERBURN.

23, Russell Court, Drury Lane.

Source: Robert Wedderburn, *The Horrors of Slavery and Other Writings by Robert Wedderburn*, ed. I. McCalman, Edinburgh, Edinburgh University Press, 1991 [1824], pp. 44–53, 58–61.

Mary Prince, *The History of Mary Prince*, 1831

Extract 9

The history of Mary Prince, a West Indian slave (Related by herself)

I WAS born at Brackish-Pond, in Bermuda, on a farm belonging to Mr Charles Myners. My mother was a household slave; and my father, whose name was Prince, was a sawyer belonging to Mr Trimmingham, a ship-builder at Crow-Lane. When I was an infant, old Mr Myners died, and there was a division of the slaves and other property among the family. I was bought along with my mother by old Captain Darrel, and given to his grandchild, little Miss Betsey Williams. Captain Williams, Mr Darrel's son-in-law, was master of a vessel which traded to several places in America and the West Indies, and he was seldom at home long together.

Mrs Williams was a kind-hearted good woman, and she treated all her slaves well. She had only one daughter, Miss Betsey, for whom I was purchased, and who was about my own age. I was made quite a pet of by Miss Betsey, and loved her very much. She used to lead me about by the hand, and call me her little nigger. This was the happiest period of my life; for I was too young to understand rightly my condition as a slave, and too thoughtless and full of spirits to look forward to the days of toil and sorrow.

My mother was a household slave in the same family. I was under her own care, and my little brothers and sisters were my play-fellows and companions. My mother had several fine children after she came to Mrs Williams, – three girls and two boys. The tasks given out to us children were light, and we used to play together with Miss Betsey, with as much freedom almost as if she had been our sister.

My master, however, was a very harsh, selfish man; and we always dreaded his return from sea. His wife was herself much afraid of him; and, during his stay at home, seldom dared to shew her usual kindness to the slaves. He often left her, in the most distressed circumstances, to reside in other female society, at some place in the West Indies of which I have forgot the name. My poor mistress bore his ill-treatment with great patience, and all her slaves loved and pitied her. I was truly attached to her, and, next to my own mother, loved her better than any creature in the world. My obedience to her commands was cheerfully given: it sprung solely from the affection I felt for her, and not from fear of the power which the white people's law had given her over me.

I had scarcely reached my twelfth year when my mistress became too poor to keep so many of us at home; and she hired me out to Mrs Pruden, a lady who lived about five miles off, in the adjoining parish, in a large house near the sea. I cried bitterly at parting with my dear mistress and Miss Betsey, and when I kissed my mother and brothers and sisters, I thought my young heart would break, it pained me so. But there was no help; I was forced to go. Good Mrs Williams comforted me by saying that I should still be near the home I was about to quit, and might come over and see her and my kindred whenever I could obtain leave of absence from Mrs Pruden. A few hours after this I was taken to a strange house, and found myself among strange people. This separation seemed a sore trial to me then; but oh! 'twas light, light to the trials I have since endured! – 'twas nothing – nothing to be mentioned with them; but I was a child then, and it was according to my strength.

I knew that Mrs Williams could no longer maintain me; that she was fain to part with me for my food and clothing; and I tried to submit myself to the change. My new mistress was a passionate woman; but yet she did not treat me very unkindly. I do not remember her striking me but once, and that was for going to see Mrs Williams when I heard she was sick, and staying longer than she had given me leave to do. All my employment at this time was nursing a sweet baby, little Master Daniel; and I grew so fond of my nursling that it was my greatest delight to walk out with him by the sea-shore, accompanied by his brother and sister, Miss Fanny and Master James. – Dear Miss Fanny! She was a sweet, kind young lady, and so fond of me that she wished me to learn all that she knew herself; and her method of teaching me was as follows: – Directly she had said her lessons to her grandmamma, she used to come running to me, and make me repeat them one by one after her; and in a few months I was able not only to say my letters but to spell many small words. But this happy state was not to last long. Those days were too pleasant to last. My heart always softens when I think of them.

At this time Mrs Williams died. I was told suddenly of her death, and my grief was so great that, forgetting I had the baby in my arms, I ran away directly to my poor mistress's house; but reached it only in time to see the corpse carried out. Oh, that was a day of sorrow, – a heavy day! All the slaves cried. My mother cried and lamented her sore; and I (foolish creature!) vainly entreated them to bring my dear mistress back to life. I knew nothing rightly about death then, and it seemed a hard thing to bear. When I thought about my mistress I felt as if the world was all gone wrong; and for many days and weeks I could think of nothing else. I returned to Mrs Pruden's; but my sorrow was too great to be comforted, for my own dear mistress was always in my mind.

Whether in the house or abroad, my thoughts were always talking to me about her.

I staid at Mrs Pruden's about three months after this; I was then sent back to Mr Williams to be sold. Oh, that was a sad sad time! I recollect the day well. Mrs Pruden came to me and said, 'Mary, you will have to go home directly; your master is going to be married, and he means to sell you and two of your sisters to raise money for the wedding.' Hearing this I burst out a crying, – though I was then far from being sensible of the full weight of my misfortune, or of the misery that waited for me. Besides, I did not like to leave Mrs Pruden, and the dear baby, who had grown very fond of me. For some time I could scarcely believe that Mrs Pruden was in earnest, till I received orders for my immediate return. – Dear Miss Fanny! how she cried at parting with me, whilst I kissed and hugged the baby, thinking I should never see him again. I left Mrs Pruden's, and walked home with a heart full of sorrow. The idea of being sold away from my mother and Miss Betsey was so frightful, that I dared not trust myself to think about it. We had been bought of Mr Myners, as I have mentioned, by Miss Betsey's grandfather, and given to her, so that we were by right *her* property, and I never thought we should be separated or sold away from her.

When I reached the house, I went in directly to Miss Betsey. I found her in great distress; and she cried out as soon as she saw me, 'Oh, Mary! my father is going to sell you all to raise money to marry that wicked woman. You are *my* slaves, and he has no right to sell you; but it is all to please her.' She then told me that my mother was living with her father's sister at a house close by, and I went there to see her. It was a sorrowful meeting; and we lamented with a great and sore crying our unfortunate situation. 'Here comes one of my poor picaninnies!' she said, the moment I came in, 'one of the poor slave-brood who are to be sold to-morrow.'

Oh dear! I cannot bear to think of that day, – it is too much. – It recalls the great grief that filled my heart, and the woeful thoughts that passed to and fro through my mind, whilst listening to the pitiful words of my poor mother, weeping for the loss of her children. I wish I could find words to tell you all I then felt and suffered. The great God above alone knows the thoughts of the poor slave's heart, and the bitter pains which follow such separations as these. All that we love taken away from us – Oh, it is sad, sad! and sore to be borne! – I got no sleep that night for thinking of the morrow; and dear Miss Betsey was scarcely less distressed. She could not bear to part with her old playmates, and she cried sore and would not be pacified.

The black morning at length came; it came too soon for my poor mother and us. Whilst she was putting on us the new osnaburgs in which we were to be sold, she said, in a sorrowful voice, (I shall never forget it!) 'See, I am *shrouding* my poor children; what a task for a mother!' – She then called Miss Betsey to take leave of us. 'I am going to carry my little chickens to market,' (these were her very words,) 'take your last look of them; may be you will see them no more.' 'Oh, my poor slaves! my own slaves!' said dear Miss Betsey, 'you belong to me; and it grieves my heart to part with you.' – Miss Betsey kissed us all, and, when she left us, my mother called the rest of the slaves to bid us good bye. One of them, a woman named Moll, came with her infant in her arms. 'Ah!' said my mother, seeing her turn away and look at her child with the tears in her eyes, 'your turn will come next.' The slaves could say nothing to comfort us; they could only weep and lament with us. When I left my dear little brothers and the house in which I had been brought up, I thought my heart would burst.

Our mother, weeping as she went, called me away with the children Hannah and Dinah, and we took the road that led to Hamble Town, which we reached about four o'clock in the afternoon. We followed my mother to the market-place, where she placed us in a row against a large house, with our backs to the wall and our arms folded across our breasts. I, as the eldest, stood first, Hannah next to me, then Dinah; and our mother stood beside, crying over us. My heart throbbed with grief and terror so violently, that I pressed my hands quite tightly across my breast, but I could not keep it still, and it continued to leap as though it would burst out of my body. But who cared for that? Did one of the many by-standers, who were looking at us so carelessly, think of the pain that wrung the hearts of the negro woman and her young ones? No, no! They were not all bad, I dare say, but slavery hardens white people's hearts towards the blacks; and many of them were not slow to make their remarks upon us aloud, without regard to our grief – though their light words fell like cayenne on the fresh wounds of our hearts. Oh those white people have small hearts who can only feel for themselves.

At length the vendue master, who was to offer us for sale like sheep or cattle, arrived, and asked my mother which was the eldest. She said nothing, but pointed to me. He took me by the hand, and led me out into the middle of the street, and, turning me slowly round, exposed me to the view of those who attended the vendue. I was soon surrounded by strange men, who examined and handled me in the same manner that a butcher would a calf or a lamb he was about to purchase, and who talked about my shape and size in like words – as if I could no more understand their meaning than the dumb beasts. I was then put up to sale. The bidding commenced at a few pounds, and gradually rose to fifty-seven,[27] when I was knocked down to the highest bidder; and the

[27] Bermuda currency: about £18 sterling.*

people who stood by said that I had fetched a great sum for so young a slave.

I then saw my sisters led forth, and sold to different owners; so that we had not the sad satisfaction of being partners in bondage. When the sale was over, my mother hugged and kissed us, and mourned over us, begging of us to keep up a good heart, and do our duty to our new masters. It was a sad parting; one went one way, one another, and our poor mammy went home with nothing.

My new master was a Captain I—, who lived at Spanish Point. After parting with my mother and sisters, I followed him to his store, and he gave me into the charge of his son, a lad about my own age, Master Benjy, who took me to my new home. I did not know where I was going, or what my new master would do with me. My heart was quite broken with grief, and my thoughts went back continually to those from whom I had been so suddenly parted. 'Oh, my mother! my mother!' I kept saying to myself, 'Oh, my mammy and my sisters and my brothers, shall I never see you again!'

Oh, the trials! the trials! they make the salt water come into my eyes when I think of the days in which I was afflicted – the times that are gone; when I mourned and grieved with a young heart for those whom I loved.

It was night when I reached my new home. The house was large, and built at the bottom of a very high hill; but I could not see much of it that night. I saw too much of it afterwards. The stones and the timber were the best things in it; they were not so hard as the hearts of the owners.[28]

Before I entered the house, two slave women, hired from another owner, who were at work in the yard, spoke to me, and asked who I belonged to? I replied, 'I am come to live here.' 'Poor child, poor child!' they both said; 'you must keep a good heart, if you are to live here.' – When I went in, I stood up crying in a corner. Mrs I— came and took off my hat, a little black silk hat Miss Pruden made for me, and said in a rough voice, 'You are not come here to stand up in corners and cry, you are come here to work.' She then put a child into my arms, and, tired as I was, I was forced instantly to take up my old occupation of a nurse. – I could not bear to look at my mistress, her countenance was so stern. She was a stout tall woman with a very dark complexion, and her brows were always drawn together into a frown. I thought of the words of the two slave women when I saw Mrs I—, and heard the harsh sound of her voice.

The person I took the most notice of that night was a French Black called Hetty, whom my master took in privateering from another vessel,

[28] These strong expressions, and all of a similar character in this little narrative, are given verbatim as uttered by Mary Prince.*

and made his slave. She was the most active woman I ever saw, and she was tasked to her utmost. A few minutes after my arrival she came in from milking the cows, and put the sweet-potatoes on for supper. She then fetched home the sheep, and penned them in the fold; drove home the cattle, and staked them about the pond side;[29] fed and rubbed down my master's horse, and gave the hog and the fed cow[30] their suppers; prepared the beds, and undressed the children, and laid them to sleep. I liked to look at her and watch all her doings, for her's was the only friendly face I had as yet seen, and I felt glad that she was there. She gave me my supper of potatoes and milk, and a blanket to sleep upon, which she spread for me in the passage before the door of Mrs I—'s chamber.

I got a sad fright, that night. I was just going to sleep, when I heard a noise in my mistress's room; and she presently called out to inquire if some work was finished that she had ordered Hetty to do. 'No, Ma'am, not yet,' was Hetty's answer from below. On hearing this, my master started up from his bed, and just as he was, in his shirt, ran down stairs with a long cow-skin[31] in his hand. I heard immediately after, the cracking of the thong, and the house rang to the shrieks of poor Hetty, who kept crying out, 'Oh, Massa! Massa! me dead. Massa! have mercy upon me – don't kill me outright.' – This was a sad beginning for me. I sat up upon my blanket, trembling with terror, like a frightened hound, and thinking that my turn would come next. At length the house became still, and I forget for a little while all my sorrows by falling fast asleep.

The next morning my mistress set about instructing me in my tasks. She taught me to do all sorts of household work; to wash and bake, pick cotton and wool, and wash floors, and cook. And she taught me (how can I ever forget it!) more things than these; she caused me to know the exact difference between the smart of the rope, the cart-whip, and the cow-skin, when applied to my naked body by her own cruel hand. And there was scarcely any punishment more dreadful than the blows I received on my face and head from her hard heavy fist. She was a fearful woman, and a savage mistress to her slaves.

There were two little slave boys in the house, on whom she vented her bad temper in a special manner. One of these children was a mulatto, called Cyrus, who had been bought while an infant in his mother's arms; the other, Jack, was an African from the coast of Guinea, whom a sailor had given or sold to my master. Seldom a day passed without these boys

[29] The cattle on a small plantation in Bermuda are, it seems, often thus staked or tethered, both night and day, in situations where grass abounds.*
[30] A cow fed for slaughter.*
[31] A thong of hard twisted hide, known by this name in the West Indies.*

receiving the most severe treatment, and often for no fault at all. Both my master and mistress seemed to think that they had a right to ill-use them at their pleasure; and very often accompanied their commands with blows, whether the children were behaving well or ill. I have seen their flesh ragged and raw with licks. – Lick – lick – they were never secure one moment from a blow, and their lives were passed in continual fear. My mistress was not contented with using the whip, but often pinched their cheeks and arms in the most cruel manner. My pity for these poor boys was soon transferred to myself; for I was licked, and flogged, and pinched by her pitiless fingers in the neck and arms, exactly as they were. To strip me naked – to hang me up by the wrists and lay my flesh open with the cow-skin, was an ordinary punishment for even a slight offence. My mistress often robbed me too of the hours that belong to sleep. She used to sit up very late, frequently even until morning; and I had then to stand at a bench and wash during the greater part of the night, or pick wool and cotton; and often I have dropped down overcome by sleep and fatigue, till roused from a state of stupor by the whip, and forced to start up to my tasks.

Poor Hetty, my fellow slave, was very kind to me, and I used to call her my Aunt; but she led a most miserable life, and her death was hastened (at least the slaves all believed and said so,) by the dreadful chastisement she received from my master during her pregnancy. It happened as follows. One of the cows had dragged the rope away from the stake to which Hetty had fastened it, and got loose. My master flew into a terrible passion, and ordered the poor creature to be stripped quite naked, notwithstanding her pregnancy, and to be tied up to a tree in the yard. He then flogged her as hard as he could lick, both with the whip and cowskin, till she was all over streaming with blood. He rested, and then beat her again and again. Her shrieks were terrible. The consequence was that poor Hetty was brought to bed before her time, and was delivered after severe labour of a dead child. She appeared to recover after her confinement, so far that she was repeatedly flogged by both master and mistress afterwards; but her former strength never returned to her. Ere long her body and limbs swelled to a great size; and she lay on a mat in the kitchen, till the water burst out of her body and she died. All the slaves said that death was a good thing for poor Hetty; but I cried very much for her death. The manner of it filled me with horror. I could not bear to think about it; yet it was always present to my mind for many a day.

After Hetty died all her labours fell upon me, in addition to my own. I had now to milk eleven cows every morning before sunrise, sitting among the damp weeds; to take care of the cattle as well as the children; and to do the work of the house. There was no end to my toils – no end to my blows. I lay down at night and rose up in the morning in fear and sorrow; and often wished that like poor Hetty I could escape from this cruel bondage and be at rest in the grave. But the hand of that God whom then I knew not, was stretched over me; and I was mercifully preserved for better things. It was then, however, my heavy lot to weep, weep, weep, and that for years; to pass from one misery to another, and from one cruel master to a worse. But I must go on with the thread of my story.

One day a heavy squall of wind and rain came on suddenly, and my mistress sent me round the corner of the house to empty a large earthen jar. The jar was already cracked with an old deep crack that divided it in the middle, and in turning it upside down to empty it, it parted in my hand. I could not help the accident, but I was dreadfully frightened, looking forward to a severe punishment. I ran crying to my mistress, 'O mistress, the jar has come in two.' 'You have broken it, have you?' she replied; 'come directly here to me.' I came trembling: she stripped and flogged me long and severely with the cow-skin; as long as she had strength to use the lash, for she did not give over till she was quite tired. – When my master came home at night, she told him of my fault; and oh, frightful! how he fell a swearing. After abusing me with every ill name he could think of, (too, too bad to speak in England,) and giving me several heavy blows with his hand, he said, 'I shall come home to-morrow morning at twelve, on purpose to give you a round hundred.' He kept his word – Oh sad for me! I cannot easily forget it. He tied me up upon a ladder, and gave me a hundred lashes with his own hand, and master Benjy stood by to count them for him. When he had licked me for some time he sat down to take breath; then after resting, he beat me again and again, until he was quite wearied, and so hot (for the weather was very sultry), that he sank back in his chair, almost like to faint. While my mistress went to bring him drink, there was a dreadful earthquake. Part of the roof fell down, and every thing in the house went – clatter, clatter, clatter. Oh I thought the end of all things near at hand; and I was so sore with the flogging, that I scarcely cared whether I lived or died. The earth was groaning and shaking; every thing tumbling about; and my mistress and the slaves were shrieking and crying out, 'The earthquake! the earthquake!' It was an awful day for us all.

During the confusion I crawled away on my hands and knees, and laid myself down under the steps of the piazza, in front of the house. I was in a dreadful state – my body all blood and bruises, and I could not help moaning piteously. The other slaves, when they saw me, shook their heads and said, 'Poor child! poor child!' – I lay there till the morning, careless of what might happen, for life was very weak in me, and I wished more than ever to die. But when we are very young, death always seems a great way off, and it would not come that night to me. The next morning I was forced by my master to rise and go about my usual work, though my body and limbs were so stiff and sore, that I could not move without the greatest pain. – Nevertheless, even after all this severe punishment, I never heard the last of that jar; my mistress was always throwing it in my face.

Some little time after this, one of the cows got loose from the stake, and eat one of the sweet-potatoe slips. I was milking when my master found it out. He came to me, and without any more ado, stooped down, and taking off his heavy boot, he struck me such a severe blow in the small of my back, that I shrieked with agony, and thought I was killed; and I feel a weakness in that part to this day. The cow was frightened at his violence, and kicked down the pail and spilt the milk all about. My master knew that this accident was his own fault, but he was so enraged that he seemed glad of an excuse to go on with his ill usage. I cannot remember how many licks he gave me then, but he beat me till I was unable to stand, and till he himself was weary.

After this I ran away and went to my mother, who was living with Mr Richard Darrel. My poor mother was both grieved and glad to see me; grieved because I had been so ill used, and glad because she had not seen me for a long, long while. She dared not receive me into the house, but she hid me up in a hole in the rocks near, and brought me food at night, after every body was asleep. My father, who lived at Crow-Lane, over the salt-water channel, last heard of my being hid up in the cavern, and he came and took me back to my master. Oh I was loth, loth to go back; but as there was no remedy, I was obliged to submit.

When we got home, my poor father said to Capt. I—, 'Sir, I am sorry that my child should be forced to run away from her owner; but the treatment she has received is enough to break her heart. The sight of her wounds has nearly broke mine. – I entreat you, for the love of God, to forgive her for running away, and that you will be a kind master to her in future.' Capt. I— said I was used as well as I deserved, and that I ought to be punished for running away. I then took courage and said that I could stand the floggings no longer; that I was weary of my life, and therefore I had run away to my mother; but mothers could only weep and mourn over their children, they could not save them from cruel masters – from the whip, the rope, and the cow-skin. He told me to hold my tongue and go about my work, or he would find a way to settle me. He did not, however, flog me that day.

For five years after this I remained in his house, and almost daily received the same harsh treatment. At length he put me on board a sloop, and to my great joy sent me away to Turk's Island. I was not permitted to see my mother or father, or poor sisters and brothers, to say good bye, though going away to a strange land, and might never see them again. Oh the Buckra people who keep slaves think that black people are like cattle, without natural affection. But my heart tells me it is far otherwise.

We were nearly four weeks on the voyage, which was unusually long. Sometimes we had a light breeze, sometimes a great calm, and the ship made no way; so that our provisions and water ran very low, and we were put upon short allowance. I should almost have been starved had it not been for the kindness of a black man called Anthony, and his wife, who had brought their own victuals, and shared them with me.

When we went ashore at the Grand Quay, the captain sent me to the house of my new master, Mr D—, to whom Captain I— had sold me. Grand Quay is a small town upon a sandbank; the houses low and built of wood. Such was my new master's. The first person I saw, on my arrival, was Mr D—, a stout sulky looking man, who carried me through the hall to show me to his wife and children. Next day I was put up by the vendue master to know how much I was worth, and I was valued at one hundred pounds currency.

My new master was one of the owners or holders of the salt ponds, and he received a certain sum for every slave that worked upon his premises, whether they were young or old. This sum was allowed him out of the profits arising from the salt works. I was immediately sent to work in the salt water with the rest of the slaves. This work was perfectly new to me. I was given a half barrel and a shovel, and had to stand up to my knees in the water, from four o'clock in the morning till nine, when we were given some Indian corn boiled in water, which we were obliged to swallow as fast as we could for fear the rain should come on and melt the salt. We were then called again to our tasks, and worked through the heat of the day; the sun flaming upon our heads like fire, and raising salt blisters in those parts which were not completely covered. Our feet and legs, from standing in the salt water for so many hours, soon became full of dreadful boils, which eat down in some cases to the very bone, afflicting the sufferers with great torment. We came home at twelve; ate our corn soup, called *blawly*, as fast as we could, and went back to our employment till dark at night. We then shovelled up the salt in large heaps, and went down to the sea, where we washed the pickle from our limbs, and cleaned the barrows and shovels from the salt. When we returned to the house, our master gave us each our allowance of raw Indian corn, which we pounded in a mortar and boiled in water for our suppers.

We slept in a long shed, divided into narrow slips, like the stalls used for cattle. Boards fixed upon stakes driven into the ground, without mat or covering, were our only beds. On Sundays, after we had washed the salt bags, and done other work required of us, we went into the bush and cut the long soft grass, of which we made trusses for our legs and feet to rest upon, for they were so full of the salt boils that we could get no rest lying upon the bare boards.

Though we worked from morning till night, there was no satisfying Mr D—. I hoped, when I left Capt. I—, that I should have been better off, but I found it was but going from one butcher to another. There was this difference between them: my former master used to beat me while raging and foaming with passion; Mr D—was usually quite calm. He would stand by and give orders for a slave to be cruelly whipped, and assist in the punishment, without moving a muscle of his face; walking about and taking snuff with the greatest composure. Nothing could touch his hard heart – neither sighs, nor tears, nor prayers, nor streaming blood; he was deaf to our cries, and careless of our sufferings. – Mr D— has often stripped me naked, hung me up by the wrists, and beat me with the cow-skin, with his own hand, till my body was raw with gashes. Yet there was nothing very remarkable in this; for it might serve as a sample of the common usage of the slaves on that horrible island.

Owing to the boils in my feet, I was unable to wheel the barrow fast through the sand, which got into the sores, and made me stumble at every step; and my master, having no pity for my sufferings from this cause, rendered them far more intolerable, by chastising me for not being able to move so fast as he wished me. Another of our employments was to row a little way off from the shore in a boat, and dive for large stones to build a wall round our master's house. This was very hard work; and the great waves breaking over us continually, made us often so giddy that we lost our footing, and were in danger of being drowned.

Ah, poor me! – my tasks were never ended. Sick or well, it was work – work – work! – After the diving season was over, we were sent to the South Creek, with large bills, to cut up mangoes to burn lime with. Whilst one party of slaves were thus employed, another were sent to the other side of the island to break up coral out of the sea.

When we were ill, let our complaint be what it might, the only medicine given to us was a great bowl of hot salt water, with salt mixed with it, which made us very sick. If we could not keep up with the rest of the gang of slaves, we were put in the stocks, and severely flogged the next morning. Yet, not the less, our master expected, after we had thus been kept from our rest, and our limbs rendered stiff and sore with ill usage, that we should still go through the ordinary tasks of the day all the same. – Sometimes we had to work all night, measuring salt to load a vessel; or turning a machine to draw water out of the sea for the salt-making. Then we had no sleep – no rest – but were forced to work as fast as we could, and go on again all next day the same as usual. Work – work – work – Oh that Turk's Island was a horrible place! The people in England, I am sure, have never found out what is carried on there. Cruel, horrible place!

Mr D— had a slave called old Daniel, whom he used to treat in the most cruel manner. Poor Daniel was lame in the hip, and could not keep up with the rest of the slaves; and our master would order him to be stripped and laid down on the ground, and have him beaten with a rod of rough briar till his skin was quite red and raw. He would then call for a bucket of salt, and fling upon the raw flesh till the man writhed on the ground like a worm, and screamed aloud with agony. This poor man's wounds were never healed, and I have often seen them full of maggots, which increased his torments to an intolerable degree. He was an object of pity and terror to the whole gang of slaves, and in his wretched case we saw, each of us, our own lot, if we should live to be as old.

Oh the horrors of slavery! – How the thought of it pains my heart! But the truth ought to be told of it; and what my eyes have seen I think it is my duty to relate; for few people in England know what slavery is. I have been a slave – I have felt what a slave feels, and I know what a slave knows; and I would have all the good people in England to know it too, that they may break our chains, and set us free.

Mr D— had another slave called Ben. He being very hungry, stole a little rice one night after he came in from work, and cooked it for his supper. But his master soon discovered the theft; locked him up all night; and kept him without food till one o'clock the next day. He then hung Ben up by his hands, and beat him from time to time till the slaves came in at night. We found the poor creature hung up when we came home; with a pool of blood beneath him, and our master still licking him. But this was not the worst. My master's son was in the habit of stealing the rice and rum. Ben had seen him do this, and thought he might do the same, and when master found out that Ben had stolen the rice and swore to punish him, he tried to excuse himself by saying that Master Dickey did the same thing every night. The lad denied it to his father, and was so angry with Ben for informing against him, that out of revenge he ran and got a bayonet, and whilst the poor wretch was suspended by his hands and writhing under his wounds, he run it quite through his foot. I was not by when he did it, but I saw the wound when I came home, and heard Ben tell the manner in which it was done.

I must say something more about this cruel son of a cruel father. – He had no heart – no fear of God; he had been brought up by a bad father in a bad path, and he delighted to follow in the same steps. There was a little old woman among the slaves called Sarah, who was nearly past work; and, Master Dickey being the overseer of the slaves just then, this poor creature, who was subject to several bodily infirmities, and was not quite right in her head, did not wheel the barrow fast enough to please him. He threw her down on the ground, and after beating her severely, he took her up in his arms and flung her among the prickly-pear bushes, which are all covered over with sharp venomous prickles. By this her naked flesh was so grievously wounded, that her body swelled and festered all over, and she died a few days after. In telling my own sorrows, I cannot pass by those of my fellow-slaves – for when I think of my own griefs, I remember theirs.

I think it was about ten years I had worked in the salt ponds at Turk's Island, when my master left off business, and retired to a house he had in Bermuda, leaving his son to succeed him in the island. He took me with him to wait upon his daughters; and I was joyful, for I was sick, sick of Turk's Island, and my heart yearned to see my native place again, my mother, and my kindred.

I had seen my poor mother during the time I was a slave in Turk's Island. One Sunday morning I was on the beach with some of the slaves, and we saw a sloop come in loaded with slaves to work in the salt water. We got a boat and went aboard. When I came upon the deck I asked the black people, 'Is there any one here for me?' 'Yes,' they said, 'your mother.' I thought they said this in jest – I could scarcely believe them for joy; but when I saw my poor mammy my joy was turned to sorrow, for she had gone from her senses. 'Mammy,' I said, 'is this you?' She did not know me. 'Mammy,' I said, 'what's the matter?' She began to talk foolishly, and said that she had been under the vessel's bottom. They had been overtaken by a violent storm at sea. My poor mother had never been on the sea before, and she was so ill, that she lost her senses, and it was long before she came quite to herself again. She had a sweet child with her – a little sister I had never seen, about four years of age, called Rebecca. I took her on shore with me, for I felt I should love her directly; and I kept her with me a week. Poor little thing! her's has been a sad life, and continues so to this day. My mother worked for some years on the island, but was taken back to Bermuda some time before my master carried me again thither.[32]

---

[32] Of the subsequent lot of her relatives she can tell but little. She says, her father died while she and her mother were at Turk's Island; and that he had been long dead and buried before any of his children in Bermuda knew it, they being slaves on other estates. Her mother died after Mary went to Antigua. Of the fate of the rest of her kindred, seven brothers and three sisters, she knows nothing further than this – that the eldest sister, who had several children to her master, was taken by him to Trinidad; and that the youngest, Rebecca, is still alive, and in slavery in Bermuda. Mary herself is now about forty-three years of age.*

After I left Turk's Island, I was told by some negroes that came over from it, that the poor slaves had built up a place with boughs and leaves, where they might meet for prayers, but the white people pulled it down twice, and would not allow them even a shed for prayers. A flood came down soon after and washed away many houses, filled the place with sand, and overflowed the ponds: and I do think that this was for their wickedness; for the Buckra men[33] there were very wicked. I saw and heard much that was very very bad at that place.

I was several years the slave of Mr D— after I returned to my native place. Here I worked in the grounds. My work was planting and hoeing sweet-potatoes, Indian corn, plaintains, bananas, cabbages, pumpkins, onions, &c. I did all the household work, and attended upon a horse and cow besides, – going also upon all errands. I had to curry the horse – to clean and feed him – and sometimes to ride him a little. I had more than enough to do – but still it was not so very bad as Turk's Island.

My old master often got drunk, and then he would get in a fury with his daughter, and beat her till she was not fit to be seen. I remember on one occasion, I had gone to fetch water, and when I was coming up the hill I heard a great screaming; I ran as fast as I could to the house, put down the water, and went into the chamber, where I found my master beating Miss D— dreadfully. I strove with all my strength to get her away from him; for she was all black and blue with bruises. He had beat her with his fist, and almost killed her. The people gave me credit for getting her away. He turned round and began to lick me. Then I said, 'Sir, this is not Turk's Island.' I can't repeat his answer, the words were too wicked – too bad to say. He wanted to treat me the same in Bermuda as he had done in Turk's Island.

He had an ugly fashion of stripping himself quite naked, and ordering me then to wash him in a tub of water. This was worse to me than all the licks. Sometimes when he called me to wash him I could not come, my eyes were so full of shame. He would then come to beat me. One time I had plates and knives in my hand, and I dropped both plates and knives, and some of the plates were broken. He struck me so severely for this, that at last I defended myself, for I thought it was high time to do so. I then told him I would not live longer with him, for he was a very indecent man – very spiteful, and too indecent; with no shame for his servants, no shame for his own flesh. So I went away to a neighbouring house and sat down and cried till the next morning, when I went home again, not knowing what else to do.

---

[33] Negro term for white people.*

After that I was hired to work at Cedar Hills and every Saturday night I paid the money to my master. I had plenty of work to do there – plenty of washing; but yet I made myself pretty comfortable. I earned two dollars and a quarter a week, which is twenty pence a day.

During the time I worked there, I heard that Mr John Wood was going to Antigua. I felt a great wish to go there, and I went to Mr D—, and asked him to let me go in Mr Wood's service. Mr Wood did not then want to purchase me; it was my own fault that I came under him, I was so anxious to go. It was ordained to be, I suppose; God led me there. The truth is, I did not wish to be any longer the slave of my indecent master.

Mr Wood took me with him to Antigua, to the town of St John's, where he lived. This was about fifteen years ago. He did not then know whether I was to be sold; but Mrs Wood found that I could work, and she wanted to buy me. Her husband then wrote to my master to inquire whether I was to be sold? Mr D— wrote in reply, 'that I should not be sold to any one that would treat me ill.' It was strange he should say this, when he had treated me so ill himself. So I was purchased by Mr Wood for 300 dollars, (or £100 Bermuda currency.)[34]

My work there was to attend the chambers and nurse the child, and to go down to the pond and wash clothes. But I soon fell ill of the rheumatism, and grew so very lame that I was forced to walk with a stick. I got the Saint Anthony's fire,[35] also, in my left leg, and became quite a cripple. No one cared much to come near me, and I was ill a long long time; for several months I could not lift the limb. I had to lie in a little old outhouse, that was swarming with bugs and other vermin, which tormented me greatly; but I had no other place to lie in. I got the rheumatism by catching cold at the pond side, from washing in the fresh water; in the salt water I never got cold. The person who lived in next yard, (a Mrs Greene,) could not bear to hear my cries and groans. She was kind, and used to send an old slave woman to help me, who sometimes brought me a little soup. When the doctor found I was so ill, he said I must be put into a bath of hot water. The old slave got the bark of some bush that was good for the pains, which she boiled in the hot water, and every night she came and put me into the bath, and did what she could for me: I don't know what I should have done, or what would have become of me, had it not been for her. – My mistress, it is true, did send me a little food; but no one from our family came near me but the cook, who used

---

[34] About £67. 10s. sterling.*

[35] Also known as erysipelas, Saint Anthony's fire was a form of eruptive fever that could attack any part of the body, and often led to gangrene, and in extreme cases, death. It was treated in the eighteenth century by blood-letting and purges.

to shove my food in at the door, and say, 'Molly, Molly, there's your dinner.' My mistress did not care to take any trouble about me; and if the Lord had not put it into the hearts of the neighbours to be kind to me, I must, I really think, have lain and died.

It was a long time before I got well enough to work in the house. Mrs Wood, in the meanwhile, hired a mulatto woman to nurse the child; but she was such a fine lady she wanted to be mistress over me. I thought it very hard for a coloured woman to have rule over me because I was a slave and she was free. Her name was Martha Wilcox; she was a saucy woman, very saucy; and she went and complained of me, without cause, to my mistress, and made her angry with me. Mrs Wood told me that if I did not mind what I was about, she would get my master to strip me and give me fifty lashes: 'You have been used to the whip,' she said, 'and you shall have it here.' This was the first time she threatened to have me flogged; and she gave me the threatening so strong of what she would have done to me, that I thought I should have fallen down at her feet, I was so vexed and hurt by her words. The mulatto woman was rejoiced to have power to keep me down. She was constantly making mischief; there was no living for the slaves – no peace after she came.

I was also sent by Mrs Wood to be put in the Cage one night, and was next morning flogged, by the magistrate's order, at her desire; and this all for a quarrel I had about a pig with another slave woman. I was flogged on my naked back on this occasion: although I was in no fault after all; for old Justice Dyett, when we came before him, said that I was in the right, and ordered the pig to be given to me. This was about two or three years after I came to Antigua.

When we moved from the middle of the town to the Point, I used to be in the house and do all the work and mind the children, though still very ill with the rheumatism. Every week I had to wash two large bundles of clothes, as much as a boy could help me to lift; but I could give no satisfaction. My mistress was always abusing and fretting after me. It is not possible to tell all her ill language. – One day she followed me foot after foot scolding and rating me. I bore in silence a great deal of ill words: at last my heart was quite full, and I told her that she ought not to use me so; – that when I was ill I might have lain and died for what she cared; and no one would then come near me to nurse me, because they were afraid of my mistress. This was a great affront. She called her husband and told him what I had said. He flew into a passion: but did not beat me then; he only abused and swore at me; and then gave me a note and bade me go and look for an owner. Not that he meant to sell me; but he did this to please his wife and to frighten me. I went to Adam White, a cooper, a free black, who had money, and asked him to buy me.

He went directly to Mr Wood, but was informed that I was not to be sold. The next day my master whipped me.

Another time (about five years ago) my mistress got vexed with me, because I fell sick and I could not keep on with my work. She complained to her husband, and he sent me off again to look for an owner. I went to a Mr Burchell, showed him the note, and asked him to buy me for my own benefit; for I had saved about 100 dollars, and hoped, with a little help, to purchase my freedom. He accordingly went to my master: – 'Mr Wood,' he said, 'Molly has brought me a note that she wants an owner. If you intend to sell her, I may as well buy her as another.' My master put him off and said that he did not mean to sell me. I was very sorry at this, for I had no comfort with Mrs Wood, and I wished greatly to get my freedom.

The way in which I made my money was this. – When my master and mistress went from home, as they sometimes did, and left me to take care of the house and premises, I had a good deal of time to myself, and made the most of it. I took in washing, and sold coffee and yams and other provisions to the captains of ships. I did not sit still idling during the absence of my owners; for I wanted, by all honest means, to earn money to buy my freedom. Sometimes I bought a hog cheap on board ship, and sold it for double the money on shore; and I also earned a good deal by selling coffee. By this means I by degrees acquired a little cash. A gentleman also lent me some to help to buy my freedom – but when I could not get free he got it back again. His name was Captain Abbot.

My master and mistress went on one occasion into the country, to Date Hill, for change of air, and carried me with them to take charge of the children, and to do the work of the house. While I was in the country, I saw how the field negroes are worked in Antigua. They are worked very hard and fed but scantily. They are called out to work before daybreak, and come home after dark; and then each has to heave his bundle of grass for the cattle in the pen. Then, on Sunday morning, each slave has to go out and gather a large bundle of grass; and, when they bring it home, they have all to sit at the manager's door and wait till he come out: often they have to wait there till past eleven o'clock, without any breakfast. After that, those that have yams or potatoes, or fire-wood to sell, hasten to market to buy a dog's worth[36] of salt fish, or pork, which is a great treat for them. Some of them buy a little pickle out of the shad barrels, which they call sauce, to season their yams and Indian corn. It is very wrong, I know, to work on Sunday or go to market; but will not God call the Buckra men to answer for this on the great day of judgment – since they will give the slaves no other day?

[36] A dog is the 72nd part of a dollar.*

219

While we were at Date Hill Christmas came; and the slave woman who had the care of the place (which then belonged to Mr Roberts the marshal), asked me to go with her to her husband's house, to a Methodist meeting for prayer, at a plantation called Winthorps. I went; and they were the first prayers I ever understood. One woman prayed; and then they all sung a hymn; then there was another prayer and another hymn; and then they all spoke by turns of their own griefs as sinners. The husband of the woman I went with was a black driver. His name was Henry. He confessed that he had treated the slaves very cruelly; but said that he was compelled to obey the orders of his master. He prayed them all to forgive him, and he prayed that God would forgive him. He said it was a horrid thing for a ranger[37] to have sometimes to beat his own wife or sister; but he must do so if ordered by his master.

I felt sorry for my sins also. I cried the whole night, but I was too much ashamed to speak. I prayed God to forgive me. This meeting had a great impression on my mind, and led my spirit to the Moravian church;[38] so that when I got back to town, I went and prayed to have my name put down in the Missionaries' book; and I followed the church earnestly every opportunity. I did not then tell my mistress about it; for I knew that she would not give me leave to go. But I felt I *must* go. Whenever I carried the children their lunch at school, I ran round and went to hear the teachers.

The Moravian ladies (Mrs Richter, Mrs Olufsen, and Mrs Sauter) taught me to read in the class; and I got on very fast. In this class there were all sorts of people, old and young, grey headed folks and children; but most of them were free people. After we had done spelling, we tried to read in the Bible. After the reading was over, the missionary gave out a hymn for us to sing. I dearly loved to go to the church, it was so solemn. I never knew rightly that I had much sin till I went there. When I found out that I was a great sinner, I was very sorely grieved, and very much frightened. I used to pray God to pardon my sins for Christ's sake, and forgive me for every thing I had done amiss; and when I went home to my work, I always thought about what I had heard from the missionaries, and wished to be good that I might go to heaven. After a while I was admitted a candidate for the holy Communion. – I had been baptized long before this, in the year 1817, by the Rev. Mr Curtin, of the

---

[37] The head negro of an estate – a person who has the chief superintendence under the manager.*

[38] The Moravians were a Protestant sect with fifteenth-century origins, who were particularly active in missionary work in the eighteenth century. They were distinguished from other missionary societies by their highly ordered social and religious regimen, and enjoyed substantial successes in the West Indies, with 5,465 recorded converts on Antigua alone by 1787.

English Church, after I had been taught to repeat the Creed and the Lord's Prayer. I wished at that time to attend a Sunday School taught by Mr Curtin, but he would not receive me without a written note from my master, granting his permission. I did not ask my owner's permission, from the belief that it would be refused; so that I got no farther instruction at that time from the English Church.[39]

Some time after I began to attend the Moravian Church, I met with Daniel James, afterwards my dear husband. He was a carpenter and cooper to his trade; an honest, hard-working, decent black man, and a widower. He had purchased his freedom of his mistress, old Mrs Baker, with money he had earned whilst a slave. When he asked me to marry him, I took time to consider the matter over with myself, and would not say yes till he went to church with me and joined the Moravians. He was very industrious after he bought his freedom; and he had hired a comfortable house, and had convenient things about him. We were joined in marriage, about Christmas 1826, in the Moravian Chapel at Spring Gardens, by the Rev. Mr Olufsen. We could not be married in the English Church. English marriage is not allowed to slaves; and no free man can marry a slave woman.

When Mr Wood heard of my marriage, he flew into a great rage, and sent for Daniel, who was helping to build a house for his old mistress. Mr Wood asked him who gave him a right to marry a slave of his? My husband said, 'Sir, I am a free man, and thought I had a right to choose a wife; but if I had known Molly was not allowed to have a husband, I should not have asked her to marry me.' Mrs Wood was more vexed about my marriage than her husband. She could not forgive me for getting married, but stirred up Mr Wood to flog me dreadfully with the horsewhip. I thought it very hard to be whipped at my time of life for getting a husband – I told her so. She said that she would not have nigger men about the yards of premises, or allow a nigger man's clothes to be washed in the same tub where hers were washed. She was fearful, I think, that I should lose her time, in order to wash and do thing for my husband; but I had then no time to wash for myself; I was obliged to put out my own clothes, though I was always at the wash-tub.

I had not much happiness in my marriage, owing to my being a slave. It made my husband sad to see me so ill-treated. Mrs Wood was always

---

[39] She possesses a copy of Mrs Trimmer's 'Charity School Spelling Book,' presented to her by the Rev. Mr Curtin, and dated August 30, 1817. In this book her name is written 'Mary, Princess of Wales' – an appellation which, she says, was given her by her owners. It is a common practice with the colonists to give ridiculous names of this description to their slaves; being, in fact, one of the numberless modes of expressing the habitual contempt with which they regard the negro race. – In printing this narrative we have retained Mary's paternal name of Prince.*

abusing me about him. She did not lick me herself, but she got her husband to do it for her, whilst she fretted the flesh off my bones. Yet for all this she would not sell me. She sold five slaves whilst I was with her; but though she was always finding fault with me, she would not part with me. However, Mr Wood afterwards allowed Daniel to have a place to live in our yard, which we were very thankful for.

After this, I fell ill again with the rheumatism, and was sick a long time; but whether sick or well, I had my work to do. About this time I asked my master and mistress to let me buy my own freedom. With the help of Mr Burchell, I could have found the means to pay Mr Wood; for it was agreed that I should afterwards serve Mr Burchell a while, for the cash he was to advance for me. I was earnest in the request to my owners; but their hearts were hard – too hard to consent. Mrs Wood was very angry – she grew quite outrageous – she called me a black devil, and asked me who had put freedom into my head. 'To be free is very sweet,' I said: but she took good care to keep me a slave. I saw her change colour, and I left the room.

About this time my master and mistress were going to England to put their son to school, and bring their daughters home; and they took me with them to take care of the child. I was willing to come to England: I thought that by going there I should probably get cured of my rheumatism, and should return with my master and mistress, quite well, to my husband. My husband was willing for me to come away, for he had heard that my master would free me, – and I also hoped this might prove true; but it was all a false report.

The steward of the ship was very kind to me. He and my husband were in the same class in the Moravian Church. I was thankful that he was so friendly, for my mistress was not kind to me on the passage; and she told me, when she was angry, that she did not intend to treat me any better in England than in the West Indies – that I need not expect it. And she was as good as her word.

When we drew near to England, the rheumatism seized all my limbs worse than ever, and my body was dreadfully swelled. When we landed at the Tower, I shewed my flesh to my mistress, but she took no great notice of it. We were obliged to stop at the tavern till my master got a house; and a day or two after, my mistress sent me down into the wash-house to learn to wash in the English way. In the West Indies we wash with cold water – in England with hot. I told my mistress I was afraid that putting my hands first into the hot water and then into the cold, would increase the pain in my limbs.

The doctor had told my mistress long before I came from the West Indies, that I was a sickly body and the washing did not agree with me.

But Mrs Wood would not release me from the tub, so I was forced to do as I could. I grew worse, and could not stand to wash. I was then forced to sit down with the tub before me, and often through pain and weakness was reduced to kneel or to sit down on the floor, to finish my task. When I complained to my mistress of this, she only got into a passion as usual, and said washing in hot water could not hurt any one; – that I was lazy and insolent, and wanted to be free of my work; but that she would make me do it. I thought her very hard on me, and my heart rose up within me. However I kept still at that time, and went down again to wash the child's things; but the English washerwomen who were at work there, when they saw that I was so ill, had pity upon me and washed them for me.

After that, when we came up to live in Leigh Street, Mrs Wood sorted out five bags of clothes which we had used at sea, and also such as had been worn since we came on shore, for me and the cook to wash. Elizabeth the cook told her, that she did not think that I was able to stand to the tub, and that she had better hire a woman. I also said myself, that I had come over to nurse the child, and that I was sorry I had come from Antigua, since mistress would work me so hard, without compassion for my rheumatism. Mr and Mrs Wood, when they heard this, rose up in a passion against me. They opened the door and bade me get out. But I was a stranger, and did not know one door in the street from another, and was unwilling to go away. They made a dreadful uproar, and from that day they constantly kept cursing and abusing me. I was obliged to wash, though I was very ill. Mrs Wood, indeed once hired a washerwoman, but she was not well treated, and would come no more.

My master quarrelled with me another time, about one of our great washings, his wife having stirred him up to do so. He said he would compel me to do the whole of the washing given out to me, or if I again refused, he would take a short course with me: he would either send me down to the brig in the river, to carry me back to Antigua, or he would turn me at once out of doors, and let me provide for myself. I said I would willingly go back, if he would let me purchase my own freedom. But this enraged him more than all the rest: he cursed and swore at me dreadfully, and said he would never sell my freedom – if I wished to be free, I was free in England, and I might go and try what freedom would do for me, and be d—d. My heart was very sore with this treatment, but I had to go on. I continued to do my work, and did all I could to give satisfaction, but all would not do.

Shortly after, the cook left them, and then matters went on ten times worse. I always washed the child's clothes without being commanded to do it, and any thing else that was wanted in the family; though still I was very sick – very sick indeed. When the great washing came round, which was every two months, my mistress got together again a great many heavy things, such as bed-ticks, bed-coverlets, &c. for me to wash. I told her I was too ill to wash such heavy things that day. She said, she supposed I thought myself a free woman, but I was not; and if I did not do it directly I should be instantly turned out of doors. I stood a long time before I could answer, for I did not know well what to do. I knew that I was free in England, but I did not know where to go, or how to get my living; and therefore, I did not like to leave the house. But Mr Wood said he would send for a constable to thrust me out; and at last I took course and resolved that I would not be longer thus treated, but would go and trust to Providence. This was the fourth time they had threatened to turn me out, and, go where I might, I was determined now to take them at their word; though I thought it very hard, after I had lived with them for thirteen years, and worked for them like a horse, to be driven out in this way, like a beggar. My only fault was being sick, and therefore unable to please my mistress, who thought she never could get work enough out of her slaves; and I told them so: but they only abused me and drove me out. This took place from two to three months, I think, after we came to England.

When I came away, I went to the man (one Mash) who used to black the shoes of the family, and asked his wife to get somebody to go with me to Hatton Garden to the Moravian Missionaries: these were the only persons I knew in England. The woman sent a young girl with me to the mission house, and I saw there a gentleman called Mr Moore. I told him my whole story, and how my owners had treated me, and asked him to take in my trunk with what few clothes I had. The missionaries were very kind to me – they were sorry for my destitute situation, and gave me leave to bring my things to be placed under their care. They were very good people, and they told me to come to the church.

When I went back to Mr Wood's to get my trunk, I saw a lady, Mrs Pell, who was on a visit to my mistress. When Mr and Mrs Wood heard me come in, they set this lady to stop me, finding that they had gone too far with me. Mrs Pell came out to me, and said, 'Are you really going to leave, Molly? Don't leave, but come into the country with me.' I believe she said this because she thought Mrs Wood would easily get me back again. I replied to her, 'Ma'am, this is the fourth time my master and mistress have driven me out, or threatened to drive me – and I will give them no more occasion to bid me go. I was not willing to leave them, for I am a stranger in this country, but now I must go – I can stay no longer to be so used.' Mrs Pell then went up stairs to my mistress, and told that I would go, and that she could not stop me. Mrs Wood was very much hurt and frightened when she found I was determined to go out that day. She said, 'If she goes the people will rob her, and then turn her adrift.' She did not say this to me, but she spoke it loud enough for me to hear; that it might induce me not to go, I suppose. Mr Wood also asked me where I was going to. I told him where I had been, and that I should never have gone away had I not been driven out by my owners. He had given me a written paper some time before, which said that I had come with them to England by my own desire; and that was true. It said also that I left them of my own free will, because I was a free woman in England; and that I was idle and would not do my work – which was not true. I gave this paper afterwards to a gentleman who inquired into my case.

I went into the kitchen and got my clothes out. The nurse and the servant girl were there, and I said to the man who was going to take out my trunk, 'Stop, before you take up this trunk, and hear what I have to say before these people. I am going out of this house, as I was ordered; but I have done no wrong at all to my owners, neither here nor in the West Indies. I always worked very hard to please them, both by night and day; but there was no giving satisfaction, for my mistress could never be satisfied with reasonable service. I told my mistress I was sick, and yet she has ordered me out of doors. This is the fourth time; and now I am going out.'

And so I came out, and went and carried my trunk to the Moravians. I then returned back to Mash the shoe-black's house, and begged his wife to take me in. I had a little West Indian money in my trunk; and they got it changed for me. This helped to support me for a little while. The man's wife was very kind to me. I was very sick, and she boiled nourishing things up for me. She also sent for a doctor to see me, and he sent me medicine, which did me good, though I was ill for a long time with the rheumatic pains. I lived a good many months with these poor people, and they nursed me, and did all that lay in their power to serve me. The man was well acquainted with my situation, as he used to go to and fro to Mr Wood's house to clean shoes and knives; and he and his wife were sorry for me.

About this time, a woman of the name of Hill told me of the Anti-Slavery Society, and went with me to their office, to inquire if they could do any thing to get me my freedom, and send me back to the West Indies. The gentlemen of the Society took me to a lawyer, who examined very strictly into my case; but told me that the laws of England could do nothing to make me free in Antigua.[40] However they did all they could for

---

[40] She came first to the Anti-Slavery Office in Aldermanbury, about the latter end of November 1828; and her case was referred to Mr George Stephen to be investigated. More of this hereafter.*

me: they gave me a little money from time to time to keep me from want; and some of them went to Mr Wood to try to persuade him to let me return a free woman to my husband; but though they offered him, as I have heard, a large sum for my freedom, he was sulky and obstinate, and would not consent to let me go free.

This was the first winter I spent in England, and I suffered much from the severe cold, and from the rheumatic pains, which still at times torment me. However, Providence was very good to me, and I got many friends – especially some Quaker ladies, who hearing of my case, came and sought me out, and gave me good warm clothing and money. Thus I had great cause to bless God in my affliction.

When I got better I was anxious to get some work to do, as I was unwilling to eat the bread of idleness. Mrs Mash, who was a laundress, recommended me to a lady for a charwoman. She paid me very handsomely for what work I did, and I divided the money with Mrs Mash; for though very poor, they gave me food when my own money was done, and never suffered me to want.

In the spring, I got into service with a lady, who saw me at the house where I sometimes worked as a charwoman. This lady's name was Mrs Forsyth. She had been in the West Indies, and was accustomed to Blacks, and liked them. I was with her six months, and went with her to Margate. She treated me well, and gave me a good character when she left London.[41]

After Mrs Forsyth went away, I was again out of place, and went to lodgings, for which I paid two shillings a week, and found coals and candle. After eleven weeks, the money I had saved in service was all gone, and I was forced to go back to the Anti-Slavery office to ask a supply, till I could get another situation. I did not like to go back – I did not like to be idle. I would rather work for my living than get it for nothing. They were very good to give me a supply, but I felt shame at being obliged to apply for relief whilst I had strength to work.

At last I went into the service of Mr and Mrs Pringle, where I have been ever since, and am as comfortable as I can be while separated from my dear husband, and away from my own country and all old friends and connections. My dear mistress teaches me daily to read the word of God, and takes great pains to make me understand it. I enjoy the great privilege of being enabled to attend church three times on the Sunday; and I have met with many kind friends since I have been here, both clergymen and others. The Rev. Mr Young, who lives in the next house, has shown me much kindness, and taken much pains to instruct me, partic-

---

[41] She refers to a written certificate which will be inserted afterwards.*

ularly while my master and mistress were absent in Scotland. Nor must I forget, among my friends, the Rev. Mr Mortimer, the good clergyman of the parish, under whose ministry I have now sat for upwards of twelve months. I trust in God I have profited by what I have heard from him. He never keeps back the truth, and I think he has been the means of opening my eyes and ears much better to understand the word of God. Mr Mortimer tells me that he cannot open the eyes of my heart, but that I must pray to God to change my heart, and make me to know the truth, and the truth will make me free.

I still live in the hope that God will find a way to give me my liberty, and give me back to my husband. I endeavour to keep down my fretting, and to leave all to Him, for he knows what is good for me better than I know myself. Yet, I must confess, I find it a hard and heavy task to do so.

I am often much vexed, and I feel great sorrow when I hear some people in this country say that the slaves do not need better usage, and do not want to be free.[42] They believe the foreign people,[43] who deceive them, and say slaves are happy. I say, Not so. How can slaves be happy when they have the halter round their neck and the whip upon their back? and are disgraced and thought no more of than beasts? – and are separated from their mothers, and husbands, and children, and sisters, just as cattle are sold and separated? Is it happiness for a driver in the field to take down his wife or sister or child, and strip them, and whip them in such a disgraceful manner? – women that have had children exposed in the open field to shame! There is no modesty or decency shown by the owner to his slaves; men, women, and children are exposed alike. Since I have been here I have often wondered how English people can go out into the West Indies and act in such a beastly manner. But when they go to the West Indies, they forget God and all feeling of shame, I think, since they can see and do such things. They tie up slaves like hogs – moor[44] them up like cattle, and they lick them, so as hogs, or cattle, or horses never were flogged; – and yet they come home and say, and make some good people believe, that slaves don't want to get out of slavery. But they put a cloak about the truth. It is not so. All slaves want to be free – to be free is very sweet. I will say the truth to English people who may read this history that my good friend, Miss S—, is now writing down for me. I have been a slave myself – I know what slaves feel – I can

[42] The whole of this paragraph especially, is given as nearly as was possible in Mary's precise words.*
[43] She means West Indians.*
[44] A West Indian phrase: to fasten or tie up.*

tell by myself what other slaves feel, and by what they have told me. The man that says slaves be quite happy in slavery – that they don't want to be free – that man is either ignorant or a lying person. I never heard a slave say so. I never heard a Buckra man say so, till I heard tell of it in England. Such people ought to be ashamed of themselves. They can't do without slaves, they say. What's the reason they can't do without slaves as well as in England? No slaves here – no whips – no stocks – no punishment, except for wicked people. They hire servants in England; and if they don't like them, they send them away: they can't lick them. Let them work ever so hard in England, they are far better off than slaves. If they get a bad master, they give warning and go hire to another. They have their liberty. That's just what *we* want. We don't mind hard work, if we had proper treatment, and proper wages like English servants, and proper time given in the week to keep us from breaking the Sabbath. But they won't give it: they will have work – work – work, night and day, sick or well, till we are quite done up; and we must not speak up nor look amiss, however much we be abused. And then when we are quite done up, who cares for us, more than for a lame horse? This is slavery. I tell it, to let English people know the truth; and I hope they will never leave off to pray God, and call loud to the great King of England, till all the poor blacks be given free, and slavery done up for evermore.

Source: Mary Prince, *The History of Mary Prince, a West Indian Slave*, ed. S. Salih, Harmondsworth, Penguin, 2000 [1831].

John Newton, William Cowper and others: the *Olney Hymns* in context

The *Olney Hymns*, published in 1779, but written over a preceding period of more than a decade, was compiled by John Newton (1725–1807), then the Anglican curate in charge of Olney in north Buckinghamshire. Of the 384 hymns in the book, 67 (indicated by a 'C' in original, by 'Cowper' here) were by Newton's friend and parishioner William Cowper (1731–1800), while the others were Newton's own compositions. The hymns were an expression of their shared Calvinist Evangelical convictions, and a reflection of their joint pastoral labours at Olney. Their publication was a landmark in the development of the English hymn, and their distinctive character is pointed up in this anthology by a few selections from earlier and later writers.

Eighteenth-century hymns

Joseph Addison,[1] 'The spacious firmament on high'

> The spacious firmament on high,
> With all the blue etherial sky,
> And spangled heav'ns, a shining frame,
> Their great Original proclaim:
> Th'unwearied Sun, from day to day,
> Does his Creator's power display,
> And publishes to every land
> The work of an Almighty hand.
>
> Soon as the evening shades prevail,
> The Moon takes up the wondrous tale,

---

[1] Joseph Addison (1672–1719) essayist, moralist and politician. This hymn originally appeared at the conclusion of a short essay in which Addison explored the best means of strengthening and confirming religious faith.

And nightly to the listning earth
Repeats the story of her birth:
Whilst all the Stars that round her burn,
And all the Planets, in their turn,
Confirm the tidings as they rowl,[2]
And spread the truth from pole to pole.

What though, in solemn silence, all
More round the dark terrestrial ball?
What tho' nor real voice nor sound
Amid their radiant orbs be found?
In Reason's ear they all rejoice,
And utter forth a glorious voice,
For ever singing, as they shine,
"The hand that made us is divine."

Source: *The Works of the Right Honourable Joseph Addison, Esq*, London, Jacob Tonson, 1721, Vol. III, pp. 574–5. Originally published in *The Spectator*, No. 465, 23 August, 1712.

Isaac Watts,[3] 'When I survey the won'drous Cross'

Crucifixion to the World, by the Cross of Christ. Gal vi.14[4]

When I survey the won'drous Cross
On which the Prince of Glory dy'd,
My richest Gain I count but Loss,
And pour Contempt on all my Pride.

Forbid it, Lord, that I should boast
Save in the Death of *Christ*[5] my God:
All the vain Things that charm me most,
I sacrifice them to his Blood.

See from his Head, his Hands, his Feet,
Sorrow and Love flow mingled down;
Did e'er such Love and Sorrow meet?
Or Thorns compose so rich a Crown?

[2] *rowl*: roll
[3] Isaac Watts (1674–1748), Independent minister.
[4] Watts's original title and biblical reference.
[5] Emphasis in the original.

His dying Crimson, like a Robe
Spreads o'er his Body on the Tree,
Then am I dead to all the Globe,
And all the Globe is dead to me.

Were the whole Realm of Nature mine,
That were a present far too small;
Love so amazing, so divine,
Demands my Soul, my Life, my All.

Source: Isaac Watts, *Hymns and Spiritual Songs*, 7th edition, London, J. H. for E. Ford, 1720 (first published 1707), Book III, No. 7, p. 289.

Charles Wesley,[6] 'And can it be'

And can it be, that I should gain
   An interest in the Saviour's blood?
Died he for me, who caused his pain!
   For me! who him to death pursued;
Amazing love, how can it be,
That thou, my God, should'st die for me?

'Tis mystery all: the immortal dies!
   Who can explore his strange design?
In vain the first-born seraph tries
   To sound the depths of love divine:
'Tis mercy all! let earth adore;
Let angel-minds enquire no more.

He left his Father's throne above,
   (So free, so infinite his grace!)
Emptied himself of all but love,
   And bled for Adam's helpless race:
'Tis mercy all, immense and free,
For, O my God, it found out me!

Long my imprisoned spirit lay,
   Fast bound in sin and nature's night:
Thine eye diffused a quickening ray;
   I woke; the dungeon flamed with light!
My chains fell off, my heart was free,
I rose, went forth, and followed thee.

[6] Charles Wesley (1707–88), younger brother of John Wesley, the founder of Methodism.

No condemnation now I dread,
   Jesus, and all in him, is mine:
Alive in him, my living head,
   And clothed in righteousness divine,
Bold I approach the eternal throne,
And claim the crown through Christ my own.

Source: A Collection of Hymns for the Use of the People called Methodists, 3rd edition, London, J. Paramore, 1782, No. 193, p. 197.

Extracts from the *Olney Hymns*

Preface

COPIES of a few of these Hymns have already appeared in periodical publications, and in some recent collections. I have observed one or two of them attributed to persons who certainly had no concern in them, but as transcribers. All that have been at different times parted with in manuscript are included in the present volume; and (if the information were of any great importance) the public may be assured, that the whole number were composed by two persons only. The original design would not admit of any other association. A desire of promoting the faith and comfort of sincere christians, though the principal, was not the only motive to this undertaking. It was likewise intended as a monument, to perpetuate the remembrance of an intimate and endeared friendship. With this pleasing view I entered upon my part, which would have been smaller than it is, and the book would have appeared much sooner, and in a very different form, if the wise, though mysterious providence of GOD, had not seen fit to cross my wishes. We had not proceeded far upon our proposed plan, before my dear friend was prevented, by a long and affecting indisposition, from affording me any farther assistance. My grief and disappointment were great; I hung my harp upon the willows, and for some time thought myself determined to proceed no farther without him. Yet my mind was afterwards led to resume the service. My progress in it, amidst a variety of other engagements, has been slow, yet in a course of years the hymns amounted to a considerable number: And my deference to the judgment and desires of others, has at length overcome the reluctance I long felt to see them in print, while I had so few of my friend's hymns to insert in the collection. Though it is possible a good judge of composition might be able to distinguish those which are his, I have thought it proper to preclude a misapplication, by prefixing the letter C to each of them. For the rest I must be responsible.

There is a stile and manner suited to the composition of hymns, which may be more successfully, or at least more easily attained by a versifier, than by a poet. They should be *Hymns*, not *Odes*, if designed for public worship, and for the use of plain people. Perspicuity, simplicity and ease, should be chiefly attended to; and the imagery and coloring of poetry, if admitted at all, should be indulged very sparingly and with great judgment. The late Dr *Watts*, many of whose hymns are admirable patterns in this species of writing, might, as a poet, have a right to say, That it cost him some labor to restrain his fire, and to accommodate himself to the capacities of common readers. But it would not become me to make such a declaration. It behoved me to do my best. But though I would not offend readers of taste by a wilful coarseness, and negligence, I do not write professedly for them. If the LORD whom I serve, has been pleased to favor me with that mediocrity of talent, which may qualify me for usefulness to the weak and the poor of his flock, without quite disgusting persons of superior discernment, I have reason to be satisfied.

As the workings of the heart of man, and of the Spirit of GOD, are in general the same, in all who are the subjects of grace, I hope most of these hymns, being the fruit and expression of my own experience, will coincide with the views of real christians of all denominations. But I cannot expect that every sentiment I have advanced will be universally approved. However, I am not conscious of having written a single line with an intention, either to flatter, or to offend any party or person upon earth. I have simply declared my own views and feelings, as I might have done if I had composed hymns in some of the newly discovered islands in the South-Sea, where no person had any knowledge of the name of JESUS, but myself. I am a friend of peace, and being deeply convinced that no one can profitably understand the great truths and doctrines of the gospel, any farther than he is taught of GOD, I have not a wish to obtrude my own tenets upon others, in a way of controversy: yet I do not think myself bound to conceal them. Many gracious persons (for many such I am persuaded there are) who differ from me, more or less, in those points which are called Calvinistic, appear desirous that the Calvinists should, for their sakes, studiously avoid every expression which they cannot approve. Yet few of them, I believe, impose a like restraint upon themselves, but think the importance of what they deem to be truth, justifies them in speaking their sentiments plainly, and strongly. May I not plead for an equal liberty? The views I have received of the doctrines of grace are essential to my peace, I could not live comfortably a day or an hour without them. I likewise believe, yea, so far as my poor attainments warrant me to speak, I know them to be friendly to holiness, and to have a direct influence in producing and maintaining a gospel conversation, and therefore I must not be ashamed of them.

The Hymns are distributed into three Books. In the first I have classed those which are formed upon select passages of Scripture, and placed them in the order of the books of the Old and New Testament. The second contains occasional Hymns, suited to particular seasons, or suggested by particular events or objects. The third Book is miscellaneous, comprising a variety of subjects relative to a life of faith in the son of GOD, which have no express reference either to a single text of Scripture, or to any determinate season or incident. These are farther subdivided into distinct heads. This arrangement is not so accurate but that several of the hymns might have been differently disposed. Some attention to method may be found convenient, though a logical exactness was hardly practicable. As some subjects in the several books are nearly co-incident, I have, under the divisions in the third book, pointed out those which are similar in the two former. And I have likewise here and there in the first and second, made a reference to hymns of a like import in the third.

This publication, which, with my humble prayer to the LORD for his blessing upon it, I offer to the service and acceptance of all who love the LORD JESUS CHRIST in sincerity, of every name and in every place, into whose hands it may come; I more particularly dedicate to my dear friends in the parish and neighbourhood of *Olney*, for whose use the hymns were originally composed; as a testimony of the sincere love I bear them, and as a token of my gratitude to the LORD, and to them, for the comfort and satisfaction with which the discharge of my ministry among them has been attended.

The hour is approaching, and at my time of life cannot be very distant, when my heart, my pen, and my tongue, will no longer be able to move in their service. But I trust, while my heart continues to beat, it will feel a warm desire for the prosperity of their souls; and while my hand can write, and my tongue speak, it will be the business and the pleasure of my life, to aim at promoting their growth and establishment in the grace of our GOD and Saviour. To this precious grace I commend them, and earnestly entreat them, and all who love his name, to strive mightily with their prayers to GOD for me, that I may be preserved faithful to the end, and enabled at last to finish my course with joy.

Olney, Bucks,
Feb. 15, 1779.
JOHN NEWTON.

Extracts from Book I, *On Select Passages of Scripture*

HYMN 3

Cowper. *Walking with* GOD. GENESIS Chap. v. 24

1 Oh! for a closer walk with GOD,
    A calm and heav'nly frame;
  A light to shine upon the road
    That leads me to the Lamb!

2 Where is the blessedness I knew
    When first I saw the LORD?
  Where is the soul-refreshing view
    Of JESUS, and his word?

3 What peaceful hours I once enjoy'd!
    How sweet their mem'ry still!
  But they have left an aching void,
    The world can never fill.

4 Return, O holy Dove, return,
    Sweet messenger of rest;
  I hate the sins that made thee mourn,
    And drove thee from my breast.

5 The dearest idol I have known,
    Whate'er that idol be;
  Help me to tear it from thy throne,
    And worship only thee.

6 So shall my walk be close with GOD,
    Calm and serene my frame;
  So purer light shall mark the road
    That leads me to the Lamb.

HYMN 7

The LORD *will provide*

1 Tho' troubles assail
  And dangers affright,
  Tho' friends should all fail
  And foes all unite;
  Yet one thing secures us,
  Whatever betide,
  The scripture assures us,
  The LORD will provide.

2   The birds without barn
    Or storehouse are fed,
    From them let us learn
    To trust for our bread:
    His saints, what is fitting,
    Shall ne'er be deny'd,
    So long as 'tis written,
    The LORD will provide.

3   We may, like the ships,
    By tempests be tost
    On perilous deeps,
    But cannot be lost.
    Tho' Satan enrages
    The wind and the tide,
    The promise engages,
    The LORD will provide.

4   His call we obey
    Like Abra'm of old,
    Not knowing our way,
    But faith makes us bold;
    For tho' we are strangers
    We have a good Guide,
    And trust in all dangers,
    The LORD will provide.

5   When Satan appears
    To stop up our path,
    And fill us with fears,
    We triumph by faith;
    He cannot take from us,
    Tho' oft he has try'd,
    This heart-cheering promise,
    The LORD will provide.

6   He tells us we'er weak,
    Our hope is in vain,
    The good that we seek
    We ne'er shall obtain;
    But when such suggestions
    Our spirits have ply'd,
    This answers all questions,
    The LORD will provide.

7   No strength of our own,
    Or goodness we claim,
    Yet since we have known
    The Saviour's great name;
    In this our strong tower
    For safety we hide,
    The LORD is our power,
    The LORD will provide.

8   When life sinks apace
    And death is in view,
    This word of his grace
    Shall comfort us thro':
    No fearing or doubting
    With CHRIST on our side,
    We hope to die shouting,
    The LORD will provide.

HYMN 28

SAUL's armor. I SAMUEL Chap. xvii. 38–40

1   When first my soul enlisted
     My Saviour's foes to fight;
   Mistaken friends insisted
     I was not arm'd aright:
   So Saul advised David
     He certainly would fail;
   Nor could his life be saved
     Without a coat of mail.

2   But David, tho' he yielded
     To put the armor on,
   Soon found he could not wield it,
     And ventur'd forth with none.
   With only sling and pebble
     He fought the fight of faith;
   The weapons seem'd but feeble,
     Yet prov'd Goliath's death.

3   Had I by him been guided,
     And quickly thrown away
   The armor men provided,
     I might have gain'd the day;

But arm'd as they advis'd me,
　　My expectations fail'd;
My enemy surpriz'd me,
　　And had almost prevail'd.

4　Furnish'd with books and notions,
　　And arguments and pride;
I practis'd all my motions,
　　And Satan's pow'r defy'd:
But soon perceiv'd with trouble,
　　That these would do no good;
Iron to him is stubble,[7]
　　And brass like rotten wood.

5　I triumph'd at a distance
　　While he was out of sight;
But faint was my resistance
　　When forc'd to join in fight:
He broke my sword in shivers,
　　And pierc'd my boasted shield;
Laugh'd at my vain endeavors,
　　And drove me from the field.

6　Satan will not be braved
　　By such a worm as I;
Then let me learn with David,
　　To trust in the Most High;
To plead the name of JESUS,
　　And use the sling of pray'r;
Thus arm'd, when Satan sees us
　　He'll tremble and despair.

HYMN 41

Faith's review and expectation. I CHRONICLES Chap. xvii. 16, 17

1　Amazing grace! (how sweet the sound)
　　That sav'd a wretch like me!
I once was lost, but now am found,
　　Was blind, but now I see.

---

[7] Job xli. 27.*

2 'Twas grace that taught my heart to fear,
   And grace my fears reliev'd;
   How precious did that grace appear,
   The hour I first believ'd!

3 Thro' many dangers, toils and snares,
   I have already come;
   'Tis grace has brought me safe thus far,
   And grace will lead me home.

4 The LORD has promis'd good to me,
   His word my hope secures;
   He will my shield and portion be,
   As long as life endures.

5 Yes, when this flesh and heart shall fail,
   And mortal life shall cease;
   I shall possess, within the vail,
   A life of joy and peace.

6 The earth shall soon dissolve like snow,
   The sun forbear to shine;
   But God, who call'd me here below,
   Will be for ever mine.

HYMN 46

None upon earth I desire besides thee. PSALM lxxiii. 25

1 How tedious and tasteless the hours,
   When JESUS no longer I see;
   Sweet prospects, sweet birds, and sweet flow'rs,
   Have lost all their sweetness with me:
   The mid-summer sun shines but dim,
   The fields strive in vain to look gay;
   But when I am happy in him,
   December's as pleasant as May.

2 His name yields the richest perfume,
   And sweeter than music his voice;
   His presence disperses my gloom,
   And makes all within me rejoice:
   I should, were he always thus nigh,
   Have nothing to wish or to fear;
   No mortal so happy as I,
   My summer would last all the year.

3   Content with beholding his face,
      My all to his pleasure resign'd;
    No changes of season or place,
      Would make any change in my mind:
    While bless'd with a sense of his love,
      A palace a toy would appear;
    And prisons would palaces prove,
      If JESUS would dwell with me there.

4   Dear LORD, if indeed I am thine,
      If thou art my sun and my song;
    Say, why do I languish and pine,
      And why are my winters so long?
    O drive these dark clouds from my sky,
      Thy soul-cheering presence restore;
    Or take me unto thee on high,
      Where winter and clouds are no more.

HYMN 52

Cowper. *Wisdom.* PROVERBS Chap. viii. 22–31

1   Ere GOD had built the mountains,
    Or rais'd the fruitful hills;
    Before he fill'd the fountains
    That feed the running rills;
    In me, from everlasting,
    The wonderful I AM,
    Found pleasures never wasting,
    And Wisdom is my name.

2   When, like a tent to dwell in,
    He spread the skies abroad;
    And swath'd about the swelling
    Of ocean's mighty flood;
    He wrought by weight and measure,
    And I was with him then;
    Myself the Father's pleasure,
    And mine, the sons of men.

3   Thus wisdom's words discover
    Thy glory and thy grace,
    Thou everlasting lover
    Of our unworthy race!
    Thy gracious eye survey'd us

Ere stars were seen above;
In wisdom thou hast made us,
And dy'd for us in love.

4   And couldst thou be delighted
With creatures such as we!
Who when we saw thee, slighted
And nail'd thee to a tree?
Unfathomable wonder,
And mystery divine!
The voice that speaks in thunder,
Says, "Sinner I am thine!"

HYMN 53

A friend that sticketh closer than a brother. PROVERBS Chap. xviii. 24

1   One there is, above all others,
Well deserves the name of friend;
His is love beyond a brother's,
Costly, free, and knows no end:
    They who once his kindness prove,
    Find it everlasting love!

2   Which of all our friends to save us,
Could or would have shed their blood?
But our JESUS dy'd to have us
Reconcil'd, in him to God:
    This was boundless love indeed!
    JESUS is a friend in need.

3   Men, when rais'd to lofty stations,
Often know their friends no more;
Slight and scorn their poor relations
Tho' they valu'd them before.
    But our Saviour always owns
    Those whom he redeem'd with grones.

4   When he liv'd on earth abased,
Friend of sinners was his name;
Now, above all glory raised,
He rejoices in the same:
    Still he calls them brethren, friends,
    And to all their wants attends.

5   Could we bear from one another,
     What he daily bears from us?
     Yet this glorious Friend and Brother,
     Loves us tho' we treat him thus:
        Tho' for good we render ill,
        He accounts us brethren still.

6   Oh! for grace our hearts to soften!
     Teach us, LORD, at length to love;
     We, alas! forget too often,
     What a Friend we have above:
        But when home our souls are brought,
        We will love thee as we ought.

HYMN 55

Cowper. *Vanity of the world.*

1   GOD gives his mercies to be spent;
     Your hoard will do your soul no good:
     Gold is a blessing only lent,
     Repaid by giving others food.

2   The world's esteem is but a bribe,
     To buy their peace you sell your own;
     The slave of a vain-glorious tribe,
     Who hate you while they make you known.

3   The joy that vain amusements give,
     Oh! sad conclusion that it brings!
     The honey of a crowded hive,
     Defended by a thousand stings.

4   'Tis thus the world rewards the fools
     That live upon her treach'rous smiles;
     She leads them, blindfold, by her rules,
     And ruins all whom she beguiles.

5   GOD knows the thousands who go down
     From pleasure, into endless woe;
     And with a long despairing grone
     Blaspheme their Maker as they go.

6   O fearful thought! be timely wise;
     Delight but in a Saviour's charms;
     And GOD shall take you to the skies,
     Embrac'd in everlasting arms.

HYMN 57

The name of JESUS. SOLOMON'S SONG Chap. i. 3

1 How sweet the name of JESUS sounds
    In a believer's ear?
  It sooths his sorrows, heals his wounds,
    And drives away his fear.

2 It makes the wounded spirit whole,
    And calms the troubled breast;
  'Tis Manna to the hungry soul,
    And to the weary rest.

3 Dear name! the rock on which I build,
    My shield and hiding place;
  My never-failing treas'ry fill'd
    With boundless stores of grace.

4 By thee my pray'rs acceptance gain,
    Altho' with sin defil'd;
  Satan accuses me in vain,
    And I am own'd a child.

5 JESUS! my Shepherd, Husband, Friend,
    My Prophet, Priest, and King;
  My LORD, my Life, my Way, my End,
    Accept the praise I bring.

6 Weak is the effort of my heart,
    And cold my warmest thought;
  But when I see thee as thou art,
    I'll praise thee as I ought.

7 'Till then I would thy love proclaim
    With ev'ry fleeting breath;
  And may the music of thy name
    Refresh my soul in death.

HYMN 60

Zion, or the city of GOD.[8] ISAIAH Chap. xxxiii. 27, 28

1   Glorious things of thee are spoken,[9]
Zion, city of our GOD!
He, whose word cannot be broken,
Form'd thee for his own abode.[10]
On the rock of ages founded.[11]
What can shake thy sure repose?
With salvation's walls surrounded[12]
Thou may'st smile at all thy foes.

2   See! the streams of living waters
Springing from eternal love;[13]
Well supply thy sons and daughters,
And all fear of want remove:
Who can faint while such a river
Ever flows their thirst t' assuage?
Grace, which like the LORD, the giver,
Never fails from age to age.

3   Round each habitation hov'ring
See the cloud and fire appear![14]
For a glory and a cov'ring,
Shewing that the LORD is near:
Thus deriving from their banner
Light by night and shade by day;
Safe they feed upon the Manna
Which he gives them when they pray.

4   Blest inhabitants of Zion,
Wash'd in the Redeemer's blood!
JESUS, whom their souls rely on,
Makes them kings and priests to God.[15]
'Tis his love his people raises

---

[8] Book II. Hymn 24.*
[9] Psalm lxxxvii. 3.*
[10] Psalm cxxxii. 14.*
[11] Matt. xvi. 16.*
[12] Isaiah xxvi. 1.*
[13] Psalm xlvi. 4.*
[14] Isaiah iv. 5, 6.*
[15] Rev. i. 6.*

Over self to reign as kings
And as priests, his solemn praises
Each for a thank-off'ring brings.

5   Saviour, if of Zion's city
I thro' grace a member am;
Let the world deride or pity,
I will glory in thy name:
Fading is the worldling's pleasure,
All his boasted pomp and show;
Solid joys and lasting treasure,
None but Zion's children know.

HYMN 65

Cowper. *The future peace and glory of the church.* ISAIAH
Chap. lx. 15–20

1   Hear what GOD the LORD hath spoken,
O my people, faint and few;
Comfortless, afflicted, broken,
Fair abodes I build for you:
Themes of heart-felt tribulation
Shall no more perplex your ways;
You shall name your walls, Salvation,
And your gates shall all be praise.

2   There, like streams that feed the garden,
Pleasures, without end, shall flow;
For the LORD, your faith rewarding,
All his bounty shall bestow:
Still in undisturb'd possession,
Peace and righteousness shall reign;
Never shall you feel oppression,
Hear the voice of war again.

3   Ye no more your suns descending,
Waning moons no more shall see;
But your griefs, for ever ending,
Find eternal noon in me:
GOD shall rise, and shining o'er you,
Change to day the gloom of night;
He, the LORD, shall be your glory,
GOD your everlasting light.

HYMN 79

Cowper. *Praise for the fountain opened.* ZECHARIAH Chap. xiii. 1

1   There is a fountain fill'd with blood
      Drawn from EMMANUEL's veins;
   And sinners, plung'd beneath that flood,
      Loose all their guilty stains.

2   The dying thief rejoic'd to see
      That fountain in his day;
   And there have I, as vile as he,
      Wash'd all my sins away.

3   Dear dying Lamb, thy precious blood
      Shall never lose its pow'r;
   Till all the ransom'd church of God
      Be sav'd, to sin no more.

4   E'er since, by faith, I saw the stream
      Thy flowing wounds supply:
   Redeeming love has been my theme,
      And shall be till I die.

5   Then in a nobler sweeter song
      I'll sing thy pow'r to save;
   When this poor lisping stamm'ring tongue
      Lies silent in the grave.

6   LORD, I believe thou hast prepar'd
      (Unworthy tho' I be)
   For me a blood-bought free reward,
      A golden harp for me!

7   'Tis strung, and tun'd, for endless years,
      And form'd by pow'r divine;
   To sound, in GOD the Father's ears,
      No other name but thine.

HYMN 85

Cowper. *The sower.* MATTHEW Chap. xiii. 3

1   Ye sons of earth prepare the plough,
      Break up your fallow ground!
   The Sower is gone forth to sow,
      And scatter blessings round.

246

2   The seed that finds a stony soil,
     Shoots forth a hasty blade;
   But ill repays the sower's toil,
     Soon wither'd, scorch'd, and dead.

3   The thorny ground is sure to baulk
     All hopes of harvest there;
   We find a tall and sickly stalk,
     But not the fruitful ear.

4   The beaten path and high-way side
     Receive the trust in vain;
   The watchful birds the spoil divide,
     And pick up all the grain.

5   But where the LORD of grace and pow'r
     Has bless'd the happy field;
   How plenteous is the golden store
     The deep-wrought furrows yield!

6   Father of mercies we have need
     Of thy preparing grace;
   Let the same hand that gives the seed,
     Provide a fruitful place.

HYMN 103

The barren fig-tree. LUKE Chap. xiii. 6–9

1   The church a garden is
   In which believers stand,
   Like ornamental trees
   Planted by GOD's own hand:
His Spirit waters all their roots,
And ev'ry branch abounds with fruits.

2   But other trees there are,
   In this enclosure grow;
   Which, tho' they promise fair,
   Have only leaves to show:
No fruits of grace are on them found,
They stand but cumb'rers of the ground.

3   The under gard'ner grieves,
   In vain his strength he spends,
   For heaps of useless leaves,

Afford him small amends:
He hears the LORD his will make known,
To cut the barren fig-trees down.

4   How difficult his post,
     What pangs his bowels move,
     To find his wishes crost,
     His labors useless prove!
His last relief is earnest pray'r,
LORD, spare them yet another year.

5   Spare them, and let me try
     What farther means may do;
     I'll fresh manure apply,
     My digging I'll renew:
Who knows but yet they fruit may yield!
If not—'tis just, they must be fell'd.

6   If under means of grace,
     No gracious fruits appear;
     It is a dreadful case,
     Tho' GOD may long forbear:
At length he'll strike the threatned blow,[16]
And lay the barren fig-tree low.

Extracts from Book II, *On Occasional Subjects*

HYMN 3

Uncertainty of life

1   See! another year is gone!
     Quickly have the seasons past!
     This we enter now upon
     May to many prove our last:
     Mercy hitherto has spar'd,
     But have mercies been improv'd?
     Let us ask, am I prepar'd?
     Should I be this year remov'd?

2   Some we now no longer see,
     Who their mortal race have run;
     Seem'd as fair for life as we,

---

[16] Book II. Hymn 26.*

When the former year begun:
Some, but who G O D only knows,
Who are here assembled now;
Ere the present year shall close,
To the stroke of death must bow.

3   Life a field of battle is,
Thousands fall within our view;
And the next death-bolt that flies,
May be sent to me or you:
While we preach, and while we hear,
Help us, L O R D, each one, to think,
Vast eternity is near,
I am standing on the brink.

4   If from guilt and sin set free,
By the knowledge of thy grace;
Welcome, then, the call will be
To depart and see thy face:
To thy saints, while here below,
With new years, new mercies come;
But the happiest year they know
Is their last, which leads them home.

HYMN 26

Travelling in birth for souls. Gal. iv. 19

1   What contradictions meet
In ministers employ!
It is a bitter sweet,
A sorrow full of joy:
No other post affords a place
For equal honor, or disgrace!

2   Who can describe the pain
Which faithful preachers feel;
Constrain'd to speak, in vain,
To hearts as hard as steel?
Or who can tell the pleasures felt,
When stubborn hearts begin to melt?

3   The Saviour's dying love,
The soul's amazing worth;
Their utmost efforts move,

And draw their bowels forth:
They pray and strive, their rest departs,
Till CHRIST be form'd in sinners hearts.

4   If some small hope appear,
     They still are not content;
     But, with a jealous fear,
     They watch for the event:
Too oft they find their hopes deceiv'd,
Then, how their inmost souls are griev'd!

5   But when their pains succeed,
     And from the tender blade
     The rip'ning ears proceed,
     Their toils are overpaid:
No harvest-joy can equal theirs,
To find the fruit of all their cares.

6   On what has now been sown
     Thy blessing, LORD, bestow;
     The pow'r is thine alone,
     To make it spring and grow:
Do thou the gracious harvest raise,
And thou, alone, shalt have the praise.

HYMN 32

Spring.

1   Bleak winter is subdu'd at length,
     And forc'd to yield the day;
   The sun has wasted all his strength,
     And driven him away.

2   And now long wish'd for spring is come,
     How alter'd is the scene!
   The trees and shrubs are drest in bloom,
     The earth array'd in green.

3   Where'er we tread, beneath our feet
     The clust'ring flowers spring;
   The artless birds, in concert sweet,
     Invite our hearts to sing.

4   But ah! in vain I strive to join,
     Oppress'd with sin and doubt;

I feel 'tis winter still, within,
    Tho' all is spring without.

5 Oh! would my Saviour from on high,
    Break thro' these clouds and shine!
  No creature then, more blest than I,
    No song more loud than mine.

6 Till then—no softly warbling thrush,
    Nor cowslip's sweet perfume;
  Nor beauties of each painted bush,
    Can dissipate my gloom.

7 To Adam, soon as he transgress'd,
    Thus Eden bloom'd in vain;
  Not paradise could give him rest,
    Or sooth his heart-felt pain.

8 Yet here an emblem I perceive
    Of what the LORD can do;
  Dear Saviour, help me to believe
    That I may flourish too.

9 Thy word can soon my hopes revive,
    Can overcome my foes;
  And make my languid graces thrive,
    And blossom like the rose.

HYMN 36

Harvest.

1 See! the corn again in ear!
  How the fields and valleys smile!
  Harvest now is drawing near
  To repay the farmer's toil:
  Gracious LORD, secure the crop,
  Satisfy the poor with food;
  In thy mercy is our hope,
  We have sinn'd but thou art good.

2 While I view the plenteous grain
  As it ripens on the stalk;
  May I not instruction gain,
  Helpful, to my daily walk?
  All this plenty of the field

Was produc'd from foreign seeds;
For the earth itself would yield
Only crops of useless weeds.

3   Tho', when newly sown, it lay
Hid awhile beneath the ground,
(Some might think it thrown away)
Now a large increase is found:
Tho' conceal'd, it was not lost,
Tho' it dy'd, it lives again;
Eastern storms, and nipping frosts
Have oppos'd its growth in vain.

4   Let the praise be all the LORD's,
As the benefit is ours!
He, in seasons, still affords
Kindly heat, and gentle show'rs:
By his care the produce thrives
Waving o'er the furrow'd lands;
And when harvest-time arrives,
Ready for the reaper stands.

5   Thus in barren hearts he sows
Precious seeds of heav'nly joy;[17]
Sin, and hell, in vain oppose,
None can grace's crop destroy:
Threat'ned oft, yet still it blooms,
After many changes past,
Death, the reaper, when he comes,
Finds it fully ripe at last.

HYMN 40

Saturday evening.

1   Safely thro' another week,
      God has brought us on our way;
    Let us now a blessing seek
      On th' approaching sabbath-day:
        Day, of all the week, the best;
        Emblem of eternal rest!

2   Mercies, multiply'd each hour,
      Thro' the week our praise demand;

[17] Hosea xiv. 7. Mark iv. 26–29.*

Guarded by almighty pow'r,
  Fed and guided by his hand:
    Tho' ungrateful we have been,
    Only made returns of sin.

3 While we pray for pard'ning grace,
     Thro' the dear Redeemer's name;
   Shew thy reconciled face,
     Shine away our sin and shame:
       From our worldly cares set free,
       May we rest, this night, with thee.

4 When the morn shall bid us rise,
     May we feel thy presence near;
   May thy glory meet our eyes,
     When we in thy house appear!
       There afford us, LORD, a taste
       Of our everlasting feast.

5 May thy gospel's joyful sound
     Conquer sinners, comfort saints;
   Make the fruits of grace abound,
     Bring relief for all complaints:
       Thus may all our sabbaths prove
       Till we join the church above!

HYMN 43

On opening a place for social prayer.

1 O Lord, our languid souls inspire,
     For here, we trust, thou art!
   Send down a coal of heav'nly fire,
     To warm each waiting heart.

2 Dear Shepherd of thy people, hear,
     Thy presence now display;
   As thou hast giv'n a place for pray'r,
     So give us hearts to pray.

3 Shew us some token of thy love,
     Our fainting hope to raise;
   And pour thy blessings from above,
     That we may render praise.

4 Within these walls let holy peace,
     And love, and concord dwell;

253

Here give the troubled conscience ease,
The wounded spirit heal.

5   The feeling heart, the melting eye,
The humble mind bestow;
And shine upon us from on high,
To make our graces grow!

6   May we in faith receive thy word,
In faith present our pray'rs;
And, in the presence of our LORD,
Unbosom all our cares.

7   And may the gospel's joyful sound
Enforc'd by mighty grace,
Awaken many sinners round,
To come and fill the place.

HYMN 44

Cowper. *Another.*

1   JESUS, wheree'er thy people meet,
There they behold thy mercy-seat;
Wheree'er they seek thee thou art found,
And ev'ry place is hallow'd ground.

2   For thou, within no walls confin'd,
Inhabitest the humble mind;
Such ever bring thee, where they come,
And going, take thee to their home.

3   Dear Shepherd of thy chosen few!
Thy former mercies here renew;
Here, to our waiting hearts, proclaim
The sweetness of thy saving name.

4   Here may we prove the pow'r of pray'r,
To strengthen faith, and sweeten care;
To teach our faint desires to rise,
And bring all heav'n before our eyes.

5   Behold! at thy commanding word,
We stretch the curtain and the cord;[18]
Come thou, and fill this wider space,
And help us with a large encrease.

[18] Isaiah liv. 2.*

6 LORD, we are few, but thou art near;
Nor short thine arm, nor deaf thine ear;
Oh rend the heav'ns, come quickly down,
And make a thousand hearts thine own!

HYMN 55

Cowper. JESUS *hasting to suffer.*

1 The Saviour! what a noble flame
Was kindled in his breast,
When hasting to Jerusalem
He march'd before the rest!

2 Good-will to men, and zeal for GOD,
His ev'ry thought engross;
He longs to be baptiz'd with blood,[19]
He pants to reach the cross.

3 With all his suff'rings full in view,
And woes, to us, unknown,
Forth to the task his spirit flew,
'Twas love that urg'd him on.

4 Lord, we return thee what we can!
Our hearts shall sound abroad
Salvation, to the dying Man,
And to the rising GOD!

5 And while thy bleeding glories here
Engage our wond'ring eyes;
We learn our lighter cross to bear,
And hasten to the skies.

HYMN 62

Cowper. *The light and glory of the word.*

1 The Spirit breathes upon the word,
And brings the truth to sight;
Precepts and promises afford
A sanctifying light.

2 A glory gilds the sacred page,
Majestic like the sun;
It gives a light to ev'ry age,
It gives, but borrows none.

[19] Luke xii. 50.*

3   The hand that gave it, still supplies
        The gracious light and heat;
    His truths upon the nations rise,
        They rise, but never set.

4   Let everlasting thanks be thine!
        For such a bright display,
    As makes a world of darkness shine
        With beams of heav'nly day.

5   My soul rejoices to pursue
        The steps of him I love;
    Till glory breaks upon my view
        In brighter worlds above.

HYMN 63

The word more precious than gold.

1   Precious Bible! what a treasure
Does the word of GOD afford?
All I want for life or pleasure,
FOOD and MED'CINE, SHIELD and SWORD:
    Let the world account me poor,
    Having this I need no more.

2   Food to which the world's a stranger,
Here my hungry soul enjoys;
Of excess there is no danger,
Tho' it fills, it never cloys:
    On a dying CHRIST I feed,
    He is meat and drink indeed!

3   When my faith is faint and sickly,
Or when Satan wounds my mind,
Cordials, to revive me quickly,
Healing MED'CINES here I find:
    To the promises I flee,
    Each affords a remedy.

4   In the hour of dark temptation
Satan cannot make me yield;
For the word of consolation

Is to me a mighty S H I E L D :
  While the scripture-truths are sure,
  From his malice I'm secure.

5 Vain his threats to overcome me,
When I take the Spirits' S W O R D ;
Then with ease I drive him from me,
Satan trembles at the word:
  'Tis a sword for conquest made,
  Keen the edge, and strong the blade.

6 Shall I envy then the miser
Doating on his golden store;
Sure I am, or should be, wiser,
I am Rich, 'tis he is Poor:
  J E S U S gives me in his word,
  F O O D and M E D ' C I N E, S H I E L D and S W O R D.

H Y M N 69

On the fire at Olney. September 22, 1799

1 Wearied by day with toils and cares,
How welcome is the peaceful night!
Sweet sleep our wasted strength repairs,
And fits us for returning light.

2 Yet when our eyes in sleep are clos'd,
Our rest may break ere well begun;
To dangers ev'ry hour expos'd
We neither can foresee nor shun.

3 'Tis of the Lord that we can sleep
A single night without alarms;
His eye alone our lives can keep
Secure, amidst a thousand harms.

4 For months and years of safety past,
Ungrateful, we, alass! have been;
Tho' patient long, he spoke at last,
And bid the fire rebuke our sin.

5 The shout of fire! a dreadful cry,
Imprest each heart with deep dismay;
While the fierce blaze and red'ning sky,
Made midnight wear the face of day.

6   The throng and terror who can speak?
     The various sounds that fill'd the air!
     The infant's wail, the mother's shriek,
     The voice of blasphemy and pray'r!

7   But pray'r prevail'd, and sav'd the town;
     The few, who lov'd the Saviour's name,
     Were hear'd, and mercy hasted down
     To change the wind, and stop the flame.

8   Oh, may that night be ne'er forgot!
     LORD, still encrease thy praying few!
     Were OLNEY left without a Lot,
     Ruin, like Sodoms', would ensue.

HYMN 85

On the eclipse of the moon. July 30, 1776

1   The moon in silver glory shone,
      And not a cloud in sight;
    When suddenly a shade begun
      To intercept her light.

2   How fast across her orb it spread,
      How fast her light withdrew!
    A circle, ting'd with languid red,
      Was all appear'd in view.

3   While many with unmeaning eye
      Gaze on thy works in vain;
    Assist me, LORD, that I may try
      Instruction to obtain.

4   Fain would my thankful heart and lips
      Unite in praise to thee;
    And meditate on thy eclipse,
      In sad Gethsemane.

5   Thy peoples guilt, a heavy load!
      (When standing in their room)
    Depriv'd thee of the light of GOD,
      And fill'd thy soul with gloom.

6   How punctually eclipses move,
      Obedient to thy will!

Thus shall thy faithfulness and love,
Thy promises fulfill.

7   Dark, like the moon without the sun,
I mourn thine absence, Lord!
For light or comfort I have none,
But what thy beams afford.

8   But lo! the hour draws near apace,
When changes shall be o'er;
Then I shall see thee face to face,
And be eclips'd no more.

Extracts from Book III, *On the Rise, Progress, Changes and Comforts of the Spiritual Life*

HYMN I

Expostulation

1   No words can declare,
No fancy can paint,
What rage and despair,
What hopeless complaint,
Fill Satan's dark dwelling,
The prison beneath;
What weeping and yelling,
And gnashing of teeth!

2   Yet sinners will choose
This dreadful abode,
Each madly persues
The dangerous road;
Tho' GOD give them warning
They onward will go,
They answer with scorning,
And onward do go.

3   How sad to behold
The rich and the poor,
The young and the old,
All blindly secure!
All posting to ruin,
Refusing to stop;
Ah! think what you're doing,
While yet there is hope!

4 How weak is your hand
   To fight with the LORD!
  How can you withstand
   The edge of his sword?
  What hope of escaping
   For those who oppose,
  When hell is wide gaping
   To swallow his foes?

5 How oft have you dar'd
   The LORD to his face!
  Yet still you are spar'd
   To hear of his grace;
  Oh pray for repentance
   And life-giving faith,
  Before the just sentence
   Consign you to death.

6 It is not too late
   To JESUS to flee,
  His mercy is great,
   His pardon is free;
  His blood has such virtue
   For all that believe,
  That nothing can hurt you,
   If him you receive.

HYMN 15

Cowper. *Light shining out of darkness.*

1 God moves in a mysterious way,
   His wonders to perform;
  He plants his footsteps in the sea,
   And rides upon the storm.

2 Deep in unfathomable mines
   Of never failing skill;
  He treasures up his bright designs,
   And works his sovereign will.

3 Ye fearful saints fresh courage take,
   The clouds ye so much dread
  Are big with mercy, and shall break
   In blessings on your head.

4 Judge not the LORD by feeble sense,
        But trust him for his grace;
    Behind a frowning providence,
        He hides a smiling face.

5 His purposes will ripen fast,
        Unfolding ev'ry hour;
    The bud may have a bitter taste,
        But sweet will be the flow'r.

6 Blind unbelief is sure to err,[20]
        And scan his work in vain;
    God is his own interpreter,
        And he will make it plain.

HYMN 17

Cowper. *Afflictions sanctified by the word.*

1 O How I love thy holy word,
    Thy gracious covenant, O LORD!
    It guides me in the peaceful way,
    I think upon it all the day.

2 What are the mines of shining wealth,
    The strength of youth, the bloom of health!
    What are all joys compar'd with those
    Thine everlasting word bestows!

3 Long unafflicted, undismay'd,
    In pleasures path secure I stray'd;
    Thou mad'st me feel thy chastning rod,[21]
    And strait I turn'd unto my GOD.

4 What tho' it pierc'd my fainting heart,
    I bless thine hand that caus'd the smart;
    It taught my tears awhile to flow,
    But sav'd me from eternal woe.

5 Oh! hadst thou left me unchastis'd,
    Thy precept I had still despis'd;
    And *still* the snare in secret laid,
    Had my unwary feet betray'd.

[20] John xiii. 7.*
[21] Psalm cxix. 71.*

6 I love thee therefore O my GOD,
   And breathe towards thy dear abode;
   Where in thy presence fully blest,
   Thy chosen saints for ever rest.

HYMN 48

Cowper. *Joy and peace in believing.*

1 Sometimes a light surprizes
       The christian while he sings;
   It is the LORD who rises
       With healing in his wings:
   When comforts are declining,
       He grants the soul again
   A season of clear shining
       To cheer it after rain.

2 In holy contemplation,
       We sweetly then pursue
   The theme of GOD's salvation,
       And find it ever new:
   Set free from present sorrow,
       We cheerfully can say,
   Ee'n let th' unknown to-morrow,[22]
       Bring with it what it may.

3 It can bring with it nothing
       But he will bear us thro';
   Who gives the lilies clothing
       Will clothe his people too:
   Beneath the spreading heavens,
       No creature but is fed;
   And he who feeds the ravens,
       Will give his children bread.

4 The vine, nor fig-tree neither,[23]
       Their wonted fruit should bear,
   Tho' all the fields should whither,
       Nor flocks, nor herds, be there:
   Yet God the same abiding,
       His praise shall tune my voice;
   For while in him confiding,
       I cannot but rejoice.

[22] Matt. vi. 34.*
[23] Habakkuk iii. 17, 18.*

HYMN 68

Cowper. *The new convert.*

1   The new-born child of gospel-grace,
    Like some fair tree when summer's nigh,
    Beneath EMMANUEL's shining face,
    Lifts up his blooming branch on high.

2   No fears he feels, he sees no foes,
    No conflict yet his faith employs,
    Nor has he learnt to whom he owes,
    The strength and peace his soul enjoys.

3   But sin soon darts its cruel sting,
    And comforts sinking day by day;
    What seem'd his own, a self-fed spring,
    Proves but a brook that glides away.

4   When Gideon arm'd his num'rous host,
    The LORD soon made his numbers less;
    And said, lest Israel vainly boast,
    "My arm procur'd me this success."

5   Thus will he bring our spirits down,
    And draw our ebbing comforts low;
    That sav'd by grace, but not our own,
    We may not claim the praise we owe.

HYMN 81

Cowper. *Grace and Providence.*

1   Almighty King! whose wond'rous hand,
    Supports the weight of sea and land;
    Whose grace is such a boundless store,
    No heart shall break that sighs for more.

2   Thy Providence supplies my food,
    And 'tis thy blessing makes it good;
    My soul is nourish'd by thy word,
    Let soul and body praise the LORD.

3   My streams of outward comfort came
    From him, who built this earthly frame;
    Whate'er I want his bounty gives,
    By whom my soul for ever lives.

4   Either his hand preserves from pain,
    Or, if I feel it, heals again;
    From Satan's malice shields my breast,
    Or overrules it for the best.

5   Forgive the song that falls so low
    Beneath the gratitude I owe!
    It means thy praise, however poor,
    An angel's song can do no more.

HYMN 83

Cowper. *I will praise the* LORD *at all times.*

1   Winter has a joy for me,
    While the Saviour's charms I read,
    Lowly, meek, from blemish free,
    In the snow-drop's pensive head.

2   Spring returns, and brings along
    Life-invigorating suns:
    Hark! the turtle's plaintive song,
    Seems to speak his dying grones!

3   Summer has a thousand charms,
    All expressive of his worth;
    'Tis his sun that lights and warms,
    His the air that cools the earth.

4   What, has autumn left to say
    Nothing, of a Saviour's grace?
    Yes, the beams of milder day
    Tell me of his smiling face.

5   Light appears with early dawn;
    While the sun makes haste to rise,
    See his bleeding beauties, drawn
    On the blushes of the skies.

6   Ev'ning, with a silent pace,
    Slowly moving in the west,
    Shews an emblem of his grace,
    Points to an eternal rest.

Source: *Olney Hymns, in Three Books*, London, Oliver, Buckland and Johnson, 1779 (Facsimile edition: Olney, Trustees of The Cowper and Newton Museum, 1979).

Early nineteenth-century hymns

Robert Grant,[24] Psalm 104 'O worship the King'

O worship the King
   All glorious above,
O gratefully sing
   His power and his love –
Our shield and defender,
   The Ancient of days,
Pavilion'd in splendour,
   And girded with praise.

O tell of his might,
   O sing of his grace,
Whose robe is the light,
   Whose canopy space.
His chariots of wrath
   Deep thunder-clouds form,
And dark is his path
   On the wings of the storm.

This earth, with its store
   Of wonders untold,
Almighty! thy power
   Hath founded of old;
Hath stablish'd it fast
   By a changeless decree,
And round it hath cast,
   Like a mantle, the sea.

Thy bountiful care
   What tongue can recite?
It breathes in the air,
   It shines in the light:
It streams from the hills,
   It descends to the plain,
And sweetly distils
   In the dew and the rain.

[24] Sir Robert Grant (1779–1838), lawyer, politician and governor of Bombay.

Frail children of dust,
  And feeble as frail,
In thee do we trust,
  Nor find thee to fail:
Thy mercies how tender!
  How firm to the end!
Our Maker, Defender,
Redeemer, and Friend!

O measureless might!
  Ineffable Love!
While angels delight
  To hymn thee above,
The humbler creation,
  Tho' feeble their lays,
With true adoration
  Shall lisp to thy praise!

Source: *Sacred Poems by the late Right Hon. Sir Robert Grant*,
London, Saunders and Otley, 1839, pp. 33–5.

Reginald Heber,[25] 'From Greenland's icy mountains'

BEFORE A COLLECTION MADE FOR THE SOCIETY FOR THE
PROPAGATION OF THE GOSPEL[26]

From Greenland's icy mountains,
  From India's coral strand,
Where Afric's sunny fountains
  Roll down their golden sand;
From many an ancient river,
  From many a palmy plain,
They call us to deliver
  Their land from error's chain!

What though the spicy breezes
  Blow soft o'er Java's isle,
And every prospect pleases,
  And only man is vile:
In vain with lavish kindness

[25] Reginald Heber (1783–1826), Anglican clergyman, bishop of Calcutta.
[26] One of the oldest missionary societies, founded in 1701.

The gifts of God are strewn,
The Heathen, in his blindness,
  Bows down to wood and stone!

Can we, whose souls are lighted
  With Wisdom from on high,
Can we to men benighted
  The lamp of life deny?
Salvation! oh Salvation!
  The joyful sound proclaim,
Till each remotest nation
  Has learn'd Messiah's name.

Waft waft ye winds his story
  And you ye waters roll,
Till like a sea of glory,
  It spreads from pole to pole:
Till o'er our ransom'd Nature,
  The Lamb for sinners slain,
Redeemer, King, Creator,
  In bliss returns to reign!

Source: Reginald Heber, *Hymns Written and Adapted to the Weekly Church Service of the Year*, London, John Murray, 1827, pp. 139–40.

James Montgomery,[27] Psalm 72 'Hail to the Lord's anointed'

Hail to the Lord's anointed!
  Great David's greater Son;
Hail, in the time appointed,
  His reign on earth begun!
He comes to break oppression
  To let the captive free;
To take away transgression,
  And rule in equity.

He comes, with succour speedy,
  To those who suffer wrong;
To help the poor and needy,
  And bid the weak be strong;

[27] James Montgomery (1771–1854), journalist and poet.

To give them songs for sighing,
   Their darkness turn to light,
Whose souls, condemn'd and dying,
   Were precious in his sight.

By such shall He be feared,
   While sun and moon endure,
Belov'd, obey'd, revered;
   For He shall judge the poor
Through changing generations,
   With justice, mercy, truth,
While stars maintain their stations,
   Or moons renew their youth.

He shall come down, like showers
   Upon the fruitful earth,
And love, joy, hope, like flowers,
   Spring in his path to birth:
Before Him, on the mountains
   Shall Peace the herald go;
And righteousness in fountains
   From hill to valley flow.

Arabia's desert-ranger
   To Him shall bow the knee;
The Ethiopian stranger
   His glory come to see;
With offerings of devotion,
   Ships from the isles shall meet,
To pour the wealth of ocean
   In tribute at his feet.

Kings shall fall down before Him
   And gold and incense bring;
All nations shall adore Him,
   His praise all people sing;
For He shall have dominion
   O'er river, sea, and shore,
Far as the eagle's pinion,
   Or dove's light wing can soar.

For Him shall prayer unceasing,
   And daily vows, ascend;
His Kingdom still increasing,

A Kingdom without end:
The mountain-dews shall nourish
A seed in weakness sown,
Whose fruit shall spread and flourish,
And shake like Lebanon.

O'er every foe victorious,
He on his throne shall rest,
From age to age more glorious,
All blessing and all-blest;
The tide of time shall never
His covenant remove;
His name shall stand for ever;
That name to us is – Love.

Source: *The Poetical Works of James Montgomery, Vol. III: Songs of Zion*, London, Longman, Rees, Orme, Brown and Green, 1828, pp. 59–63.

William Wilberforce

Selections from three publications by William Wilberforce (1759–1833) serve to illuminate his religious ideas and their social and political implications. The *Practical View* is an extended critique of the nominal Christianity of late eighteenth-century England against the backdrop of war with revolutionary France. Wilberforce presents Evangelical Christianity as the only secure base for the salvation of individuals and the stability of the nation. The extracts from two works on slavery have been chosen to illustrate the religious dimensions and motivations of Wilberforce's activities in this field. The *Letter on the Abolition of the Slave Trade* was addressed to Wilberforce's Yorkshire constituents, and was published as the lengthy parliamentary campaign was at last within sight of success. It reviewed the arguments used over the last two decades. The *Appeal . . . in Behalf of the Negro Slaves* was written at the end of Wilberforce's active career and helped to launch the campaign for the emancipation of slaves in the British colonies, which was eventually successful in 1833.

Extracts from *Practical View of the Prevailing Religious System of Professed Christians . . . Contrasted with Real Christianity*, 1797

INTRODUCTION

It has been, for several years, the earnest wish of the writer of the following pages to address his countrymen on the important subject of Religion; but the various duties of his public station, and a constitution incapable of much labour, have obstructed the execution of his purpose. Long has he been looking forward to some vacant season, in which he might devote his whole time and attention to this interesting service, free from the interruption of all other concerns; and he has the rather wished for this opportunity of undistracted and mature reflection, from a desire that what he might send into the world might thus be rendered less undeserving of the public eye. Meanwhile life is wearing away, and he daily becomes more and more convinced, that he might wait in vain for this season of complete vacancy. He must, therefore, improve such occasional intervals of leisure as may occur to him in the course of a busy life, and throw himself on the Reader's indulgence for the pardon of such imperfections as the opportunity of undiverted and more mature attention might have enabled him to discover and correct.

But the plea here suggested is by no means intended as an excuse for the opinions which he shall express, if they be found mistaken. Here, if he be in an error, it is however a deliberate error. He would indeed account himself unpardonable, if he were to intrude his first thoughts upon the Public on a question of such importance; and he can truly declare, that what he shall offer will be the result of much reading, observation, and inquiry, and of long, serious, and repeated consideration.

It is not improbable that he may be accused of deviating from his proper line, and of impertinently interfering in the concerns of a profession to which he does not belong. If it were necessary, however, to defend himself against this charge, he might shelter himself under the authority of many most respectable examples. But surely to such an accusation it may be sufficient to reply, that it is the duty of every man to promote the happiness of his fellow-creatures to the utmost of his power; and that he who thinks he sees many around him, whom he esteems and loves, labouring under a fatal error, must have a cold heart, or a most confined notion of benevolence, if he could refrain from endeavouring to set them right, lest in so doing he should be accused of stepping out of his proper walk, and expose himself on that ground to the imputation of officiousness.

But he might also allege as a full justification, not only that Religion is the business of every one, but that its advancement or decline in any country is so intimately connected with the temporal interests of society, as to render it the peculiar concern of a political man; and that what he may presume to offer on the subject of Religion may perhaps be perused with less jealousy and more candour, from the very circumstance of its having been written by a Layman, which must at least exclude the idea (an idea sometimes illiberally suggested to take off the effect of the works of Ecclesiastics) that it is prompted by motives of self-interest, or of professional prejudice.

But if the writer's apology be not found in the work itself, and in his avowed motive for undertaking it, he would in vain endeavour to satisfy his readers by any excuses he might assign; therefore, without farther preamble, he will proceed to the statement and execution of his purpose.

The main object which he has in view is, not to convince the Sceptic, or to answer the arguments of persons who avowedly oppose the fundamental doctrines of our Religion; but to point out the scanty and erroneous system of the bulk of those who belong to the class of orthodox Christians, and to contrast their defective scheme with a representation of what the author apprehends to be real Christianity. Often has it filled him with deep concern, to observe in this description of persons, scarcely any distinct knowledge of the real nature and principles of the religion which they profess. The subject is of infinite importance; let it not be driven out of our minds by the bustle or dissipations of life. This present scene, and all its cares and all its gaieties, will soon be rolled away, and "we must stand before the judgment seat of Christ." This aweful consideration will prompt the writer to express himself with greater freedom than he should otherwise be disposed to use. This consideration he trusts, also, will justify his frankness, and will secure him a serious and patient perusal. But it would be trespassing on the indulgence of the reader to detain him with introductory remarks. Let it only be farther premised, that if what shall be stated should to any appear needlessly austere and rigid, the writer must lay in his claim not to be condemned without a fair inquiry whether or not his statements accord with the language of the sacred writings. To that test he refers with confidence; and it must be conceded by those who admit the authority of Scripture (such only he is addressing) that from the decision of the word of God there can be no appeal.

[. . .]

CHAPTER IV.

SECT. VI.

Grand defect.—Neglect of the peculiar Doctrines of Christianity.

But the grand radical defect in the practical system of these nominal Christians, is their forgetfulness of all the peculiar doctrines of the Religion which they profess—the corruption of human nature—the atonement of the Saviour—and the sanctifying influence of the Holy Spirit.

Here then we come again to the grand distinction between the Religion of Christ and that of the bulk of nominal Christians in the present day. The point is of the utmost *practical importance*, and we would therefore trace it into its actual effects.

There are, it is to be apprehended, not a few, who having been for some time hurried down the stream of dissipation in the indulgence of all

272

their natural appetites (except perhaps that they were restrained from very gross vice by a regard to character, or by the yet unsubdued voice of conscience) and who, having all the while thought little, or scarce at all, about Religion, "living," to use the emphatical language of Scripture, "without God in the world," become in some degree impressed with a sense of the infinite importance of Religion. A fit of sickness, perhaps, or the loss of some friend or much loved relative, or some other stroke of adverse fortune, damps their spirits, awakens them to a practical conviction of the precariousness of all human things, and turns them to seek for some more stable foundation of happiness than this world can afford. Looking into themselves ever so little, they become sensible that they must have offended God. They resolve accordingly to set about the work of reformation.—Here it is that we shall recognize the fatal effects of the prevailing ignorance of the real nature of Christianity, and the general forgetfulness of its grand peculiarities. These men *wish* to reform, but they know neither the real *nature* of their distemper nor its true remedy. They are aware, indeed, that they must cease to do evil, and learn to do well; that they must relinquish their habits of vice, and attend more or less to the duties of Religion; but having no conception of the actual malignity of the disease under which they labour, or of the perfect cure which the Gospel has provided for it, or of the manner in which that cure is to be effected,

"They do but skin and film the ulcerous place,
While rank corruption, mining all within,
Infects unseen."

It often happens therefore but too naturally in this case, that where they do not soon desist from their attempt at reformation, and relapse into their old habits of sin, they take up with a partial and scanty amendment, and fondly flatter themselves that it is a thorough change. They now conceive that they have a right to take to themselves the comforts of Christianity. Not being able to raise their practice up to their standard of right, they lower their standard to their practice; they sit down for life contented with their present attainments, beguiled by the complacencies of their own minds, and by the favourable testimony of surrounding friends; and it often happens, particularly where there is any degree of strictness in formal and ceremonial observances, that there are no people more jealous of their character for Religion.

Others perhaps go farther than this. The dread of the wrath to come has sunk deeper into their hearts; and for a while they strive with all their might to resist their evil propensities, and to walk without stumbling in the path of duty. Again and again they resolve; again and again they break their resolutions. All their endeavours are foiled, and they become more and more convinced of their own moral weakness, and of the strength of their indwelling corruption. Thus groaning under the enslaving power of sin, and experiencing the futility of the utmost efforts which they can use for effecting their deliverance, they are tempted (sometimes it is to be feared they yield to the temptation) to give up all in despair, and to acquiesce under their wretched captivity, conceiving it impossible to break their chains. Sometimes, probably, it even happens that they are driven to seek for refuge from their disquietude in the suggestions of infidelity, and to quiet their troublesome consciences by arguments which they themselves scarcely believe, at the very moment in which they suffer themselves to be lulled asleep by them. In the mean time while this conflict has been going on, their walk is sad and comfortless, and their couch is nightly watered with tears. These men are pursuing the right object, but they mistake the way in which it is to be obtained. *The path in which they are now treading is not that which the Gospel has provided for conducting them to true holiness, nor will they find in it any solid peace.*

Persons under these circumstances naturally seek for religious instruction. They turn over the works of our modern Religionists, and as well as they can collect the advice addressed to men in their situation, the substance of it is, at the best, of this sort. "Be sorry indeed for your sins, and discontinue the practice of them, but do not make yourselves so uneasy. Christ died for the sins of the whole world. Do your utmost; discharge with fidelity the duties of your stations, not neglecting your religious offices, and fear not but that in the end all will go well, and that having thus performed the conditions required on your part, you will at last obtain forgiveness of our merciful Creator through the merits of Jesus Christ, and be aided, where your own strength shall be insufficient, by the assistance of his Holy Spirit. Meanwhile you cannot do better than read carefully such books of practical divinity as will instruct you in the principles of a Christian life. We are excellently furnished with works of this nature; and it is by the diligent study of them that you will gradually become a proficient in the lessons of the Gospel."

But the holy Scriptures, and with them the Church of England, call upon those who are in the circumstances above-stated, to *lay afresh the whole foundation of their Religion.* In concurrence with the Scripture, that Church calls upon them, in the first place, gratefully to adore that undeserved goodness which has awakened them from the sleep of death; to prostrate themselves before the Cross of Christ with humble penitence and deep self-abhorrence, solemnly resolving to forsake all their sins, but relying on the Grace of God alone for power to keep their resolution. Thus, and thus only, she assures them that all their crimes will be blotted out, and that they will receive from above a new living principle of holiness. She produces from the Word of God the ground and warrant of her counsel; "Believe in the Lord Jesus Christ, and thou shalt be saved."—"No man," says our blessed Saviour "cometh unto the Father but by me."—"I am the true vine. As the branch cannot bear fruit of itself except it abide in the vine, no more can ye except ye abide in me."—"He that abideth in me and I in him, the same bringeth forth much fruit; for without (or severed from) me ye can do nothing."—"By grace ye are saved through faith, and that not of yourselves, it is the gift of God; not of works, lest any man should boast, for we are his workmanship, created in Christ Jesus unto good works."

Let us not be thought tedious, or be accused of running into needless repetitions, in pressing this point with so much earnestness. It is in fact a point which can never be too much insisted on. It is the cardinal point on which the whole of Christianity turns; on which it is peculiarly proper in this place to be perfectly distinct. There have been some who have imagined that the wrath of God was to be deprecated, or his favour conciliated, by austerities and penances, or even by forms and ceremonies, and external observances. But all men of enlightened understandings, who acknowledge the moral government of God, must also acknowledge, that vice must offend and virtue delight him. In short they must, more or less, assent to the Scripture declaration, "without holiness no man shall see the Lord." But the grand distinction which subsists between the true Christian and all other Religionists (the class of persons in particular whom it is our object to address) is concerning the *nature* of this holiness, and the *way in which it is to be obtained.* The views entertained by the latter, of the *nature* of holiness, are of all degrees of inadequateness; and they conceive it is to be *obtained* by their own natural unassisted efforts; or if they admit some vague indistinct notion of the assistance of the Holy Spirit, it is unquestionably obvious, on conversing with them, that this does not constitute the *main practical* ground of their dependence. *But the nature of the holiness to which the desires of the true Christian are directed, is no other than the restoration of the image of God; and as to the manner of acquiring it, disclaiming with indignation every idea of attaining it by his own strength, all his hopes of possessing it rest altogether on the divine assurances of the operation of the Holy Spirit, in those who cordially embrace the Gospel of Christ. He knows therefore that this holiness is not to* PRECEDE *his reconciliation to God, and be its* CAUSE, *but to* FOLLOW *it, and be its* EFFECT. *That in short it is by* FAITH IN CHRIST *only that he is to be justified in the sight of God; to be delivered from the condition of a child of wrath, and a slave of Satan; to be adopted into the family of God; to become an heir of God and a joint heir with Christ, entitled to all the privileges which belong to this high relation; here, to the Spirit of Grace, and a partial renewal after the image of his Creator; hereafter, to the more perfect possession of the Divine likeness, and an inheritance of eternal glory.*

And as it is in this way, that in obedience to the dictates of the Gospel, the true Christian must originally become possessed of the vital Spirit and living principle of universal holiness, so, in order to grow in grace, he must also study in the same school; finding in the consideration of the peculiar doctrines of the Gospel, and in the contemplation of the life and character and sufferings of our blessed Saviour, the elements of all practical wisdom, and an inexhaustible storehouse of instructions and motives, no otherwise to be so well supplied. From the neglect of these peculiar doctrines arise the main practical errors of the bulk of professed Christians. These gigantic truths retained in view, would put to shame the littleness of their dwarfish morality. It would be impossible for them to make these harmonize with their low conceptions of the wretchedness and danger of their natural state, which is represented in Scripture as having so powerfully called forth the compassion of God, that he sent his only begotten Son to rescue us. Where *now* are their low conceptions of the worth of the soul, when means like these were taken to redeem it? Where *now* their inadequate conceptions of the guilt of sin, for which in the divine councils it seemed requisite that an atonement no less costly should be made, than that of the blood of the only begotten Son of God? How can they reconcile their low standard of Christian practice with the representation of our being "temples of the Holy Ghost?" Their cold sense of obligation, and scanty grudged returns of service, with the glowing gratitude of those who, having been "delivered from the power of darkness, and translated into the kingdom of God's dear Son," may well conceive that the labours of a whole life will be but an imperfect expression of their thankfulness.

The peculiar doctrines of the Gospel being once admitted, the conclusions which have been now suggested are clear and obvious deductions of reason. But our neglect of these important truths is still less pardonable, because they are distinctly and repeatedly applied in Scripture to the very purposes in question, and the whole superstructure of Christian morals is grounded on their deep and ample basis.

[. . .]

CHAPTER VI.

Brief Inquiry into the present State of Christianity in this Country, with some of the Causes which have led to its critical Circumstances. Its Importance to us as a political Community, and practical Hints for which the foregoing Considerations give occasion.

It may not be altogether improper to remind the reader, that hitherto, our discussion has been concerning the prevailing Religious opinions merely of *professed Christians*; no longer confining ourselves to persons of this description, let us now extend our inquiry, and briefly investigate the *general* state of Christianity in this country.

The tendency of Religion in general to promote the temporal well-being of political communities, is a fact which depends on such obvious and undeniable principles, and which is so forcibly inculcated by the history of all ages, that there can be no necessity for entering into a formal proof of its truth. It has indeed been maintained, not merely by School-men and Divines, but by the most celebrated philosophers, and moralists, and politicians of every age.

The peculiar excellence in this respect also of Christianity, considered independently of its truth or falsehood, has been recognized by many writers, who, to say the least, were not disposed to exaggerate its merits. Either or both of these propositions being admitted, the state of Religion in a country at any given period, not to mention its connection with the eternal happiness of the inhabitants, immediately becomes a question of great *political* importance; and in particular it must be material to ascertain whether Religion be in an advancing or in a declining state; and if the latter be the case, whether there be any practicable means for preventing at least its farther declension.

If the representations contained in the preceding chapters, of the state of Christianity among the bulk of professed Christians, be not very erroneous, they may well excite serious apprehension in the mind of every reader, when considered merely in a political view. And this apprehension would be increased, if there should appear reason to believe that, for some time past, Religion has been on the decline amongst us, and that it continues to decline at the present moment.

When it is proposed, however, to inquire into the actual state of Religion in any country, and in particular to compare that state with its condition at any former period, there is one preliminary observation to be made, if we would not be liable to gross error. There exists, established by tacit consent, in every country, what may be called a general standard or tone of morals, varying in the same community at different periods, and different at the same period in different ranks and situations in

society. Whoever falls below this standard, and not unfrequently, whoever also rises above it, offending against this general rule, suffers proportionably in the general estimation. Thus a regard for character,
which, as was formerly remarked, is commonly the grand governing
principle among men, becomes to a certain degree, though no farther, an
incitement to morality and virtue. It follows of course, that where the
practice does no more than come up to the required level, it will be no
sufficient evidence of the existence, much less will it furnish any just
measure of the force, of a real internal principle of Religion. Christians,
Jews, Turks, Infidels and Heretics, persons of ten thousand different
sorts of passions and opinions, being members at the same time of the
same community, and all conscious that they will be examined by this
same standard, will regulate their conduct accordingly, and, with no
great difference, will all adjust themselves to the required measure.

It must also be remarked, that the causes which tend to raise or to
depress this standard, commonly produce their efforts by slow and
almost insensible degrees; and that it often continues for some time
nearly the same, when the circumstances, by which it was fixed, have
materially altered.

It is a truth which will hardly be contested, that Christianity, whenever
it has at all prevailed, has raised the general standard of morals to a
height before unknown. Some actions, which among the ancients were
scarcely held to be blemishes in the most excellent characters, have been
justly considered by the laws of every Christian community, as meriting
the severest punishments. In other instances, virtues formerly rare have
become common, and in particular a merciful and courteous temper has
softened the rugged manners, and humanized the brutal ferocity preva-
lent among the most polished nations of the heathen world. But from
what has been recently observed, it is manifest, that so far as external
appearances are concerned, these effects, when once produced by Christianity, are produced alike in those who deny and in those who admit her
divine original; I had almost said in those who reject and those who cordially embrace the doctrines of the Gospel: and those effects might and
probably would remain for a while, without any great apparent alteration, however her spirit might languish, or even her authority decline.
[. . .] When we are inquiring therefore into the real state of Christianity
at any period, if we would not be deceived in this important investiga-
tion, it becomes us to be so much the more careful not to take up with
superficial appearances.

It may perhaps help us to ascertain the advancing or declining state of
Christianity in Great Britain at the present moment, and still more to
discover some of the causes by which that state has been produced, to

employ a little time in considering what might naturally be expected to be its actual situation; what advantages or disadvantages such a religion might be expected to derive from the circumstances in which it has been placed among us, and from those in which it still continues.

Experience warrants, and reason justifies and explains the assertion, that Persecution generally tends to quicken the vigour and extend the prevalence of the opinions which she would eradicate. For the peace of mankind, it has grown at length almost into an axiom, that "her devilish engine back recoils upon herself." Christianity especially has always thriven under persecution. At such a season she has no lukewarm professors; no adherents concerning whom it is doubtful to what party they belong. The Christian is then reminded at every turn, that his Master's kingdom is not of this world. When all on earth wears a black and threatening aspect, he looks up to heaven for consolation; he learns practically to consider himself as a pilgrim and stranger. He then cleaves to fundamentals, and examines well his foundation, as at the hour of death. When Religion is in a state of external quiet and prosperity, the contrary of all this naturally takes place. The soldiers of the church militant then forget that they are in a state of warfare. Their ardour slackens, their zeal languishes. Like a colony long settled in a strange country,[1] they are gradually assimilated in features, and demeanour, and language, to the native inhabitants, till at length almost every vestige of peculiarity dies away.

If, in general, persecution and prosperity be productive respectively of these opposite effects, this circumstance alone might teach us what expectations to form concerning the state of Christianity in this country, where she has long been embodied in an establishment, which is intimately blended, and is generally and justly believed to have a common interest with our civil institutions; which is liberally, though by no means too liberally endowed, and, not more favoured in wealth than dignity, has been allowed "to exalt her mitred front in courts and parliaments:" an establishment—the offices in which are extremely numerous, and these, not like the priesthood of the Jews, filled up from a particular race, or, like that of the Hindoos, held by a separate cast in entailed succession, but supplied from every class and branching by its widely extended ramifications into almost every individual family in the community: an establishment—of which the ministers are not, like the Roman Catholic clergy, debarred from forming matrimonial ties, but are allowed to unite themselves, and multiply their holdings to the general mass of the community by the close bonds of family connection; not like some of the

---

[1] The author must acknowledge himself indebted to Dr. OWEN for this illustration.*

severer of the religious orders, immured in colleges and monasteries, but, both by law and custom, permitted to mix without restraint in all the intercourses of society.

Such being the circumstances of the pastors of the church, let the community in general be supposed to have been for some time in a rapidly improving state of commercial prosperity; let it also be supposed to have been making no unequal progress in all those arts, and sciences, and literary productions, which have ever been the growth of a polished age, and are the sure marks of a highly finished condition of society. It is not difficult to anticipate the effects likely to be produced on *vital* Religion, both in the clergy and the laity, by such a state of external prosperity as has been assigned to them respectively. And these effects would be infallibly furthered, where the country in question should enjoy a free constitution of government. We formerly had occasion to quote the remark of an accurate observer of the stage of human life, that a much looser system of morals commonly prevails in the higher, than in the middling and lower orders of society. Now, in every country, of which the middling classes are daily growing in wealth and consequence, by the success of their commercial speculations, and, most of all, in a country having such a constitution as our own, where the acquisition of riches is the possession also of rank and power; with the comforts and refinements, the vices also of the higher orders are continually descending, and a mischievous uniformity of sentiments, and manners, and morals, gradually diffuses itself throughout the whole community. The multiplication of great cities also, and above all, the habit, ever increasing with the increasing wealth of the country, of frequenting a splendid and luxurious metropolis, would powerfully tend to accelerate the discontinuance of the religious habits of a purer age, and to accomplish the substitution of a more relaxed morality. And it must even be confessed, that the commercial spirit, much as we are indebted to it, is not naturally favourable to the maintenance of the religious principle in a vigorous and lively state.

In times like these, therefore, the strict precepts and self-denying habits of Christianity naturally slide into disuse, and even among the better sort of Christians, are likely to be softened, so far at least as to be rendered less abhorrent, from the general disposition to relaxation and indulgence. In such prosperous circumstances, men, in truth, are apt to think very little about religion. Christianity, therefore, seldom occupying the attention of the bulk of nominal Christians, and being scarcely at all the object of their study, we should expect, of course, to find them extremely unacquainted with its tenets. Those doctrines and principles indeed, which it contains in common with the law of the land, or which are sanctioned by the general standard of morals formerly described, being brought into continual notice and mention by the common occurrences of life, might continue to be recognized. But whatever she contains peculiar to herself, and which should not be habitually brought into recollection by the incidents of every day, might be expected to be less and less thought of, till at length it should be almost wholly forgotten. Still more might this be naturally expected to become the case, if the peculiarities in question should be, from their very nature, at war with pride, and luxury, and worldly mindedness, the too general concomitants of rapidly increasing wealth; and this would particularly happen among the laity, if the circumstance of their having been at any time abused to purposes of hypocrisy or fanaticism should have prompted even some of the better disposed of the clergy, perhaps from well intentioned though erroneous motives, to bring them forward less frequently in their discourses on religion.

When so many should thus have been straying out of the right path, some bold reformer might, from time to time, be likely to arise, who should not unjustly charge them with their deviation; but, though right perhaps in the main, yet deviating himself also in an opposite direction, and creating disgust by his violence, or vulgarity, or absurdities, he might fail, except in a few instances, to produce the effect of recalling them from their wanderings.

Still, however, the Divine Original of Christianity would not be professedly disavowed; partly from a real, and more commonly from a political deference for the established faith, but most of all, from the bulk of mankind being not yet prepared, as it were, to throw away the scabbard, and to venture their eternal happiness on the issue of its falsehood. Some bolder spirits, indeed, might be expected to despise the cautious moderation of these timid reasoners, and to pronounce decisively, that the Bible was a forgery, while the generality, professing to believe it genuine, should, less consistently, be satisfied with remaining ignorant of its contents, and when pressed, should discover themselves by no means to believe many of the most important particulars contained in it.

When, by the operation of causes like these, any country has at length grown into the condition which has been here stated, it is but too obvious, that in the bulk of the community, Religion, already sunk very low, must be hastening fast to her entire dissolution. Causes, energetic and active like these, though accidental hindrances may occasionally thwart their operation, will not at once become sluggish and unproductive. Their effect is sure; and the time is fast approaching, when Christianity will be almost as openly disavowed in the language, as in fact it is already supposed to have disappeared from the conduct of men; when infidelity will be held to be the necessary appendage of a man of fashion, and *to believe* will be deemed the indication of a feeble mind and a contracted understanding.

Something like what have been here premised are the conjectures which we should naturally be led to form concerning the state of Christianity in this country, and its probable issue, from considering her own nature, and the peculiar circumstances in which she has been placed. That her real condition differs not much from the result of this reasoning from probability, must, with whatever regret, be confessed by all who take a careful and impartial survey of the actual situation of things among us. But our hypothetical delineation, if just, will have approved itself to the reader's conviction, as we have gone along, by suggesting its archetypes; and we may therefore be spared the painful and invidious task of pointing out, in detail, the several particulars wherein our statements are justified by facts. Every where we may actually trace the effects of increasing wealth and luxury, in banishing one by one the habits, and new-modelling the phraseology of stricter times, and in diffusing throughout the middle ranks those relaxed morals and dissipated manners, which were formerly confined to the higher classes of society. We meet, indeed, with more refinement, and more generally with those amiable courtesies which are its proper fruits: those vices also have become less frequent, which naturally infest the darkness of a ruder and less polished age, and which recede on the approach of light and civilization.

[. . .]

But with these grossnesses, Religion, on the other hand, has also declined; God is forgotten; his providence is exploded; his hand is lifted up, but we see it not; he multiplies our comforts, but we are not grateful; he visits us with chastisements, but we are not contrite. The portion of the week set apart to the service of Religion, we give up, without reluctance, to vanity and dissipation. [. . .]

It has also been a melancholy prognostic of the state to which we are progressive, that many of the most eminent of the literati of modern times have been professed unbelievers; and that others of them have discovered such lukewarmness in the cause of Christ, as to treat with especial good will, and attention, and respect, those men, who, by their avowed publications, were openly assailing, or insidiously undermining the very foundations of the Christian hope; considering themselves as more closely united to them by literature, than severed from them by the widest religious differences. Can it then occasion surprise, that under all these circumstances, one of the most acute and most forward of the professed unbelievers[2] should appear to anticipate, as at no great distance,

---

[2] Mr. HUME.*

the more complete triumph of his sceptical principles; and that another author of distinguished name,[3] not so openly professing those infidel opinions, should declare of the writer above alluded to, whose great abilities had been systematically prostituted to the open attack of every principle of Religion, both natural and revealed, "that he had always considered him, both in his life-time and since his death, as approaching as nearly to the idea of a perfectly wise and virtuous man as perhaps the nature of human frailty will permit?"

Can there then be a doubt, whither tends the path in which we are travelling, and whither at length it must conduct us? If any should hesitate, let them take a lesson from experience. In a neighbouring country, several of the same causes have been in action; and they have at length produced their full effect. Manners corrupted, morals depraved, dissipation predominant, above all, Religion discredited, and infidelity grown into repute and fashion,[4] terminated in the public disavowal of every religious principle which had been used to attract the veneration of mankind. The representatives of a whole nation publicly witnessing, not only without horror, but to say the least, without disapprobation, an open unqualified denial of the very existence of God; and at length, as a body, withdrawing their allegiance from the Majesty of Heaven.

There are not a few, perhaps, who may have witnessed with apprehension, and may be ready to confess with pain, the gradual declension of Religion, but who at the same time may conceive that the writer of this tract is disposed to carry things too far. They may even allege, that the degree of Religion for which he contends is inconsistent with the ordinary business of life, and with the well-being of society; that if it were generally to prevail, people would be wholly engrossed by Religion, and all their time occupied by prayer and preaching. Men not being sufficiently interested in the pursuit of temporal objects, agriculture and commerce would decline, the arts would languish, the very duties of common life would be neglected, and, in short the whole machine of civil society would be obstructed, and speedily stopped.

[. . .]

In reply to this objection it might be urged, that though we should allow it for a moment to be in a considerable degree well founded, yet this admission would not warrant the conclusion intended to be drawn from it. The question would still remain, whether our representation of what

---

[3] Vide Dr. A. Smith's Letter to W. Strahan, Esq.*

[4] What is here stated must be acknowledged by all, be their political opinions concerning French events what they may; and it makes no difference in the writer's view of the subject, whether the state of morals was or was not, quite, or nearly as bad, before the French revolution.*

Christianity requires be agreeable to the word of God. For if it be, surely it must be confessed to be a matter of small account to sacrifice a little worldly comfort and prosperity, during the short span of our existence in this life, in order to secure a crown of eternal glory, and the enjoyment of those pleasures which are at God's right hand for evermore. [. . .] But in truth the objection on which we have now been commenting, is not only groundless, but the very contrary to it is the truth. If Christianity, such as we have represented it, were generally to prevail, the world, from being such as it is, would become a scene of general peace and prosperity, and abating the chances and calamities "which flesh is inseparably heir to," would wear one unwearied face of complacency and joy.

On the first promulgation of Christianity, it is true, some of her early converts seem to have been in danger of so far mistaking the genius of the new Religion, as to imagine that in future they were to be discharged from an active attendance on their secular affairs. But the Apostle most pointedly guarded them against so gross an error, and expressly and repeatedly enjoined them to perform the particular duties of their several stations with increased alacrity and fidelity, that they might thereby do credit to their Christian profession.[5] [. . .] It must indeed be confessed that Christianity would not favour that vehement and inordinate ardor in the pursuit of temporal objects, which tends to the acquisition of immense wealth, or of widely spread renown; nor is it calculated to gratify the extravagant views of those mistaken politicians, the chief object of whose admiration, and the main scope of whose endeavours for their country are, extended dominion, and commanding power, and unrivalled affluence, rather than those more solid advantages of peace, and comfort, and security. These men would barter comfort for greatness. In their vain reveries they forget that a nation consists of individuals, and that true national prosperity is no other than the multiplication of particular happiness.

But in truth, so far is it from being true that the prevalence of *real* Religion would produce a stagnation in life; a man, whatever might be his employment or pursuit, would be furnished with a new motive to prosecute it with alacrity, a motive far more constant and vigorous than any human prospects can supply; at the same time, his solicitude being not so much to succeed in whatever he might be engaged in, as to act from a pure principle and leave the event to God, he would not be liable to the same disappointments as men who are active and laborious from a desire of worldly gain or of human estimation. Thus he would possess the true secret of a life at the same time useful and happy. Following peace also

---

[5] Wilberforce probably has in mind St Paul's exhortations in II Thessalonians 3:6–13.

with all men, and looking upon them as members of the same family, entitled not only to the debts of justice, but to the less definite and more liberal claims of fraternal kindness, he would naturally be respected and beloved by others, and be in himself free from the annoyance of those bad passions, by which they who are actuated by worldly principles are so commonly corroded. If any country were indeed filled with men, each thus diligently discharging the duties of his own station without breaking in upon the rights of others, but on the contrary endeavouring, so far as he might be able, to forward their views and promote their happiness, all would be active and harmonious in the goodly frame of human society. There would be no jarrings, no discord. The whole machine of civil life would work without obstruction or disorder, and the course of its movements would be like the harmony of the spheres.

Such would be the happy state of a truly Christian nation within itself. Nor would its condition with regard to foreign countries form a contrast to this its internal comfort. Such a community, on the contrary, peaceful at home, would be respected and beloved abroad. General integrity in all its dealings would inspire universal confidence; differences between nations commonly arise from mutual injuries, and still more from mutual jealousy and distrust. Of the former there would be no longer any ground for complaint; the latter would find nothing to attach upon. But if, in spite of all its justice and forbearance, the violence of some neighbouring state should force it to resist an unprovoked attack, for hostilities strictly defensive are those only in which it would be engaged, its domestic union would double its national force, while the consciousness of a good cause, and of the general favour of Heaven, would invigorate its arm, and inspirit its efforts.

[. . .]

It must be confessed, that many of the good effects of which Religion is productive to political societies would be produced even by a false Religion, which should prescribe good morals, and should be able to enforce its precepts by sufficient sanctions. Of this nature are those effects which depend on our calling in the aid of a Being who sees the heart, in order to assist the weakness, and in various ways to supply the inherent defects of all human jurisprudence. But the superior excellence of Christianity in this respect must be acknowledged, both in the superiority of her moral code, and in the powerful motives and efficacious means which she furnishes for enabling us to practise it; and in the tendency of her doctrines to provide for the observance of her precepts, by producing tempers of mind which correspond with them.

But, more than all this, it has not perhaps been enough remarked, that true Christianity, from her essential nature, appears peculiarly and powerfully adapted to promote the preservation and healthfulness of political communities. What is in truth their grand malady? The answer is short; Selfishness. This is that young disease received at the moment of their birth, "which grows with their growth, and strengthens with their strength," and through which they at length expire, if not cut off prematurely by some external shock or intestine convulsion.

The disease of selfishness, indeed, assumes different forms in the different classes of society. In the great and the wealthy, it displays itself in luxury, in pomp and parade, and in all the frivolities of a sickly and depraved imagination, which seeks in vain its own gratification, and is dead to the generous and energetic pursuits of an enlarged heart. In the lower orders, when not motionless under the weight of a superincumbent despotism, it manifests itself in pride, and its natural offspring, insubordination, in all its modes. But though the external effects may vary, the internal principle is the same; a disposition in each individual to make self the grand center and end of his desires and enjoyments; to over-rate his own merits and importance, and of course to magnify his claims on others, and in return to under-rate theirs on him; a disposition to under-value the advantages, and overstate the disadvantages of his condition in life. Thence spring rapacity, and venality, and sensuality. Thence imperious nobles and factious leaders, and an unruly commonalty, bearing with difficulty the inconveniences of a lower station, and imputing to the nature or administration of their government the evils which necessarily flow from the very constitution of our species, or which perhaps are chiefly the result of their own vices and follies. The opposite to selfishness is public spirit, which may be termed, not unjustly, the grand principle of political vitality, the very *life's breath* of states, which tends to keep them active and vigorous, and to carry them to greatness and glory. [. . .]

I might here enlarge with pleasure on the unrivalled excellence, in this very view, of the constitution under which we live in this happy country; and point out how, more perhaps than any which ever existed upon earth, it is so framed, as to provide at the same time for keeping up a due degree of public spirit, and yet for preserving unimpaired the quietness, and comfort, and charities of private life; how it even extracts from selfishness itself many of the advantages which, under less happily constructed forms of government, public spirit only can supply. But such a political discussion, however grateful to a British mind, would here be out of place. It is rather our business to remark, how much Christianity in every way sets herself in direct hostility to selfishness, the mortal distemper of political communities, and consequently, how their welfare must be inseparable from her prevalence. It might, indeed, be almost stated as the main object and chief concern of Christianity, to root out our natural selfishness, and to rectify the false standard which it imposes on us, with views, however, far higher than any which concern merely our temporal and social well-being; to bring us to a just estimate of ourselves, and of all around us, and to a due impression of the various claims and obligations resulting from the different relations in which we stand. Benevolence, enlarged, vigorous, operative benevolence, is her master principle. Moderation in temporal pursuits and enjoyments, comparative indifference to the issue of worldly projects, diligence in the discharge of personal and civil duties, resignation to the will of God, and patience under all the dispensations of his Providence, are among her daily lessons. Humility is one of the essential qualities, which her precepts most directly and strongly enjoin, and which all her various doctrines tend to call forth and cultivate; and humility, as has been before suggested, lays the deepest and surest grounds for benevolence. In whatever class or order of society Christianity prevails, she sets herself to rectify the particular faults, or, if we would speak more distinctly, to counteract the particular mode of selfishness, to which that class is liable. Affluence she teaches to be liberal and beneficent; authority, to bear its faculties with meekness, and to consider the various cares and obligations belonging to its elevated station, as being conditions on which that station is conferred. Thus, softening the glare of wealth, and moderating the insolence of power, she renders the inequalities of the social state less galling to the lower orders, whom also she instructs, in their turn, to be diligent, humble, patient; reminding them that their more lowly path has been allotted to them by the hand of God; that it is their part faithfully to discharge its duties, and contentedly to bear its inconveniences; that the present state of things is very short; that the objects about which worldly men conflict so eagerly, are not worth the contest; that the peace of mind, which Religion offers to all ranks indiscriminately, affords more true satisfaction than all the expensive pleasures which are beyond the poor man's reach; that in this view, however, the poor have the advantage, and that if their superiors enjoy more abundant comforts, they are also exposed to many temptations from which the inferior classes are happily exempted; that "having, food and raiment, they should be therewith content," for that their situation in life, with all its evils, is better than they have deserved at the hand of God; finally, that all human distinctions will soon be done away, and the true followers of Christ will all, as children of the same father, be alike admitted to the possession of the same heavenly inheritance. Such are the blessed effects of Christianity on the temporal well-being of political communities.

But the Christianity which can produce effects like these must be real, not nominal, deep, not superficial. Such then is the Religion we should cultivate, if we would realize these pleasing speculations, and arrest the progress of political decay. But in the present circumstances of this country, it is a farther reason for endeavouring to cultivate this vital Christianity, still considering its effects merely in a political view, that, according to all human appearance, we must either have this or none; unless the prevalence of this be in some degree restored, we are likely not only to lose all the advantages which we might have derived from true Christianity, but to incur all the manifold evils which would result from the absence of all religion.

In the first place, let it be remarked, that a weakly principle of Religion, and even such an one, in a political view, is productive of many advantages, though its existence may be prolonged if all external circumstances favour its continuance, can hardly be kept alive, when the state of things is so unfavourable to vital Religion, as it must be confessed to be in our condition of society. Nor is it merely the ordinary effects of a state of wealth and prosperity to which we here allude. Much also may justly be apprehended from that change which has taken place in our general habits of thinking and feeling, concerning the systems and opinions of former times. At a less advanced period of society, indeed, the Religion of the state will be generally accepted, though it be not felt in its vital power. It was the Religion of our forefathers. With the bulk it is on that account entitled to reverence, and its authority is admitted without question. The establishment in which it subsists pleads the same prescription, and obtains the same respect. But in our days, things are very differently circumstanced. Not merely the blind prejudice in favour of former times, but even the proper respect for them, and the reasonable presumption in their favour, has abated. Still less will the idea be endured, of any system being kept up, when the imposture is seen through by the higher orders, for the sake of retaining the common people in subjection. A system, if not supported by a real persuasion of its truth, will fall to the ground.

[. . .]

The kind of Religion which we have recommended, whatever opinion may be entertained concerning its truth, and to say nothing of the agency of Divine Grace, must at least be conceded to be the only one which is at all suited to make impression upon the lower orders, by strongly interesting the passions of the human mind. If it be thought that a system of ethics may regulate the conduct of the higher classes, such an one is altogether unsuitable to the lower, who must be worked upon by their affections, or they will not be worked upon at all. The ancients were wiser than ourselves, and never thought of governing the community in general by their lessons of philosophy. These lessons were confined to the schools of the learned, while for the million, a system of Religion, such as it was, was kept up, as alone adapted to their grosser natures. If this reasoning fail to convince, we may safely appeal to experience. Let the Socinian[6] and the moral teacher of Christianity come forth, and tell us what effects *they* have produced on the lower orders. They themselves will hardly deny the inefficacy of their instructions. But, blessed be God, the Religion which we recommend has proved its correspondence with the character originally given of Christianity, that it was calculated for the poor, by changing the whole condition of the mass of society in many of the most populous districts in this and other countries; and by bringing them from being scenes of almost unexampled wickedness and barbarism, to be eminent for sobriety, decency, industry, and, in short, for whatever can render men useful members of civil society.

If indeed through the blessing of Providence, a principle of true Religion should in any considerable degree gain ground, there is no estimating the effects on public morals, and the consequent influence on our political welfare. These effects are not merely negative; though it would be much, merely to check the farther progress of a gangrene which is eating out the very vital principles of our social and political existence. The general standard of morality formerly described, would be raised, it would at least be sustained and kept for a while from farther depression. The esteem which religious characters would personally attract, would extend to the system which they should hold, and to the establishment of which they should be members. These are all merely natural consequences. But to those who believe in a superintending Providence, it may be added, that the blessing of God might be drawn down upon our country, and the stroke of his anger be for a while suspended.

Let us be spared the painful talk of tracing, on the contrary, the fatal consequences of the extinction of Religion among us. They are indeed such as no man, who is ever so little interested for the welfare of his country, can contemplate without the deepest concern. The very loss of our church establishment, though, as in all human institutions, some defects may be found in it, would in itself be attended with the most fatal consequences. No prudent man dares hastily pronounce how far its destruction might not greatly endanger our civil institutions. It would not be difficult to prove, that the want of it would also be in the highest degree injurious to the cause of Christianity, and still more, that it would take away what appears from experience to be one of the most probable means of its revival. To what a degree might even the avowed principles

---

[6] One who stresses the unity of the godhead, and is hence at variance with mainstream Christian emphasis on the divinity of Jesus Christ. Otherwise known as Uniforians.

of men, not altogether without Religion, decline, when our inestimable Liturgy should no longer remain in use; a Liturgy justly inestimable, which continually sets before us a faithful model of the Christian's belief, and practice, and language, restraining us, as far as restraint is possible, from excessive deviations; furnishing us with abundant instruction when we would return into the right path; affording an advantage ground of no little value to such instructors as still adhere to the good old principles of the Church of England; in short, daily shaming us, by preserving a living representation of the opinions and habits of better times, as some historical record, which reproaches a degenerate posterity, by exhibiting the worthier deeds of their progenitors. In such a state of things, to what a depth public morals might sink, may be anticipated by those who consider what would then be the condition of society; who reflect how bad principles and vicious conduct mutually aid each other's operation, and how, in particular, the former make sure the ground which the latter may have gained; who remember, that in the lower orders, the system of honour, and the responsibility of character, are wanting, which in the superior classes, in some poor degree supply the place of higher principles. It is well for the happiness of mankind, that such a community could not long subsist. The cement of society being no more, the state would soon be dissolved into individuality.

Let it not be vainly imagined, that our state of civilization must prevent the moral degeneracy here threatened. A neighbouring nation has lately furnished a lamentable proof, that superior polish and refinement may well consist with a very large measure of depravity.

[. . .]

What then is to be done? The inquiry is of the first importance, and the general answer to it is not difficult.—The causes and nature of the decay of Religion and morals among us sufficiently indicate the course, which, on principles of sound policy, it is in the highest degree expedient for us to pursue. The distemper of which, as a community, we are sick, should be considered rather as a moral than a political malady. How much has this been forgotten by the disputants of modern times; and accordingly, how transient may be expected to be the good effects of the best of their publications! We should endeavour to tread back our steps. Every effort should be used to raise the depressed tone of public morals. This is a duty particularly incumbent on all who are in the higher walks of life; and it is impossible not to acknowledge the obligations which in this respect we owe as a nation to those exalted characters whom God in his undeserved mercy to us still suffers to continue on the throne, and who set to their subjects a pattern of decency and moderation rarely seen in their elevated station.

But every person of rank, and fortune, and abilities, should endeavour in like manner to exhibit a similar example, and recommend it to the imitation of the circle in which he moves. It has been the opinion of some well-meaning people, that by giving, as far as they possibly could with innocence, into the customs and practices of irreligious men, they might soften the prejudices too frequently taken up against Religion, of its being an austere gloomy service, and thus secure a previous favourable impression against any time when they might have an opportunity of explaining or enforcing their sentiments. This is always a questionable, and, it is to be feared, a dangerous policy. Many mischievous consequences necessarily resulting from it might easily be enumerated. But it is a policy particularly unsuitable to our inconsiderate and dissipated times, and to the lengths at which we are arrived. In these circumstances, the most likely means of producing the *revulsion* which is required, must be boldly to proclaim the distinction between "the adherents of God and Baal." The expediency of this conduct in our present situation is confirmed by another consideration, to which we have before had occasion to refer. It is this—that when men are aware that something of difficulty is to be effected, their spirits rise to the level of the encounter; they make up their minds to bear hardships and brave dangers, and to persevere in spite of fatigue and opposition: whereas in a matter which is regarded as of easy and ordinary operation, they are apt to slumber over their work, and to fail in what a small effort might have been sufficient to accomplish, for want of having called up the requisite degree of energy and spirit. Conformably to the principle which is hereby suggested, in the circumstances in which we are placed, the line of demarcation between the friends and the enemies of Religion should now be made clear; the separation should be broad and obvious. Let him then, who wishes well to his country, no longer hesitate what course of conduct to pursue. The question now is not, in what liberties he might warrantably indulge himself in another situation, but what are the restraints on himself which the exigencies of the present times render it adviseable for him to impose. Circumstanced as we now are, it is more than ever obvious, that *the best man is the truest patriot.*

Nor is it only by their personal conduct, though this mode will always be the most efficacious, that men of authority and influence may promote the cause of good morals. Let them in their several stations encourage virtue and discountenance vice in others. Let them enforce the laws by which the wisdom of our forefathers has guarded against the grosser infractions of morals [. . .] Let them favour and take part in any plans which may be formed for the advancement of morality. Above all things, let them endeavour to instruct and improve the rising generation, that, if it be possible, an antidote may be provided for the malignity of that venom which is storing up in a neighbouring country. This has long been to my mind the most formidable feature of the present state of things in France, where, it is to be feared, a brood of moral vipers, as it were, is now hatching, which, when they shall have attained to their mischievous maturity, will go forth to poison the world. But fruitless will be all attempts to sustain, much more to revive, the fainting cause of morals, unless you can in some degree restore the prevalence of Evangelical Christianity. It is in morals as in physics; unless the source of practical principles be elevated, it will be in vain to attempt to make them flow on a high level in their future course. You may force them for a while into some constrained position, but they will soon drop to their natural point of depression. By all, therefore, who are studious of their country's welfare, more particularly by all who desire to support our ecclesiastical establishment, every effort should be used to revive the Christianity of our better days.

Source: William Wilberforce, *Practical View of the Prevailing Religious System of Professed Christians . . . Contrasted with Real Christianity*, London, T. Cadell & W. Davies, 1797, pp. 1–5, 320–30, 364–422.

Extracts from *A Letter on the Abolition of the Slave Trade; addressed to the Freeholders and Other Inhabitants of Yorkshire*, 1807

No efforts have been made for the religious and moral improvement of the Negroes, and any plans of that kind, when adopted by others, have been considered as chimerical, if not dangerous. This is the more extraordinary, because an example on a large scale, has been of late years furnished in the little Danish islands, and in one settlement, at least, of our own smaller islands, of the happiest effects resulting from such endeavours: so that men of great knowledge and experience in West Indian affairs, in estimating the effects of the labours of the missionaries, who were employed in this benevolent service, by a pecuniary standard, declared, that a Slave, by becoming one of their converts, was worth half as much more than his former value, on account of his superior morality, sobriety, industry, subordination, and general good conduct. [. . .]

Might we not then have expected that our own West Indian Proprietors would be prompted, not only by considerations of self-interest, but by motives of a still higher order, to pay some attention to the religious instruction of their Negroes? Might not mere humanity have enforced the same important duty? Might we not have hoped that the Slaves of this Protestant and free nation, might have had some compensation made to them, for the evils of their temporal bondage, by a prospect being opened to them of a happier world hereafter, a world of light and liberty? But alas! no such cheering prospects are pointed out to them. It is left, alas! to Paganism to administer to them, I had almost said happily, a faint intimation of that more animating hope which Christianity should impart; and these poor beings are comforted by the idea, that death will once more restore them to their native land; on which account it is, that, as we learn from respectable testimony, the negro funerals in the West Indies are seasons of joy and triumph, whereas in Africa, they are accompanied with the usual indications of dejection and sorrow. [. . .]

Slavery, we know, existed among the ancients; and according to the savage maxims of Pagan warfare, (too strikingly agreeing with the mode of carrying on war which the Slave Trade has produced in Africa), not only the soldiery of an enemy, but the peaceable inhabitants of conquered countries were commonly sold as Slaves. But what an idea does it convey of the abhorred system, which, with coadjutors abler than myself, I have been so long endeavouring to abolish; that, just as in Africa, it has forced Christianity to acknowledge the superior power of Mahometanism, in rooting out the nature superstitions, and in instructing and civilizing the inhabitants – so in our possessions in the western hemisphere, it combines the profession of the Christian faith with a description of slavery, in many respects more bitter in its sufferings, than that which the very darkness of Paganism itself could scarcely tolerate.

This is the more grievous to those who duly venerate and love our most pure and excellent form of Christian faith, because to have first mitigated the evils of slavery, and at great length to have abolished the institution itself, have been numbered among the peculiar glories of Christianity; and because, what we deem a corrupted system of Christianity, has produced highly beneficial effects on the negro slaves of our Roman Catholic neighbours in the same quarter [. . .]

Forgive me if I seem to linger; if I appear unwilling to conclude. When I call to mind the number and magnitude of the interests which are at stake, I know not how to desist, while any fresh argument remains to be used, while any consideration not as yet suggested occurs to me, by which I may enforce my intercession in behalf of the most injured of the human race. But though the mind be naturally led to the Africans as the greatest sufferers, yet, unless the Scripture be a forgery, it is not their cause only that I am pleading, but the cause of my Country. Yet let me not here be misconceived. It is not that I expect any visible and supernatural effects of the Divine vengeance; that, not to listen with seriousness to the accounts which have been brought us of late years from the western hemisphere, as to a probable intimation of the Divine displeasure would be to resolve to shut our ears against the warning voice of Providence. To mention now other particulars, a disease new in its kind, and almost without example destructive in its ravages, has been for some time raging in those very colonies which are the chief supporters of the traffic in human beings; a disease concerning which we scarcely know any thing, but that it does not affect the Negro race, and that we first heard of it after the horrors of the Slave Trade has been completely developed in the House of Commons, but developed in vain [. . .]

Thus it is, that, most commonly by the operation of natural causes, and in the way of natural consequences, Providence governs the world. But if we are not blind to the course of human events, as well as utterly deaf to the plain instructions of Revelation, we must believe that a continued course of wickedness, oppression and cruelty, obstinately maintained in spite of the fullest knowledge and the loudest warnings, must infallibly bring down upon us the heaviest judgments of the Almighty. We may ascribe our fall to weak councils, or unskilful generals; to a factious and overburthened people; to storms which waste our fleets, to diseases which thin our armies; to mutiny among our soldiers and sailors, which may even turn against us our own force; to the diminution of our revenues and the excessive increase of our debt: men may complain on one side of a venal ministry, on the other of a factious opposition; while amid mutual recriminations the nation is gradually verging to its fate. Providence will easily provide means for the accomplishment of its own purposes. It cannot be denied, that there are circumstances in the situation of this Country, which, reasoning from experience, we must call marks of a declining empire; but we have, as I firmly believe, the means within ourselves of arresting the progress of this decline. We have been eminently blessed; we have been long spared; let us not presume too far on the forbearance of the Almighty.

Source: W. Wilberforce, *A Letter on the Abolition of the Slave Trade; addressed to the Freeholders and Other Inhabitants of Yorkshire*, London, J. Hatchard and Son, 1807, pp. 124–9, 348–51.

Extracts from *An Appeal to the Religion, Justice and Humanity of the Inhabitants of the British Empire, in Behalf of the Negro Slaves in the West Indies*, 1823

Woe unto him that buildeth his house by unrighteousness, and his chambers by wrong; that useth his neighbour's service without wages, and giveth him not for his work. JEREMIAH

Do justice and love mercy. MICAH[7]

To all the inhabitants of the British Empire, who value the favour of God, or are alive to the interests or honour of their country – to all who have any respect for justice, or any feelings of humanity, I would solemnly address myself. I call upon them, as they shall hereafter answer, in the great day of account, for the use they shall have made of any power and influence with which Providence may have entrusted them, to employ their best endeavours, by all lawful and constitutional means, to mitigate, and, as soon as it may be safely done, to terminate the Negro Slavery of the British Colonies; a system of the grossest injustice, of the most heathenish irreligion and immorality, of the most unprecedented degradation, and unrelenting cruelty.

At any time, and under any circumstances, from such a heavy load of guilt as this oppression amounts to, it would be our interest no less than our duty to absolve ourselves. But I will not attempt to conceal, that the present embarrassments and distress of our country – a distress, indeed, in which the West Indians themselves have largely participated – powerfully enforce on me the urgency of the obligation under which we lie, to commence, without delay, the preparatory measures for putting an end to a national crime of the deepest moral malignity. [. . .]

[Wilberforce surveys the evils of slavery, noting particularly its inherent injustice, and the tendency for slaves to be overworked and undernourished and hence to have high mortality. These, however, 'to a Christian eye, . . . shrink almost into insignificance when compared with the moral evils that remain behind' (p. 9). The slaves are morally degraded by being treated as chattels who can be bought and sold, by the fact that their evidence is inadmissible against a free person in a court of law, and by being driven with whips and otherwise maltreated, like animals, in their

---

[7] Two quotations from Old Testament prophets on the title-page of the pamphlet highlight Wilberforce's sense of a religious basis for the campaign.

work. No attempts have been made to introduce 'the Christian institution of marriage' (p. 17) and hence 'promiscuous intercourse . . . is nearly universal' (p. 20).]

In my estimate of things, however, and I trust in that of the bulk of my countrymen, though many of the physical evils of our colonial slavery are cruel, and odious, and pernicious, the almost universal destitution of religious and moral instruction among the slaves is the most serious of all the vices of the West Indian system; and had there been no other, this alone would have most powerfully enforced on my conscience the obligation of publicly declaring my decided conviction, that it is the duty of the legislature of this country to interpose for the mitigation and future termination of a state in which the ruin of the moral man, if I may so express myself, has been one of the sad consequences of his bondage.

It cannot be denied, I repeat, that the slaves, more especially the great body of the field Negroes, are practically strangers to the multiplied blessings of the Christian Revelation.

What a consideration is this! A nation, which besides the invaluable benefit of an unequalled degree of true civil liberty, has been favoured with an unprecedented measure of religious light, with its long train of attendant blessings, has been for two centuries detaining in a state of slavery, beyond example rigorous, and in some particulars worse than pagan darkness and depravity, hundreds of thousands of their fellow creatures, originally torn from their native land by fraud and violence. Generation after generation have thus been pining away; and in this same condition of ignorance and degradation they still, for the most part, remain. This I am well aware is an awful charge; but it undeniably is too well founded, and scarcely admits of any exception beyond what has been effected by those excellent, though too commonly traduced and persecuted men, the Christian missionaries. They have done all that it has been possible for them to do; and through the divine blessing they have indeed done much, especially in the towns, and among the household slaves, considering the many and great obstacles with which they have had to contend. [. . .]

In all that I state concerning the religious interests of the slaves, as well in every other instance, I must be understood to speak only of the *general* practice. There are, I know, resident in this country, individual owners of slaves, and some, as I believe, even in the colonies, who have been sincerely desirous that their slaves should enjoy the blessings of Christianity: though often, I lament to say, where they have desired it, their pious endeavours have been of little or no avail. So hard is it, especially for absent proprietors, to stem the tide of popular feeling and practice, which sets strongly in every colony against the religious instruction of slaves. So hard also, I must add, is it to reconcile the necessary means of such instruction with the harsh duties and harsher discipline to which these poor beings are subjected. The gift even of the rest of the Sabbath is more than the established economics of a sugar plantations permit even the most independent planter to confer, while the law tacitly sanctions its being wholly withheld from them.

Generally speaking, throughout the whole of our West Indian islands, the field slaves, or common labourers, instead of being encouraged or even permitted to devote the Sunday to religious purposes, are employed either in workin their provision-grounds for their own and their families' subsistence, or are attending, often carrying heavy loads to, the Sunday markets, which frequently in Jamaica, are from ten or fifteen miles distant from their abodes [. . .]

The insensibility of the planters, even to the temporal good effects of Christianity on their slaves, is the more surprising, because, besides their having been powerfully enforced by self-interest [. . .] in restraining a licentious intercourse between the sexes, they were strongly recommended, especially in the great island of Jamaica, by another consideration of a very peculiar nature. The Jamaica planters long imputed the most injurious effects on the health and even the lives of their slaves, to the African practice of Obeah, or witchcraft. The agents for Jamaica declared to the privy council, in 1788, that they "ascribed a very considerable portion of the annual mortality among the Negroes in that island to that fascinating mischief." I know that of late, ashamed of being supposed to have punished witchcraft with such severity it has been alleged, that the professors of Obeah used to prepare and administer poison to the subjects of their spells: but any one who will only examine the laws of Jamaica against these practices, or read the evidence of the agents, will see plainly that this was not the view that was taken of the proceedings of the Obeah-men, but that they were considered as impostors, who preyed on their ignorant countrymen by a pretended intercourse with evil spirits, or by some other pretences to supernatural powers. The idea of rooting out any form of pagan superstition by severity of punishment, especially in wholly uninstructed minds, like that of extirpating Christianity by the fire and the faggot, has long been exploded among the well-informed; and it has even been established that the devilish engine of persecution recoils back on its employers, and disseminates the very principles it would suppress. Surely then it might have been expected, that, if from no other motive, yet that for the purpose of rooting a pagan superstition out of the minds of the slaves, the aid of Christianity would have been called in, as the safest species of knowledge? and it was strange if the Jamaica gentlemen were ignorant of the indubitable fact, that Christianity never failed to chase away these vain terrors of darkness and paganism. No sooner did a Negro become a Christian, than the Obeah-man despaired of bringing him into subjection. [. . .]

If anything were wanting to add the last finishing tint to the dark colouring of this gloomy picture, it would be afforded by a consideration which still remains behind. However humiliating the statement must be to that legislature which exercises its superintendency over every part of the British Empire; it is nevertheless true, that, low in point of morals as the Africans may have been in their own country, their descendants, who have never seen the continent of Africa, but are sprung from those who for several successive generations have been resident in the Christian colonies of Great Britain, are still lower. Nay, they are universally represented as remarkable in those colonies for vices which are directly opposite to the character which has been given of the Africans by several of the most intelligent travellers who have visited the interior of their native country. In proof of this assertion, I refer not to any delineations of the African character by what might be supposed to be partial hands. Let any one peruse the writings of authors who opposed the abolition of the Slave Trade, more especially the Travels of Mr. Parke and M. Golberry,[8] both published since the commencement of the Slave Trade contest. It is not unworthy of remark, that many of the Africans in their own country are raised, by not being altogether illiterate, far above the low level to which the entire want of all education depresses the field slaves in the West Indies. It is stated by Mr. Parke, who took his passage from Africa to the West Indies in a slave-ship, that of one hundred and thirty slaves which the vessel conveyed, about twenty-five of them, who, as he supposes, had been of free conditions, could most of them write a little Arabic. The want, however, of this measure of literature is of small account: but compare the moral nature of the Africans, while yet living in their native land, and in all the darkness and abominations of paganism, with the character universally given of the same Africans in our West Indian colonies. He will find that the Negroes, who while in Africa were represented to be industrious, generous, eminent for truth, seldom chargeable with licentiousness, distinguished for their domestic affections, and capable at times of acts of heroic magnanimity, are described as being in the West Indies the very opposite in all particulars; selfish, indolent, deceitful, ungrateful, – and above all, in whatever respects the intercourse between the sexes, incurably licentious.

---

[8] Mungo Park (1771–1806) travelled in West Africa from 1795 to 1797 and published his account of his journeys in 1799. The *Travels in Africa* by Sylvain Meinrad Xavier de Golbéry (1742–1822), a French soldier, appeared in English translation in 1802.

And now, without a farther or more particular delineation of slavery of the British colonies, what a system do we behold!! Is it too much to affirm, that there never was, certainly never before in a Christian country, a mass of such aggravated enormities?

That such a system should so long have been suffered to exist in any part of the British Empire will appear, to our posterity, almost incredible. It had, indeed, been less surprising, if its seat had been in regions, like those of Hindostan,[9] for instance, where a vast population had come into our hands in all the full-blown enormity of heathen institutions; where the bloody superstitions, and the unnatural cruelties and immoralities of paganism, had established themselves in entire authority, and had produced their natural effects in the depravity and moral degradation of the species; though even in such a case as that, our excuse would hold good no longer than for the period which might be necessary for reforming the native abuses by those mild and reasonable means which alone are acknowledged to be just in principle, or practically effectual to their purpose. But that in communities formed from their very origins by a Christian people, and in colonies containing no Pagan inhabitants but those whom we ourselves had compulsorily brought into it, – inhabitants too, who, from all the circumstances of their case, had the strongest possible claims on us, both for the reparation of their wrongs, and the relief of their miseries, – such a system should have been continued for two centuries, and by a people who may, nevertheless, I trust, be affirmed to be the most moral and humane of nations, is one of those anomalies which, if it does not stagger the belief, will, at least, excite the astonishment of future ages. [. . .]

[Wilberforce responds to arguments used in defence of slavery.]

Indeed, the West Indians, in the warmth of argument, have gone still farther, and have even distinctly told us, again and again, and I am shocked to say that some of their partizans in this country have re-echoed the assertion, that these poor degraded beings, the Negro slaves, are as well or even better off than our British peasantry – a proposition so monstrous, that nothing can possibly exhibit in a stronger light the extreme force of the prejudices which much exist in the minds of its assertors. A Briton to compare the state of a West Indian slave with that of an English freeman, and to give the former the preference! It is to imply an utter insensibility of the native feelings and moral dignity of man, no less than of the rights of Englishmen!! I will not condescend to argue this question, as I might, on the ground of comparative feeding and clothing, and lodging, and medical attendance. Are these the only claims? Are these the

---

[9] India.

chief privileges of a rational and immortal being? Is the consciousness of personal independence nothing? Are self-possession and self-government nothing? Is it of no account that our persons are inviolate by any private authority, and that the whip is placed only in the hands of the public executioner? Is it of no value that we have the power of pursuing the occupation and the habits of life which we prefer; that we have the prospect, or at least the hope, of improving our condition, and of rising, as we have seen others rise, from poverty and obscurity to comfort, and opulence, and distinction? Again, are all the charities of the heart, which arise out of the domestic relations, to be considered as nothing; and, I may add, all their security too among men who are free agents, and not vendible chattels, liable continually to be torn from their dearest connections, and sent into a perpetual exile? Are husband and wife, parent and child, terms of no meaning? Are willing services, or grateful returns for voluntary kindnesses, nothing? But, above all, is Christianity so little esteemed among us, that we are to account as of no value the hope, "full of immortality," the light of heavenly truth, and all the consolations and supports by which religion cheers the hearts and elevates the principles, and dignifies the conduct of multitudes of our labouring classes in this free and enlightened country? Is it nothing to be taught that all human distinctions will soon be at an end; that all the labours and sorrows of poverty and hardship will soon exist no more; and to know, on the express authority of Scripture, that the lower classes, instead of being an inferior order in the creation, are even the preferable objects of the love of the Almighty? [. . .]

[No confidence can be placed in the capacity of the colonial legislatures to reform slavery. The experience of the colony for freed slaves in Sierra Leone demonstrates that Africans can become industrious and moral Christians if their human dignity and autonomy is restored to them.]

Are these important lessons to be read to us without producing any influence on our minds? Ought they not to enforce on us, as by a voice from heaven, that we have been most cruelly and inexcusably degrading, to the level of brutes, those whom the Almighty had made capable of enjoying our own civil blessings in this world, not less clearly that he has fitted them to be heirs of our common immortality?

But while we are loudly called on by justice and humanity to take measures without delay for improving the condition of our West Indian slaves, self-interest also inculcates the same duty, and with full as clear a voice. It is a great though common error, that notwithstanding we must, on religious and moral grounds, condemn the West Indian system, yet, that in a worldly view, it has been eminently gainful both to individuals and to the community at large. On the contrary, I believe it might be proved to any inquiring and unprejudiced mind, that taking in all considerations of political economy, and looking to the lamentable waste of human life among our soldiers and seamen, raised and recruited at a great expence, as well as to the more direct pecuniary charge of protecting the sugar colonies, no system of civil polity was ever maintained at a greater price, or was less truly profitable either to individuals or to the community, than that of our West Indian settlements. Indeed, it would have been a strange exception to all those established principles which Divine Providence has ordained for the moral benefit of the world, if national and personal prosperity were generally and permanently to be found to arise from injustice and oppression. There may be individual instances of great fortunes amassed by every species of wrong doing. A course, ruinous in the long run, may, to an individual, or for a time, appear eminently profitable; nevertheless, it is unquestionably true, that the path of prosperity rarely diverges long and widely from that of integrity and virtue; or, to express it in a familiar adage, – that honesty is the best policy. [. . .]

[Fears of economic ruin from slave emancipation are unfounded, but the danger of a slave revolt if nothing is done is all too real.]

Here, indeed, is danger, if we observe the signs of the times, whether we take our lesson from the history of men, or form our conclusions from natural reason or from the revealed will of God.

But raise these poor creatures from their depressed condition, and if they are not yet fit for the enjoyment of British freedom, elevate them at least from the level of the brute creation into that of rational nature – dismiss the driving whip, and thereby afford place for the development of the first rudiments of civil character – implant in them the principle of hope – let free scope be given for their industry, and for their raising in life by their personal good conduct – give them an interest in defending the community to which they belong – teach them the lesson which Christianity alone can truly inculcate, that the present life is but a short and uncertain span, to which will succeed an eternal existence of happiness or misery – inculcate on them, on the authority of the sacred page, that the point of real importance is not what is the rank or the station men occupy, but how they discharge the duties of life – how they use the opportunities they may enjoy of providing for their everlasting happiness. Taught by Christianity, they will sustain with patience the sufferings of their actual lot, while the same instructress will rapidly prepare them for a better; and instead of being objects at one time of contempt, and at another of terror, (a base and servile passion, which too naturally degenerates into hatred,) they will soon be regarded as a grateful peasantry, the strength of the communities in which they live, – of which they have hitherto been the weakness and the terror, sometimes the mischief and the scourge.

To the real nature of the West Indian system, and still more to the extent of its manifold abuses, the bulk even of well-informed men in this country are, I believe, generally strangers. May it not be from our having sinned in ignorance that we have so long been spared? But ignorance of a duty which we have had abundant means of knowing to be such, can by no one be deemed excusable. Let us not presume too far on the for-bearance of the Almighty. Favoured in an unequalled degree with Christian light, with civil freedom, and with a greater measure of national blessings than perhaps any other country upon earth ever before enjoyed, what a return would it be for the goodness of the Almighty, if we were to continue to keep the descendants of the Africans, whom we have ourselves wrongfully planted in the western hemisphere, in their present state of unexampled darkness and degradation!

While efforts are making to rescue our country from this guilt and this reproach, let every one remember that he is answerable for any measure of assistance which Providence has enabled him to render towards the accomplishment of the good work. In a country in which the popular voice has a powerful and constitutional influence on the government and legislation, to be silent when there is a question of reforming abuses repugnant to justice and humanity, is to share their guilt. Power always implies responsibility; and the possessor of it cannot innocently be neutral, when by his exertion moral good may be promoted, or evil lessened or removed. [. . .]

Source: W. Wilberforce, *An Appeal to the Religion, Justice, and Humanity of the Inhabitants of the British Empire, in Behalf of the Negro Slaves in the West Indies*, London, J. Hatchard and Son, 1823, pp. 1–2, 24–33, 45–7, 68–9, 73–4.

Index